W0016795

Faulkner and Hemingway

Edited by Christopher Rieger
and Andrew B. Leiter

Faulkner and Hemingway
Edited by Christopher Rieger and Andrew B. Leiter
Copyright: 2018 by Southeast Missouri State University Press

Published for the Center for Faulkner Studies by
Southeast Missouri State University Press
One University Plaza, MS 2650
Cape Girardeau, MO 63701
www.semopress.com

ISBN: 978-0-9979262-93

Cover image: "Trout Fishing On the Yellowstone, Yellowstone National Park"
Creator(s): Detroit Co., 1905. Image courtesy Library of Congress Prints & Photographs Division, Washington, DC.
Cover design: Maggie Fruehwirth

Faulkner and Hemingway

Edited by Christopher Rieger
and Andrew B. Leiter

SOUTHEAST MISSOURI
STATE UNIVERSITY · 1873

Published for the Center for Faulkner Studies
by Southeast Missouri State University Press | 2018

Acknowledgements

The editors are extremely grateful to Southeast Missouri State University's Office of the Provost, College of Liberal Arts, Department of English, Kent Library, Catapult Creative House, and University Center for their support of the Faulkner and Hemingway Conference that produced the essays printed in this volume.

We also extend our thanks to Haley Albert, Taylor Bryant, Janna Harner, and David Farris, graduate assistants in the Center for Faulkner Studies, for their work corresponding with contributors and editing essays, as well as helping plan and run the conference. Roxanne Dunn and her team from Special Collections and Archives, especially Tyson Koenig, were tremendously helpful at every stage of the conference as well. Special thanks to the professors from the Art Department, especially Chris Wubbena and Hannah Sanders, for their hard work organizing the Faulkner and Hemingway art show. We also thank Leah Powers at Catapult Creative House for hosting the art show and Lisa Essmyer and her students for providing the food for the reception.

We owe a huge debt to James Brubaker and his students at the University Press. In particular, we thank Maggie Fruehwirth, who put together the cover and helped layout the book's interior. Only through their dedication and work is this book possible. Carrie Walker at the Press also put in a lot of time and effort, and we thank her.

Finally, we must thank Bob Hamblin and L.D. Brodsky without whom the Center for Faulkner Studies would not exist. We try to carry on what Bob started at the Center and to honor L.D.'s memory and legacy.

Contents

Notes on the Conference

The Faulkner and Hemingway Conference was hosted by the Center for Faulkner Studies October 20-22, 2016, on the campus of Southeast Missouri State University in Cape Girardeau, Missouri. This conference attracted fifty-four scholars from twenty different states and six foreign countries (China, Japan, South Korea, Canada, France, and England).

Scholars presented their work on Thursday, Friday, and Saturday of the conference. The essays in this volume represent the diverse approaches and new insights typified by the panel presentations as a whole. Joseph Fruscione's keynote address on Thursday evening was followed by an opening banquet at Port Cape Girardeau Restaurant, where conference attendees enjoyed fried catfish and where the winners of the conference's undergraduate writing contest were honored.

Following the panel presentations on Friday, Catapult Creative House hosted a reception for conference goers in their gallery space. On display were works of art from a Faulkner and Hemingway national juried art show. Artists from around the country created works in a variety of media that related to the Faulkner and Hemingway theme of the conference. Professors Chris Wubbena and Hannah Sanders from the Art Department at Southeast Missouri State University organized the show. Prof. Sanders and her students printed t-shirts featuring original Faulkner and Hemingway designs as part of the reception, while Prof. Lisa Essmyer's students provided food for the event.

Following the panel presentations on Saturday, Dr. Mark Cirino (University of Evansville), one of the co-authors of *Hidden Hemingway: Inside the Ernest Hemingway Archives of Oak Park* (Kent State UP, 2016), discussed the newly published book and provided a fascinating look at never-before-seen items from the Hemingway archives, such as family photos, teenage diaries, bullfighting tickets, and love letters. After Dr. Cirino's presentation, Dr. Christopher Rieger, director of the Center for Faulkner Studies, and Roxanne Dunn, head of the university's Special Collections and Archives, conducted a tour of the Rare Book Room and the L.D. Brodsky Collection of William Faulkner materials.

Dr. Fruscione's keynote address to kick off the conference extended research done for his seminal book *Faulkner and Hemingway: Biography of a Literary Rivalry* (2012). Dr. Fruscione chose to conduct a more interactive talk rather than a traditional lecture and included a discussion with the audience as part of his address. A paraphrased transcript of that portion of the talk (created by Fruscione) is included below.

Before we got to the important summer of 1947, we had an interactive interlude. Ordinarily, when a speaker asks "What's next?" the audience expects to be told the state of the field or subfield, as well as be given new directions to explore. In this case, I only asked the question. I wanted to know what's next, and I wanted the graduate students, established and emerging scholars, and others to share their ideas. It went great. Afterward, several people complimented this approach because it both gave them something different and encouraged their participation in creating the keynote. A junior scholar thanked me for soliciting the audience's input. "People don't always ask what us younger scholars are doing," she told me. Reversing the usual Q & A dynamic made for an engaging, memorable talk.

We started with these questions:

- For those of you who've read my book, what did I miss or not discuss fully? What did I leave out or underanalyze. What else did you want to hear about?
- What teaching opportunities are there with these authors? Who's taught them together?
- How can emerging scholars "do" Hemingway and Faulkner work when the profession doesn't always welcome author studies? How can younger scholars make their work with

Hemingway and Faulkner match what the profession currently wants?

- How can they be interdisciplinary? Who's done this kind of work?
- Besides William Faulkner on the Web, what other kinds of digital humanities opportunities are there? Permissions issues aside for the moment, what would you like to see digitized?
- How do you respond to scholars whose reaction to these writers (especially Hemingway) is "ugh" or an awkward "oh, *them*..."? (We've all probably heard this at some point.) See the fantastic essay on women researching and teaching Hemingway by Hilary Justice.[1] She discusses her work in Hemingway studies and getting "The Question" from scholars and students: "How do you, as a woman, justify working on Hemingway?"
- What's left to say about two such studied, written about, and taught authors?

The audience gave some great answers to start showing what's next for teaching and research:

- how they're read, taught, and currently received in England, China, and elsewhere;
- their rich, sometimes underanalyzed humor;
- their usefulness in creative writing, history, and other interdisciplinary contexts;
- translation into Chinese and other languages;
- their international presence as global (not just regional) writers;
- teachers' ways of explaining the authors' references to American history to international students;
- the development of how different schools of criticism work with the authors.

This was a great start to exploring new research and teaching directions for these writers. It's always been my hope that writing the first book on these authors would help a wide readership understand their work, their relationship, and their evolving relevance in the 21st century. Mine won't be the last word on this evolving subject, if the audience's responses are any indication.

Notes

1. See Hilary Kovar Justice, "Katie and the Pink Highlighter: Teaching Post-'Hemingway' Hemingway," *Teaching Hemingway and Gender*, ed. Verna Kale (Kent State UP, 2016), 153-64.

Introduction

In the winter of 1918-1919, Ernest Hemingway and William Faulkner returned to their respective homes of Oak Park, Illinois, and Oxford, Mississippi, in the wake of the Armistice of 11 November 1918 and the conclusion of the Great War. Both young men were sporting limps. In Faulkner's case, the limp was a spurious injury meant to aggrandize his limited service and flight training with the Canadian Royal Air Force. Hemingway, on the other hand, had been severely injured by shrapnel on the Austro-Italian front while serving as a Red Cross ambulance driver, although he, too, was prone to exaggerating his military service.[1] World War I was the seminal event of their generation, ushering in the modern era with its disillusionment and angst, the reflexive hedonism of the Jazz Age, and pervasive anxieties over shifting racial and gender dynamics in American culture. Not surprisingly, the conflict was a major thematic intersection of their literary careers and the brutal prism through which they broached fiction as aspiring authors. Three of Hemingway's classics from the 1920s, *In Our Time* (1925), *The Sun Also Rises* (1926), and *A Farewell to Arms* (1929), feature the war and/or its psychological toll on the individual. Faulkner's first novel, *Soldiers' Pay* (1926), and third novel, *Sartoris/Flags in the Dust* (1929), address physically and psychologically wounded veterans, and Faulkner returned to WWI with *A Fable* (1954), which he excruciated over for years and thought would be a masterpiece, although critics have generally disagreed with that assessment. *A Farewell to Arms* and *A Fable* feature the war most directly and are equally bleak in their presentation of military failures, conflict without meaning, and the general inhumanity of war. Likewise, shorter works such as Hemingway's "A Natural History of the Dead" (1933) and Faulkner's "Crevasse" (1931) are brutally graphic in their depictions of the corporeal horrors of war.

While the war featured prominently in their fiction, the trajectories of their literary careers as well as their biographies had numerous parallels and intersections. Before turning fully to fiction, Hemingway and Faulkner had early aspirations as poets and were published together in an edition of the avant-garde, New Orleans-based *Double Dealer* in 1922. Both were mentored by the elder literary statesman Sherwood Anderson who helped facilitate the publication of their early fiction with Boni & Liveright, and with whom both would break. While Hemingway's distancing from Anderson came in the form of *The Torrents of Spring* (1926), a rather mean-spirited parody of Anderson's *Dark Laughter* (1925), Faulkner's separation was less cruel and he would later make amends with Anderson, crediting him as "the father of all of my generation" who "has still to receive his rightful place in American letters" (*Faulkner in the University* 281). Faulkner and Hemingway rose to national literary prominence more or less simultaneously in the late 1920s with Hemingway's most enduring classic *The Sun Also Rises* appearing three years before Faulkner's most famous novel, *The Sound and the Fury* (1929). They would remain in the literary limelight for the remainder of their lives even as Hemingway endured creative droughts and Faulkner struggled financially. Both won Pulitzer Prizes: Hemingway in 1953 for *The Old Man and the Sea* (1952) and Faulkner in 1955 for *A Fable* and in 1963 for *The Reivers* (1962). Both would also receive international acclaim as Nobel Laureates with Faulkner winning the award for 1949 and Hemingway for 1954.

Both authors were avid sportsmen who hunted and fished throughout their lives, and in Hemingway's case these activities were very much a part of his public persona as well as a staple of his writing. In his safari memoir *Green Hills of Africa* (1935), Hemingway details his passion for big game hunting, a thematic interest which would also shape short stories like "The Snows of Kilimanjaro" (1936) and "The Short Happy Life of Francis Macomber" (1936). Novels such as *To Have and Have Not* (1937), *The Old Man and the Sea*, and *Islands in the Stream* (1970) are organized in part or entirely around sport and commercial fishing in the Caribbean or Gulf of Mexico, while trout fishing serves as a reprieve from the psychological strains of the modern world in *In Our Time* and *The Sun Also Rises*.

Faulkner, likewise, hunted with regularity in the Mississippi Delta region, and later in life he took up fox hunting in Virginia. Hunting informs a variety of his short stories and novels, most particularly, *Go Down, Moses* (1942) which takes its organizational structure from the multiple hunts in the novel. If one includes the numerous manhunts in such Faulkner works as "Red Leaves" (1930), *Light in August* (1932), *Absalom, Absalom!* (1936), and *The Unvanquished* (1938), the hunt motif appears as nearly pervasive in Faulkner's work as in Hemingway's. Joseph Fruscione has argued in *Faulkner and Hemingway: Biography of a Literary Rivalry* that the sporting life was a fundamental aspect of the two authors' masculine identities, and valuable critical avenues remain to explore how these traditionally masculine endeavors intertwine and shape the authors' attention to racial and gender identities as well as to ecological transitions in modern America.

Hemingway's interests in war, hunting, and fishing, as well as boxing, bullfighting, and other sports, was such that his writing is for many readers synonymous with modern masculinity and prob- lematically so for some. Hemingway cultivated a public image that mirrored his protagonists' masculine personas and, even considering his frequent flirtations with danger, he was peculiarly accident prone. In addition to his injuries in WWI, Hemingway survived multi- ple car crashes (one from which he was reported dead to his son), consecutive airplane crashes in Africa (from which he was again mistakenly reported as dead), and a self-inflicted gunshot wound while fishing off Key West. Excepting his return from the Canadian Royal Air Force, Faulkner did not adopt a similarly masculine public persona to that of Hemingway; however, he, too, shared dangerous proclivities with one of his early protagonists in Bayard Sartoris, the suicidal Royal Air Force veteran of *Sartoris/Flags in the Dust*. As Carl Rollyson contends in his essay for this collection, Faulkner's lifelong obsession with flight and its dangers has much in common with Hemingway's courting of danger. Later in life, Faulkner was also accident prone, enduring numerous falls from horseback that severely damaged his back. While these patterns in the authors' lives speak to a mutual desire to test their physicality and courage, they also suggest, perhaps, a similar self-destructive streak in their personalities, one that manifested at a slower drip in their respective alcoholism. Hemingway's boozing contributed, together with his many injuries, to his physical decline late in life, while Faulkner's severe binges led to hospitalizations and, in one case, third degrees burns on his back when he passed out against a hotel heater. The alcohol flows through their fiction, and in various works—*The Sun Also Rises*, *The Sound and the Fury*, and *Sanctuary* (1931)—they highlight the self-destructive patterns of behavior extending from their characters' drunkenness.

If their alcoholism was indicative of troubled personal lives, so too were their respective marriages. Faulkner's marriage to the sweetheart of his youth, Estelle Oldham, endured until his death but was strained by financial concerns and by his extended extramarital affairs. Hemingway was married four times with his extramarital affairs tending to lead him from one marriage to the next. Their personal relationships with women have informed, at times, the most abiding critical concerns with their fiction in terms of gender depictions. Both men were fascinated by the shift in gender roles they perceived in the New Women's emergence as more sexually liberated and socially assertive than their Victorian predecessors, and much of Faulkner's and Hemingway's fiction might be understood as studies of modern masculinity in crisis relative to new gender roles. This sense of masculine crisis appears most familiarly in Quentin Compson's psychological impotence in the face of Caddy's sexuality in *The Sound and the Fury* and Jake Barnes's war wound that leaves him incapable of performing sexually with Brett Ashley in *The Sun Also Rises*. Such attention to what female sexuality means for male protagonists lends itself to—perhaps even necessitates—the objectification of female characters, and critics have widely noted the limitations of female representation in both authors' work. At their most perceptive in terms of gender roles, Faulkner and Hemingway are self-aware and critical of the objectification and the masculine desire to control female sexuality, revealing complex gender relations that call into question the very basis of masculine identity. At worst—and this is particularly problematic in Hemingway's works— the women appear as mere projections of machismo fantasy.

Similar to gender roles, the racial dynamics in Faulkner's and

Hemingway's fiction reveal much about what it means to be a white male in modern America, but the racial presentations are limited by the white male perspective. Faulkner offers some of the most perceptive commentaries on race in American letters in *Light in August*, *Absalom, Absalom!*, and *Go Down, Moses*, and his fiction less ostensibly attending to racial issues is often informed in profound ways by racialized American culture. Yet Faulkner's great contributions to fathoming America's racial complexity deal primarily with race as it exists in white minds as he addresses slavery and segregation, as well as African American and Native American people, in terms of their fundamental impact on what it means to be white. He certainly highlights the injustices of American society and brutalities against black bodies; however, his nonwhite characters often descend into stereotype and rarely broach the complexities of African American or Native American life. The presence of nonwhite characters in Hemingway's fiction also tends to reveal more about the nature of white identity than it does about those nonwhite characters. He was not as widely invested in centering racial conflict in his fiction as Faulkner was, but Native American characters appear in important roles throughout his early short stories, and minority characters appear throughout his fiction. Whether it is the Indian husband who commits suicide in "Indian Camp" (1924), the Jewish antagonist Robert Cohn in *The Sun Also Rises*, or a black deckhand in *To Have and Have Not*, these characters are problematic stereotypes who exist primarily to develop the protagonists' attributes. As Toni Morrison argues in *Playing in the Dark* with regard to the latter novel, "a discredited Africanism" is essential to understanding the white characters' "claims to fully embodied humanity" (80).

For all of Faulkner and Hemingway's similarities, there remains a palpable difference in the ambience and artistry of their fiction. Hemingway tended toward international settings while Faulkner's best work is mostly set in his fictional Mississippi county of Yoknapatawpha and, of course, no one is likely to mistake one's prose for the other's prose. As the two most influential American prose stylists of the twentieth century, Faulkner and Hemingway expressed similar confidence in their distinctive aesthetics which were predicated on very different philosophies. Their contrasting prose styles have been characterized most concisely by Donald Kartiganer as Hemingway's "art of exclusion" and Faulkner's "art of inclusion" (54). Hemingway's succinct, clear prose and his principle of the iceberg—in which only the tip is revealed while the mass is submerged—runs counter to Faulkner's expansive verbosity and his effort "to put all mankind's history in one sentence" (Cowley 17). Each was attuned to the other's career, and their literary prominence led to a sustained rivalry that has been outlined by George Monteiro in his essay "The Faulkner-Hemingway Rivalry" and developed in full detail by Fruscione's *Faulkner and Hemingway*. When this competition devolved at various times into the authors sniping at one another, their attacks often turned on the flaws they perceived in each other's aesthetics. At a University of Mississippi class session, Faulkner famously and publicly assessed Hemingway as unwilling to take any risks as a writer or "to use a word that might cause the reader to check with a dictionary" (Faulkner, *Conversations* 71). Hemingway, meanwhile, frequently denigrated Faulkner's verbosity and compared *A Fable* and its convoluted prose to the "night soil [human waste] of Chungking" (qtd. in Meyers 361).

Despite the occasional disparagement of each other's work, Hemingway and Faulkner recognized each other as among the best writers of their generation, and they shared a dedication to craft and the pursuit of artistic perfection as an antidote of sorts to one's mortality. Hemingway's Nobel address acknowledges the Sisyphean nature of that pursuit: "For a true writer, each book should be a new beginning where he tries again for something that is beyond his attainment" (qtd. in Mellow 590). Likewise, Faulkner compared writing *The Sound and the Fury* to "mak[ing] myself a vase like that which the old Roman kept at his bedside and wore the rim slowly away with kissing it," and yet he also famously described the novel as his "most splendid failure" (Faulkner, Introduction 299-300; *Faulkner in the University* 77). When Faulkner wrote to Hemingway to apologize for his comments at the University of Mississippi, he did not—as Fruscione notes in his essay for this collection—retract his comments on Hemingway's aversion to risk or his ranking of him as an author; instead, he apologized by complimenting Hemingway's short story, "Alpine Idyll" (1926): "It's finished, complete, all the trash hacked off and thrown away, 3 dimensions and solid like a block of ice or marble; nothing more than even God could do to it; it's hard, durable, the same anywhere in fluid time" (qtd. in Fruscione 140). Without commenting on Hemingway's oeuvre, Faulkner had offered the highest accolade one consummate artist could offer another: perfection.

This collection addresses a variety of intersections in Faulkner and Hemingway studies through biographical, theoretical, and textual approaches. The essays offer new avenues for understanding the authors in terms of their rivalry, their aesthetics, and their influence on each other and subsequent authors, as well as the complexities of gender, race, masculinity, and national and regional identities as embodied in the fiction. Joseph Fruscione's keynote address, "Hemingway and Faulkner: Reflecting on a Rivalry," positions the two most influential American modernists as self-consciously in competition with one another. Engaging the fallout from Faulkner's comment in a University of Mississippi classroom that Hemingway "has no courage" among other epistolary intersections in their careers, Fruscione illuminates their competition as grounded in grudging admiration, splenetic personal attacks (particularly by Hemingway), a similar sense of masculinity, and, most importantly, assertions of their aesthetic superiority. In a comparative analysis of "Big Two-Hearted River" (1925) and *The Sound and the Fury*, Terrell Tebbetts' essay, "Hemingway's Nick and Faulkner's Quentin: A More than Accidental Similarity," identifies Nick Adams as a prototype of sorts for Quentin Compson. Concentrating on the similarities in the characters' psychological wounding and their efforts to establish order in their worlds as a means of addressing their respective traumas, Tebbetts contends that Faulkner likely read Nick as struggling with suicidal tendencies and that, through Quentin, Faulkner "replies to and revises Hemingway's portrayal."

In "From Hemingway to Faulkner via Evans: 'One Trip Across,' 'Sepulture South,' and the Visual Aesthetics of Writing," Yuko Yamamoto examines the intersections of Hemingway's and Faulkner's careers with photographer Walker Evans and his impact on the development of their aesthetics. Specifically, she examines Evans' Cuban photographs as contributing to Hemingway's short story "One Trip Across" (1934) and to his visual emphasis in his subsequent political writings of the 1930s. Similarly, Yamamoto argues that Evans' photography influenced Faulkner's lyrically visual aesthetics in his short fictional memoir "Sepulture South" (1954), and this Evans-Hemingway-Faulkner nexus speaks to the mixed-media stylistic experimentation of the modern era. In "Authorial Irresponsibility: Hemingway's 'The Battler' and Faulkner's 'Barn Burning,'" Michael Wainwright applies Jacques Derrida's reading of Beaudelaire's "La fausse monnaie" (1869) and the "surrender of authorial control" to his analysis of "The Battler" (1925) and "Barn Burning" (1939). Studying the tension between inviolable and conditional secrets within the two short stories, Wainwright argues that the authors cede interpretation to the reader during the protagonists' initiatory moments and in the function of racial alterity as it permeates their "rites of passage."

Carl Rollyson's essay, "Faulkner's Shadow: Hollywood, Hemingway, and *Pylon*," examines *Pylon* (1935) and its connections to Faulkner's screenwriting in Hollywood, as well as how it may have influenced *Absalom, Absalom!* Specifically, Rollyson's essay links Faulkner's reporter character to Hollywood prototypes and analyzes the film version of the novel, *The Tarnished Angels* (1957). Rollyson employs a biographical approach to link Faulkner's love of flying to the novel, as well as to suggest why Hemingway named it as his favorite Faulkner novel. Andrew Leiter's essay, "Rotten Logs and Mud Holes: *Bildungsroman*, Sex, and the Other in Faulkner and Hemingway," pairs Faulkner's last novel *The Reivers* with Hemingway's Nick Adams stories to examine the way in which the authors position sex and the racial Other as seminal aspects of white male maturation. He argues that, although they similarly associate the Other with the natural world as a site of primal sexuality, Hemingway turns to this association as a positive release from Victorian sexual norms while Faulkner espouses reservations about such an abandonment of "white" norms.

In "'He could do so much more': Hemingway and Faulkner's Androcentric Treatment of Gynocentric Trauma," Eden Wales Freedman analyzes representations of fetal and maternal death in *A Farewell to Arms* and "The Wild Palms." She argues that Faulkner, in both "The Wild Palms" and *As I Lay Dying* (1930) is more empathetic in his depiction of women, whereas Hemingway's Catherine Barkley is significant only in relation to Frederic Henry's development. In "'Mississippi on the Potomac': Sutpen's Hundred as Washington, D.C.," Barry Hudek finds numerous compelling similarities between Thomas Sutpen's plantation in *Absalom, Absalom!* and the nation's capital. He argues that Sutpen's Hundred allegorically represents the founding of Washington, D.C., and he sees Faulkner as "writing back" to the national culture from his marginalized position as a Southerner.

In "Courage and Verbena, Sartoris and Macomber," C.D. Albin's comparison of Hemingway's "The Short Happy Life of Francis Macomber" and Faulkner's "An Odor of Verbena" (1938) examines the verbena motif relative to the authors' respective studies of masculine courage. He argues that the females of the stories reify conventional societal standards of masculine courage which the male protagonists must navigate in order to assert their identities and, furthermore, that while Macomber lives up to those traditional standards, Bayard Sartoris transcends and transforms those cultural expectations. In "Absurdity and Grace Under Pressure: Faulkner and Hemingway as Progenitors of Ellison's *Invisible Man* and Himes's *A Rage in Harlem*," Pennie Pflueger studies Hemingway's "aesthetics of masculinity" and Faulkner's presentation of the absurd as influences on the fiction of Ralph Ellison and Chester Himes, and she argues that the younger African American authors reconstitute these elements from a black perspective in *Invisible Man* (1952) and *A Rage in Harlem* (1957). In doing so Ellison and Himes delineate the limitations of fictional white masculinity while simultaneously revitalizing black masculinity, and they illuminate the absurdity of black life as a basic reality of racialized American society. In "'A Damned Big Book': Ken Kesey's *Sometimes a Great Notion* as Faulkner-Hemingway Synthesis," Matthew D. Sutton argues that Kesey's second novel is "both a conscious and unconscious synthesis of Faulkner and Hemingway." Sutton traces the two Nobel Prize winners' influences on Kesey in general, as well as draws striking parallels among characters, style, and themes to show how the author of *Sometimes a Great Notion* (1964) and *One*

Flew Over the Cuckoo's Nest (1962) attempts to occupy the space left by the deaths of his modernist predecessors.

Han Qiqun's essay, "Faulkner's Mink Snopes, Material Places, and 'The Material Turn,'" uses a materialist approach and thing theory to analyze the Snopes Trilogy as a record of the transition to a modern South. She sees Mink Snopes, in particular, as a human reduced to an object, a thing, a human waste product in an urban, modern, industrialized world. Mink's time in prison, she argues, leaves him as an anachronism in this new world, and Faulkner is entirely unsympathetic to his plight. In her essay "'Like Nurse Shark': The Racial Economy in Hemingway's *To Have and Have Not*," Rachel Betts tackles a critical dispute about an infamous line from the novel. Toni Morrison famously reads Hemingway's comparison of an African American woman to a shark as an example of racial stereotyping prevalent in American literature. Betts provides a fresh perspective on this critical debate, combining ecocritical and economic analysis to argue for a different interpretation of this crucial passage. In "Cultivating Curses: Plants and African American Folklore in *The Sound and the Fury*," Renee Mattos employs an ecocritical approach to *The Sound and the Fury* but takes a different approach than previous scholars. She specifically analyzes the role of African American folklore as it relates to plants. From jimson weed to cedar trees, Mattos reveals how understanding African American folk beliefs and practices regarding the many references to flora in the novel can illuminate new meanings about Faulkner's portrayals of race and of his characters.

Notes

1. On their respective exaggerations, see Blotner 225-32, Karl 116-19, Mellow 60-63, and Reynolds 18-21.

Works Cited

Blotner, Joseph. *Faulkner: A Biography*. Vol. 1, Random House, 1974.

Cowley, Malcolm. *The Faulkner-Cowley File: Letters and Memories, 1944-1962*. Viking, 1966.

Faulkner, William. *Conversations with William Faulkner*, edited by M. Thomas Inge, UP of Mississippi, 1999.

—. *Faulkner in the University*, edited by Frederick L. Gwynn and Joseph L. Blotner, 1959, UP of Virginia, 1995.

—. Introduction to *The Sound and the Fury*. *Essays, Speeches & Public Letters*, edited by James B. Meriwether, Modern Library, 2004, pp. 296-300.

Fruscione, Joseph. *Faulkner and Hemingway: Biography of a Literary Rivalry*. Ohio State UP, 2012.

Karl, Frederick R. *William Faulkner: American Writer*. Weidenfeld and Nicolson, 1989.

Kartiganer, Donald M. "'Getting Good at Doing Nothing': Faulkner, Hemingway, and the Fiction of Gesture." *Faulkner and His Contemporaries: Faulkner and Yoknapatawpha, 2002*, edited by Joseph R. Urgo and Ann J. Abadie, UP of Mississippi, 2004, pp. 54-73.

Mellow, James R. *Hemingway: A Life Without Consequences*. Da Capo, 1992.

Meyers, Jeffrey. *Hemingway: A Biography*. 1985, Da Capo, 1999.

Monteiro, George. "The Faulkner-Hemingway Rivalry." *Faulkner and His Contemporaries: Faulkner and Yoknapatawpha, 2002*, edited by Joseph R. Urgo and Ann J. Abadie, UP of Mississippi, 2004, pp. 74-92.

Morrison, Toni. *Playing in the Dark: Whiteness and the Literary Imagination*. 1992, Vintage, 1993.

Reynolds, Michael. *The Young Hemingway*. W.W. Norton, 1986.

Joseph Fruscione

Hemingway and Faulkner: Reflecting on a Rivalry

This was not a traditional keynote. I changed careers to freelance editing in 2014, so I no longer teach or produce scholarly writing. My book on the Faulkner-Hemingway rivalry will be my most substantial contribution to studies of the two authors. I have said what I have to say about them, and I wanted to involve the audience in my keynote. Midway through, I asked the audience of 120 people to share what is next for researching and teaching these authors. By design, my talk asked more questions than it answered. I wanted them to discuss their professional experiences teaching writers whose reputations very much precede them. As this essay and the collection as a whole will show, there are valuable new directions to take with these authors and their era.

Given time and funding limits when I was a graduate student and fresh post-doc, I could only do archival research at the Kennedy Library. Several archives own the authors' correspondence and other papers, and the ongoing Collected Letters project is gathering Hemingway's correspondence from archives and private collections. Perhaps they exchanged more letters besides those in the summer of 1947 which I discuss below. With at least ten more volumes of Cambridge University Press's Hemingway Letters Project due in the future, there might be more comments about Faulkner to study. I have always wanted to mine the authors' copies of each other's books for marginalia or annotations, though this would require time and funds to visit archives in the U.S. and Cuba. Some detective work is also needed to decide if, when, where, and why the authors met in person. In a letter from July 1952, Hemingway refers to meeting Faulkner once, but he did not specify the place or occasion. In a comment after Hemingway's death, Faulkner refers to "the last time I saw him," but likewise does not specify when or where (Fruscione 178, 205).[1] As of now, this is a rich literary moment waiting to be discovered. There is a lot more to say about them, and there is much that we still do not know.

I say to the reader now what I said to the audience that evening in Cape Girardeau: it is your job now to show your students and fellow scholars what is next for working with two such complicated, debated, and influential writers. This book might give you some new thoughts or directions for your work, and it would be nice to see someone study the materials I could not when researching my book. Regardless of the scholarly setting or current professional ethos, Faulkner and Hemingway will always reward further reading.

I start with neither Faulkner nor Hemingway, but with Martha Gellhorn—Hemingway's third wife:

> What in hell is the matter with writers? Why do they have to be so goddamn <u>touchy</u>: I remember all E's touchiness and phobias and enemies and what-not. It seems such a furious waste of time. I find myself being a kind of Pollyanna and telling them to leave things alone and forget it, one hasn't time in life to be so full of resentments and angers. Or rather, one shouldn't have them personally: one should use up that set of emotions on causes and try to be a jolly person in normal life. (Moorhead 177)

Gellhorn wrote to Charles Scribner in late July 1945, on the verge of officially ending her tumultuous marriage to Hemingway. She had seen—and often been the target of—Hemingway's "touchiness," "phobias," and competitiveness: to him, after all, *he* was the writer of the family, regardless of Gellhorn's journalistic credentials and aspirations.

Hemingway's "resentments and angers" toward other writers is well known. Of his mentors, only Joyce and Pound were spared from his hyper-competitive writerly persona. Of his contemporaries, Faulkner was his most common—and maddening—target. In a July 1952 letter to an editor at *Time* magazine, for instance, Hemingway discussed his approach to *The Old Man and the Sea* (1952), particularly its genuine experience and tight prose. Praising himself for not cluttering his work with verbiage and insincere action is, however, an indirect criticism of Faulkner. Hemingway was then preparing the novel for publication. (I will return to this summer of 1952 shortly when we see how Hemingway reacted to a Faulkner comment about the book.) He paints himself as the dutiful, honest craftsman, unlike Faulkner and others who he thought bogged their writing down with false emotion and overwrought prose. Especially after *Requiem for a Nun* (1951) and *A Fable* (1954), Hemingway regularly criticized Faulkner in this regard. This letter contains one of many oblique references the writers made to each other in which they passed judgment by *their own* artistic standards.

Reading the authors' correspondence was the richest and most enlightening aspect of my research. I mined hundreds of Hemingway's letters at the Kennedy Library in Boston and combed through many of Faulkner's published letters. The authors' correspondence from the 1930s to the 1950s reveals much: their strong senses of masculinity, writerly self-confidence, competitive awareness of each other and the larger literary field, and occasional self-revelation. One late Hemingway letter, for instance, blasphemously riffs on the Hail Mary prayer to criticize Faulkner's *A Fable*. Another shows him writing a mock-Faulkner passage about a mutual acquaintance, the *Times Book Review* critic Harvey Breit.[2] Hemingway also once referred to Faulkner as "old corn-drinking mellifluous" to disparage him as prose stylist and alcoholic writer.[3] Faulkner's letters lack the memorable barbs of Hemingway's, but those I've read reveal his feelings of superiority to Hemingway and their peers. Based on the located correspondence, there are more letters by Hemingway about Faulkner than the reverse, which says much about who needled the other more. Despite their individual successes and self-esteem, both authors felt the pull of each other's example and professional standing. Their correspondence, among other venues, bears this out richly and, sometimes, humorously.

The authors' prodigious correspondence was a valuable element of this project, which began as my PhD dissertation in 2000 and was published in 2012 as *Faulkner and Hemingway: Biography of a Literary Rivalry*. Their letters—by turns competitive, humorous, self-effacing, and self-aggrandizing—help tell the story of a rich, nuanced, and often vexed rivalry. In Hemingway's case, his letter-writing style is highly analyzable: his corrections, strikethroughs, marginal continuations, and quality of hand- or typewriting under-score his professional self-image—and anxieties. When I did most of my archival research in 2003, it got harder to decipher Hemingway's handwriting in his later letters. Age, time, and mental instability had taken their toll on him by the late 1950s.

Their relationship embodied various attitudes: one-upmanship, respect, criticism, praise, and intellectual exchange. The relation-ship evolved over decades and across various types of texts: from Hemingway's *Death in the Afternoon* (1932) to his late "The Art of the Short Story" (1959) and Faulkner's class sessions at West Point (April 1962). They sparred over the forms, directions, and styles of American modernism. Each thought his own mode was superior, as their many comments about each other demonstrate. My central argument in the book is this: their mixed feelings *and* close reading of each other's works helped create a narrative of intense rivalry, psychological influence, and differing masculinities. I do not simply catalogue their references to or broadsides against each other in my book. I argue for how they influenced and shaped each other as seen through their direct and indirect references in letters, fiction, Nobel addresses, public remarks, and personal libraries.[4]

A few particular moments in this narrative illustrate what I mean. The early 1950s marked the tense interim between their Nobel Prizes: Faulkner won his in 1950, Hemingway his in 1954. Much of Hemingway's correspondence from this period shows a strong-willed but self-pitying writer. He was preoccupied with particular aspects of Faulkner's life and work that needled him: the Nobel Prize (which he hoped portended a loss of creativity—it did not), the religious themes of *Requiem for a Nun* and *A Fable*, Faulkner's alcoholism, and Faulkner's ranking of Hemingway as America's fourth best writer in comments he made in 1947. Some of this cor-respondence shows respect and feelings of camaraderie. Much more of it shows language of competition and masculine conflict, such as boxing, baseball, and horseracing metaphors, or—in one case—a duel between them.

A particularly complex episode stemmed from a simple request that critic Harvey Breit made of Faulkner. They met in New York in 1952 after Faulkner returned from Europe, and Breit asked him to review *The Old Man and the Sea*. What seemed like a simple task turned out to be anything but. Faulkner turned down Breit's offer but took the page proofs back to Mississippi. Upon his return to Oxford, he wrote a statement and sent it to Random House.[5] He gave reserved praise of *A Farewell to Arms* (1929), *Men without Women* (1927), and *For Whom the Bell Tolls* (1940), but—as always—assumed a loftier place: as if he (as a recent Nobel laureate) was throwing a bone to a writer dealing with creative struggles and tepid reviews of *Across the River and into the Trees* (1950). Breit had good intentions of creating dialogue between the writers, so he forwarded Faulkner's comments to Hemingway—who, predictably, overreacted. Consider two Hemingway letters from late June. On June 27, he gave guarded praise of *As I Lay Dying* (1930), *Pylon* (1935), and a handful of unspecified stories. He then criticized Faulkner's lengthy sentences in *Requiem for a Nun*, likening such showiness to maverick baseball executive Bill Veeck who was well known for his promotional gimmicks. As he often did in his late correspondence, he then took a shot at Faulkner's alcoholism, which, to his mind, weakened his handling of English (Fruscione 176-77).

Hemingway's mood was no better two days later. He continued to use Breit as his anti–Faulkner sounding board on June 29, noting that Faulkner's work was flawed because it could not be reread effectively. When rereading Faulkner, Hemingway argued, readers see how he tricked them with a showy style, whereas his own writing maintained a certain mystery. Later in this letter, Hemingway noted: "As it was it was damned good but as always I felt the lack of discipline and of character and the boozy courage of corn whiskey. When I read Faulkner I can tell exactly when he gets tired and does it on corn" (Baker 772). These and several other letters give us a model of writing and competition that the authors embraced. Here, baseball and boxing references bespeak Hemingway's gender-heavy competitiveness and view of Faulkner as a threat to his professional ego. In rich and sometimes entertaining ways, they intertwined masculinity and the writing life—both for their characters and themselves.

Seven years before this dust-up over *The Old Man and the Sea*, horseracing was the metaphor of choice. In the fall of 1945, Hemingway corresponded with the critic Malcolm Cowley about a number of literary matters, including Cowley's important work on what became *The Portable Faulkner* in 1946:

> I'd no idea Faulkner was in that bad shape and very happy you are putting together the Portable of him. He has the most talent of anybody and he just needs a sort of conscience that isn't there. [....] But he will write absolutely perfectly straight and then go on and on and not be able to end it. I wish the christ I owned him like you'd own a horse and train him like a horse and race him like a horse—only in writing. How beautifully he can write and as simple or as complicated as autumn or as spring.
>
> I'll try and write him and cheer him up. (Baker 602-04)

Faulkner knew of Random House's suggestion that Hemingway write the preface to the *Portable*, and both he and Cowley objected. Cowley thought it would be "in dubious taste" (87). Faulkner shared his objections in March 1946:

> I am opposed to asking Hemingway to write the preface. It seems to me in bad taste to ask him to write a preface to my stuff. It's like asking a horse in the middle of a race to broadcast a blurb on another horse in the same running field. A preface should be done by a preface writer, not a fictioneer; certainly not by one man on another in his own limited field. [....]
>
> The woods are full of people who like to make a nickel expressing opinions on the work of novelists. Cant you get one of them? (Blotner 229-30)

Whether seeing themselves as trainers or racing thoroughbreds,

Hemingway and Faulkner often juxtaposed their senses of writing and manhood as competition. Each saw—and continued to see—himself as autonomous and superior to the other: Hemingway wanted to enact a trainer or editor role as the more disciplined craftsman, whereas Faulkner wanted to out-race the field as the more experimental writer, which he would attempt to do a year later.

About a year after Hemingway wanted to train Faulkner and Faulkner wanted to outrace Hemingway, Faulkner was at the University of Mississippi and sparked *the* defining moment in their relationship. In this case, Faulkner sounded a lot more confrontational than he intended to sound, or perhaps more so than he wanted to *seem*. While answering questions in an Ole Miss writing class in April 1947, he was asked to rank his contemporaries.[6] After being asked by a student to include himself in the names, he gave a memorable answer:

> 1. Thomas Wolfe: he had much courage and wrote as if he didn't have long to live; 2. William Faulkner; 3. [John] Dos Passos; 4. Ernest Hemingway: he has no courage, has never crawled out on a limb. He has never been known to use a word that might cause the reader to check with a dictionary to see if it is properly used; 5. John Steinbeck: at one time I had great hopes for him—now I don't know. (Inge 71)

Faulkner's agreement with the English Department to the contrary, faculty were present, students took notes, and his comments were not restricted to the classroom. Instead, the New York *Herald Tribune* picked up the university's press release for these sessions. Hemingway received his copy in Cuba a few weeks later. Faulkner's ostensibly private remark was private no longer.

As we might guess, Hemingway's reaction to Faulkner's ranking—especially the courage remark—was one of aggression. Faulkner's remarks caught Hemingway at a tense moment: his longtime editor Max Perkins had recently died, his wife Mary had a bad case of the flu, and his son Patrick was severely ill and suffering from a concussion. Biographies of both authors have discussed this rich and lively episode. Each wrote two letters to the other: two have been published (Blotner 251; Inge 623-25), and two, which I discuss here, are archived in the Hemingway Collection.

Given Hemingway's persona of bravado and conflict, he mobilized his war-time friend General Buck Lanham to write Faulkner and vouch for Hemingway's battlefield composure in the European theater. Lanham also seems to have sent Faulkner a copy of Hemingway's Bronze Star citation, which he received from the Army in mid-June. (If we remember that Faulkner only invented his own combat experience in World War I, we can imagine that this citation resonated for him.) In his reply, Faulkner was apologetic and contrite: he stressed that his remarks were incompletely printed and not meant as an attack. One sees similar civility in Hemingway's reply from July 16, 1947—along with a particularly *un*civil suggestion that they have an old-fashioned gentlemen's duel. Hemingway opened cordially, thanked Faulkner for writing, and apologized for having Buck Lanham write on his behalf. (This last part is somewhat disingenuous, given that Hemingway requested that Lanham contact Faulkner.) Hemingway was at his most conflicted in the third paragraph, noting that Faulkner's comments no longer stung. In the next sentence, he recognized Faulkner's right to criticize him, but then reiterated his own right to disagree. He then—playfully, one hopes—said he would be eager to have a duel over the issue, although he wished his shot would not hit Faulkner. (Translation: he would shoot at Faulkner anyway and hope for the best.) He ended on a note of civility and camaraderie. He wished Faulkner and his family well and suggested that they meet up, drink, and talk. It seems they never did so (Fruscione 138).

Three days later, Faulkner replied, again with a note of civility— but without retracting his ranking or taking back his "no courage" comment. "Dear Brother H," he opened:

> Thank you for your letter. I feel much better, not completely all right; I owed Lanham an apology and I hope he accepted it but the bloke I'm still eating shit to is Faulkner. I cringe a little at my own name in printed gossip; I hate like hell to have flung any other man's into it. Damn stupid business, one of those trivial things you throw off just talking, a

nebulous idea of no value anyway, that you test by saying it.

[...] Take a thing like Madame Bovary (not the woman: the book) or your Alpine Idyll or that one of Joyce's about the woman playing the piano. [...] It's finished, complete, all the trash hacked off and thrown away, 3 dimensions and solid like a block of ice or marble; nothing more than even God could do to it; it's hard, durable, the same anywhere in fluid time; you can write another as hard and durable if you are good enough but you can't beat it.

[....] I wish I'd said it that way. But even then it would have been misquoted probably, as most things not worth saying in the first place usually are. But what I wish most is I'd never said it at all, or that I could forget having done so, which perhaps I could and would if it had not been about a first rate man. (Faulkner)

Faulkner learned of his comment's release and seemed anxious to clarify what he had said...or *meant* to say...or wanted to *appear* to have said about Hemingway. He attempted clarification here in part by putting Hemingway on par with Joyce, Flaubert, and others. He had to revisit this episode in New York, Japan, and Virginia over the next decade-plus, although he never took back what he said.

Not surprisingly, Faulkner did not address Hemingway's comment about their mock duel. One wonders what he was thinking when he read it. Faulkner's different attitudes reveal a fascinating split in his persona: his reserved side wanted to avoid open confrontation with a writer as truculent as Hemingway; his private, more competitive side, however, may have wanted to disparage Hemingway's literary worth and elevate his own. Faulkner's placement of himself second becomes somewhat misleading when we remember that Thomas Wolfe had been dead since 1938. So, by Faulkner's logic, the most important living writer was Faulkner himself. He felt himself to be the better writer, as his subsequent commentary on this incident *and* his never retracting his ranking reveal. At some level, Faulkner shared Hemingway's sense of competitiveness and masculinity, but not his ways of performing or expressing it. So far, this remains the only direct correspondence located between these writers.

Let us move ahead a decade or so after this exchange of letters and guarded praise. In the late 1950s, Hemingway was struggling to complete a number of projects, among them *The Dangerous Summer*.[7] In this nonfiction text about two rival matadors (who were also brothers-in-law) competing during the summer of 1959, Hemingway again viewed professional life competitively. As with most of his nonfiction, the Hemingway persona frames the story. At one point, we get this observation:

> Bullfighting is worthless without rivalry. But with two great bullfighters it becomes a deadly rivalry. Because when one can do something, and do it regularly, that no one else can do and it is not a trick but a deadly dangerous performance only made possible by perfect nerves, judgment, courage, and art and this one increases its deadliness steadily, then the other, if he has any temporary failure of nerves or judgment, will be gravely wounded or killed if he tries to equal or surpass it. He will have to resort to tricks and when the public learns to tell the tricks from the true thing he will be beaten in the rivalry and he will be very lucky if he is still alive or in the business. (64)

Not surprisingly, the language of competition and conflict predominate. But, imagine this passage starting *"Writing* is worthless without rivalry. But with two great *writers* it becomes a deadly rivalry" and so on. This was Hemingway's go-to move: that is, framing writing as a contest of wills, discipline, and talent. For him, competition between artists of all kinds was creatively valuable. Such one-upmanship could lead to more innovation and chance-taking. Early- and mid-career, he spoke in letters of taking on Melville, Dostoyevsky, Cervantes, Henry James, and others. Faulkner was also competitive and driven, yet more understatedly so because of his healthier professional ego, different mode of masculinity, and less dominating public image. Particularly in the 1950s, Faulkner was more successful and heralded with the Nobel Prize, a Pulitzer, and two National Book Awards, among other honors. Except for Faulkner's Pulitzer for *The Reivers*, Hemingway knew he received these late awards, which further upset an artist who had not published a novel since *The Old Man and the Sea* and could not seem to get past the editor's block hampering his creativity.

Remember Martha Gellhorn's questions from the beginning: "What in hell is the matter with writers? Why do they have to be so goddamn <u>touchy</u>?" Of the two, Hemingway was clearly the more "touchy" writer, as seen in his tense interactions with Faulkner, Gertrude Stein, F. Scott Fitzgerald, and virtually anyone else who influenced or threatened him. Less may have been "the matter with him" than with Hemingway, but Faulkner felt the pull of Hemingway's celebrity and literary example. He did not dedicate the same time or energy to engaging with another contemporary in the way he did with Hemingway, and he seemed to welcome Hemingway as a point of comparison for his own work—so long as his looked better.

Although I wrote the first book on this subject, I will not have the last word on it. I did not say or research all there is to address about these writers, their relationship, and their complex importance to American literature. Selfishly, I am grateful for both writers' competitiveness and touchiness, or else my book never would have been written. Like all such projects, mine was *work*...but it was also engaging, interesting, and often fun. I have read these letters many times, and some of their barbs still make me laugh: such as Hemingway wanting to "own" Faulkner "like a horse," or his comments about *Requiem for a Nun*'s long, showy sentences. I could go on, of course. But I will leave that to a new generation of teacher–scholars.

Notes

1. See also Stoneback, 203-19, for a discussion of Hemingway's September 1947 visit to Oxford to meet Faulkner.

2. Due to permissions issues, I am unable to quote from unpublished

letters here. For passages from this and other archival correspondence, see my *Faulkner and Hemingway: Biography of a Literary Rivalry*, 190, 193-94.

3. Ibid., 192.

4. Hemingway's library had *Absalom, Absalom!, As I Lay Dying, Big Woods, Collected Stories, A Fable, Go Down, Moses, The Wild Palms, Light in August, The Mansion, The Portable Faulkner, Pylon, Sanctuary, Soldiers' Pay*, and *The Unvanquished*. Faulkner's was more selective, it seems: *The Fifth Column, Green Hills of Africa, The Short Stories*, and *To Have and Have Not*. See *Faulkner and Hemingway: Biography of a Literary Rivalry*, 4.

5. "A few years ago, I forget what the occasion was, Hemingway said that writers should stick together just as doctors, lawyers, and wolves do. I think there is more wit in that than truth or necessity either, at least in Hemingway's case, since the sort of writers who need to band together willy nilly or perish, resemble the wolves who are wolves only in pack and, singly, are just another dog." See *Selected Letters*, 333-34.

6. His initial list: 1. Wolfe 2. Dos Passos 3. Hemingway 4. Cather 5. Steinbeck.

7. This bullfighting text dovetails with Hemingway's first, *Death in the Afternoon*, which has his comments about Faulkner being "prolific" and hiding the harsh elements of *Sanctuary* behind obscure language and imagery.

Works Cited

Baker, Carlos, editor. *Ernest Hemingway: Selected Letters, 1917-1961*. Scribner's, 1981.

Blotner, Joseph, editor. *Selected Letters of William Faulkner*. Random House, 1977.

Cowley, Malcolm. *The Faulkner-Cowley File: Letters and Memories, 1944-1962*. Viking, 1966.

Faulkner, William. Letter to Ernest Hemingway, July 19, 1947. Hemingway Collection at John F. Kennedy, Boston Massachusetts.

Fruscione, Joseph. *Faulkner and Hemingway: Biography of a Literary Rivalry*. Ohio State UP, 2012.

Hemingway, Ernest. *The Dangerous Summer*. Simon and Schuster, 1997.

Inge, M. Thomas, editor. *Conversations with William Faulkner*. UP of Mississippi, 1999.

Moorhead, Caroline, editor. *Selected Letters of Martha Gellhorn*. Henry Holt, 2007.

Stoneback, H.R. "Freedom and Motion, Place and Placelessness: On the Road in Hemingway's America." *Hemingway and the Natural World*, edited by Robert Fleming, U of Idaho P, 1999, pp. 203–19.

Terrell Tebbetts

Hemingway's Nick and Faulkner's Quentin: A More than Accidental Similarity

Joseph Fruscione's 2012 *Faulkner and Hemingway* has given new impetus to the study of these key twentieth-century writers' "intertextual relationship" (2), one in which "Faulkner and Hemingway impacted each other's work" (7). Fruscione, of course, is not the first to investigate the relationship. In particular, Jackson Benson in 1982 observed that Quentin Compson is "reminiscent" of Nick Adams, though he did not develop that observation. More recently, Mark Cirino has gone just a bit further with this tantalizing intertextual connection between Nick and Quentin, suggesting that Nick and Quentin share a similar "quest for simplicity" (120). Though Cirino goes no further, he joins Benson in prompting post-Fruscione readers to consider how much the two young, male protagonists share. Broadly speaking, for example, both young men grow up in dysfunctional families in which their parents' relationships are distant and even antagonistic. More specifically, in two of their works, *In Our Time*'s "Big Two-Hearted River" (1925) and *The Sound and the Fury*'s "June 2, 1910" (1929), Nick and Quentin in many ways seem to be two versions of the same character. Plot alone provides some striking similarities. Both young men travel by rail and then walk through the day, explicitly or implicitly hoping to have "left behind" matters that trouble them (*IOT* 179). On their journeys, both stare at trout from a bridge, Quentin noting how one hangs "delicate and motionless" in the stream (*SF* 117), Nick observing several "keeping themselves steady in the current" (*IOT* 177). These clues and others I will explore in this essay suggest that Faulkner was mining "Big Two-Hearted River" as he wrote his novel four years after *In Our Time*'s publication. Stephen Ross and Noel Polk apparently think so, offering that the "image of looking over a bridge railing at a fish . . . may have been familiar to Faulkner from Hemingway's "Big Two-Hearted River" (103). Like Benson and Cirino, Ross and Polk go no further after noting the similarity. The intertextual connections between Nick and Quentin, so frequently noted but little explored, call for examination. They suggest that Faulkner was Hemingway's best early reader, seeing in Hemingway's portrayal of Nick a wounded psychological state that he expands and develops in his own rendering of Quentin Compson, a depiction that replies to and revises Hemingway's portrayal.

I. Wounded Men

An investigation of Nick's and Quentin's psychological states is particularly important, for Hemingway and Faulkner have made characterization the most riveting element in their two stories. Eschewing tense external conflicts and surprising twists, the stories get readers interested in the internal conflicts driving Nick and Quentin as they try to leave their troubles behind. Those conflicts seem to arise from the wounds both young protagonists carry and have every reason to wish they could indeed leave behind, both being what Donald Kartiganer has called "traumatized young men" (66). Nick carries a wound from the front of World War I. He has seen the larger world explode in the raging holocaust of that war, as the time of the story and its placement at the end of *In Our Time* attest. As Robert Paul Lamb has observed, the sense that Nick's experience in war has rendered him a "shell-shocked veteran" with a "war wound" has been established since Philip Young's 1952 *Ernest Hemingway: A Reconsideration* ("Currents," 167). The devastation of Seney and the surrounding countryside presents a microcosm of the vast devastation Nick has experienced. Certainly some critics offer additional understandings of what Seney's devastation represents; Michael Reynolds points to Nick's (and Hemingway's) family pressures, money problems, and publishing difficulties (203), while Debra Moddelmog points to Nick's (and Hemingway's) difficulty writing (607). They are surely right that such difficulties have been weighing on Nick and are part of the "everything" and the "other needs" Nick is happy to be leaving behind (179). But we must not confuse these secondary difficulties with the primary one. The whole of *In Our Time* supports the sense that the devastation of Seney primarily represents the devastation of war and that Nick's departure for his pristine fishing camp is his attempt to recover from its trauma and the psychic wound he still carries.

Quentin has likewise experienced "scenes of trauma" (Polk, *Children* 110). But he endured them on the home front, his trauma and ensuing wound experienced in what Kartiganer calls "destructive parenting" (66), specifically by his father's insistence that all social, intellectual, and moral orders and all of the truths underpinning them are as "arbitrary" as the "mechanical hands" on the watch his father hands him (*SF* 77). Quentin recalls Father saying that battles are never won and victories never achieved (76). He has learned that even the worst of faults is not "worth the changing of it" (78). While studying a year at Harvard, he has recalled his father's assurance that higher education represents the "reducto absurdum of all human experience" and thus cannot ever "fit [his] individual needs" (76), for its every truth is already dead, "cling[ing] like dead ivy vines upon old dead brick" (95). As I have argued elsewhere, Quentin's wound results from confronting what we now can call "the void described by postmodernism" (Tebbetts 134), for although Father has presented Quentin with the instability of language, arguing that people merely use "themselves and each other so much by words" (118), and thus that all truths and orders asserted in language are unstable, the lot of them merely cluttering "dusty shelves" with "ordered certitudes long divorced from reality" (125), Quentin cannot fully accept that there is not "anything" that matters and that "it doesn't matter" that this is so (78). In particular, he struggles to believe that the promiscuity of his beloved sister Caddy "doesn't matter," though that would have been just the first great crisis he would have faced in dealing with his father's lessons had he lived. His father, not his sister, is the ultimate source of Quentin's trauma. He dwells on his father's lessons with all the agony of a man suffering from festering physical wounds. As I shall argue below, he leaves Cambridge on the day of his suicide with a perhaps unrealized desire to heal his postmodern wound by re-establishing certitude and the control that flows from it. But first Nick.

II. Getting Control

Nick deals with his wound not just by leaving "everything behind, the need for thinking, the need to write, other needs" (179), but also by using this time away to try to establish full and exact control over himself and his environment. Nick clearly intends to control the world about him as much as he can. In making his camp, for instance, he carefully picks a space between "two jack pines [where] the ground was quite level," removes projecting roots and "sweet fern bushes," smooths "the sandy soil with his hand," and lays out his blankets (185), all precisely and intentionally aimed at conforming his camp to his needs. After pitching his tent over the prepared ground, Nick feels it is a "good place" (186), a place he can call his "home" (187). Nick even rids his tent of the pesky mosquito threatening its own kind of aerial bombardment, a "satisfying hiss" ending its invasion of his new home (192). As Joseph Flora has noted, Nick is playing the role of Jehovah in the opening chapter of Genesis in these actions (157), forming his small universe according to his command and thus controlling it completely. In doing so, Nick makes a home utterly unlike the chaotic battlefields of war, where bullets and shells cross no man's land and bombs fall from above. Having shaped and thus controlled this new home, Nick thinks it "good" because his meticulous control of its elements has ensured that it meets all his needs and ends. He has succeeded in leaving the battlefield behind as he has created a completely opposite environment.

Nick is restoring control over himself as well as the world about him. He shows his intent to do so from the beginning of the story when he stands on the bridge and watches the trout below. As Fredrik Brogger has recognized, Nick admires the trout holding itself steady under Seney's bridge because of his own "obsession with control" (22). Nick may even identify with that trout, its steadiness and control in the current demonstrating the personal steadiness and self-control Nick wants, needs, and intends to regain on his retreat. Nick may also identify with the black grasshoppers he encounters on his hike, feeling that the trauma of war has affected him as Seney's fire has affected them, bringing them their own "traumatized state," as Cirino puts it (123). Nick may even sense that, though they have turned "sooty black" as they adapted a new camouflaging color in the ravaged countryside (181), their unusual color will not serve them well as the countryside turns green once more and their new color makes them highly visible prey. Perhaps Nick senses that, though adapted to the horror of war, he must now re-adapt lest he be lost in the peacetime that has returned. He must regain control over all the instincts, reflexes, and impulses that war produced and restore other characteristics that peaceful society will inevitably demand. As Nick attempts to create a controllable world and to restore the self-control he possessed before he went to war, he must be able to control the fear, the anxiety, the despair, the aggression, and other inner turmoil with which war scars its survivors. Only in controlling such wartime emotions will Nick be able to leave them behind.

Thus Nick controls his impulses at every turn. Leaving the burned-over town, he begins a long, hot, uncomfortable trek, carrying a pack that is "much too heavy" and encountering "hard work walking up-hill" (179), yet he refuses to "strike the river [at once] by turning off to his left," disciplining himself to keep "on toward the north to hit the river as far upstream as he could go in one day's walking" (183), even though he knows that there are "plenty of good places to camp" all along the river (188-89). When he gets as far as he intends to go, he disciplines himself to "make his camp" before cooking supper, even though he is "very hungry" from his long hike (185). Even after cooking, Nick restrains himself from eating too quickly lest his "beans and spaghetti" burn his tongue (188). On the next morning, he shows the same control over his appetite, not restraining it this time but making himself eat even though he feels "too hurried to eat breakfast" (195). He even makes himself tidy up his camp before getting to the river and beginning the fishing he is so eager to enjoy (198). From the first day to the second, Nick has kept himself from acting on his appetites and emotions, restraining them and controlling every action.

In his fishing, Nick unites the two controls he has been exercising, his control of both his environment and himself. He unites them in the expertise he brings to the sport. Feeling "professionally happy with all his equipment hanging from him" (199), he goes to the river in full command of what lies ahead. There, he applies his expertise to his every action. He picks his spots carefully, for example, turning away first from shallows where he is "certain he could catch small trout" (202), and then from deeper holes where there are "always trout," knowing that he "would get hooked in the branches" there (208). He lets his first catch go, judging it too small, and in doing so he is careful not to touch it with "a dry hand" lest the touch lead to a deadly fungus (201). Over the morning, he reels in two trout he is fully satisfied with and cleans them expertly, the "insides clean and compact, coming out all together" (212). He even knows how to dispose of the waste, tossing the "offal ashore for the minks to find" (212). In all of these circumstances, it is clear that Nick does "not want to rush his sensations" (204). How different this is from scenes of war, where every sensation is rushed. Here Nick can leave the scenes of war behind, along with all his wounds because, in this "obsessively controlled activity" (Kartiganer 58), he can measure and direct every action and every sensation according to his will, fitting himself perfectly into a world he is at home in.

In exercising this control, Nick has repeatedly *delayed* actions—delayed reaching a campsite, delayed fixing supper, delayed eating it, delayed beginning his fishing in the morning, delayed making his catches. In focusing his self-control on delays, Nick tacitly suggests a reason, perhaps the primary reason, he is seeking control. He needs to delay matters beyond the fishing camp as well as within it, matters that could have a "tragic" consequence, one that Faulkner may have sensed when he created Quentin, as I will discuss later in this essay.

Like Nick, Quentin seeks a kind of control as he leaves Cambridge for the countryside, although his internal conflict regarding control is much more evident than Nick's. He both seeks control and denies its possibility, not surprising given that his wound stems from his father's insistence on the meaninglessness of life and all actions therein, an insistence he both accepts and denies.

On the one hand, Quentin accepts the impossibility of control. He does this in trying to eschew clock time, the imposition of an arbitrary order on an otherwise fluid flow of events. He breaks the hands off his watch (77), and he enters the jeweler's shop intent on confirming that "not any of those watches in the window are right"

(84), just as none of the certitudes of philosophical, political, moral, or religious systems attempting to control the world stand on self-evident and universal truth. As his father has taught him, he seems to believe that any struggle to fit oneself and others into any controlling system of any master narrative is futile. He has reached the postmodern state described by Doreen Fowler, seeing life as uncontrollably "fluid" and all truths merely "human construction" (106).

On the other hand, Quentin still wants control and exhibits much of the same self-control that Nick exhibits. As Noel Polk has pointed out, he does so partly in his language, his desire for "control" manifesting itself as he "minutely and preciously puts into words every possible sensation, every possible observation of the present moment, to try to control" his memories of "something painful back home" (*Children* 111-12). Polk explicitly finds Quentin to be "very much like Hemingway's Nick Adams" in this drive for a perfectly controlled language (*Children* 111).

Quentin shows as much desire for control in his actions as he does in his language. In the morning, he does so in his grooming and packing. He lays out extra clothing in which to dress his anticipated corpse. He bathes and carefully dresses for the day in his "new suit" (81), attiring himself formally enough to pass for the son of "a congregational minister" (143). He carefully packs his remaining clothes into his trunk for shipping home. That night, he continues creating a precise order, cleaning his suit and brushing his teeth just before he walks toward the bridge to his well-planned death. Throughout the day, he has shown his drive for self-control in his obsession with clock time. Though he has broken the hands from his watch, he listens to the "watch tick[ing] on" (80), keeping time even without the hands, and when the campus clock sounds the "quarter hour," he "stop[s] and listen[s] to it until the chimes" cease (81), as if the sound of time provides an order by which he can direct himself even if the sight of the broken watch face no longer can. As the day wears on, he continues to "hear my watch" (137), and in lieu of chimes, he asks the boys if there is a nearby factory that would sound "one oclock whistles" (119).

Most persistently, Quentin tracks "clock" time and its controlling power by repeatedly turning his environment and even himself into sundials. At his dormitory, he tells time by using the shadows on the sash as he awakens and on the stoop as he leaves the building (77, 81). He notes the shadows of a bridge (116), of the "broken façade" of a building (130), and of Mrs. Bland's car on a wall (147). When the environment provides no ready sundial, he turns himself into one, "consulting his shadow to tell the time" (Tebbetts 134). Before he begins his trek, he leans on the bridge's rail both "hearing my watch" and "watching my shadow" (92), the play on words indicating how fully Quentin is turning his shadow into a watch. Later, hearing more chimes as he prepares to leave Cambridge, he stands "in the belly of my shadow" (100). In the countryside, he "walk[s] upon my shadow" (120), notes it "pacing" him and then "behind" him (133), and soon thereafter tricking it into a larger shadow (134). As Taylor Hagood asserts, each "shadow marks [Quentin's] progression through his life, counting down the hours of that day" (135). As he counts the hours by turning himself and his environment into sundials, Quentin shows how fully his whole being demands a system of control despite his intellectual acceptance of his father's denial that any system offers control worth pursuing or attempting to achieve.

Quentin further exhibits a Nick-like desire to control his environment in his interactions with the little Italian girl. Though his father has refused any attempt to control Caddy and has discouraged Quentin's attempts, and though Quentin has failed when he tried to do so by confronting Dalton Ames, he nevertheless tries to watch over the little girl he identifies as "Sister" and turn her over to the control of local authority, the marshal Anse (130), and, failing that, to return her to the walls of her house and the control of her family. Whether this attempt at control represents a frustrated but continuing desire to provide external control over Caddy's sexual behavior or to provide internal control over his own psychic trauma, Quentin's internal conflict over the very possibility of control perfectly exhibits what Judith Sensibar calls the "nuanced psychosexual and psychosocial tensions informing the novel" (472). He wants to control himself and his world even as he believes such control arbitrary, meaningless, and ultimately impossible to achieve.

Quentin implicitly expresses this desire for control in the

admiration for the trout that he shares with Nick. Just as Nick observes several trout "keeping themselves steady in the current" and then changing positions "only to hold steady in the fast current again" (177), Quentin observes his trout hanging "delicate and motionless" in its current (117). Just as Nick focuses on one "big trout" that appears only as a "shadow," noting its "shadow" three times in one long sentence before it "seemed to float down the stream" (178), Quentin first sees his big trout as a "shadow" (116), then follows the shadow "among the wavering shadows of the stream" (117), and finally sees the "shadow" of the trout "fade slowly downstream" (118). Clearly, Faulkner's text echoes Hemingway's. Just as clearly, Faulkner's character, who has tracked his own shadow all day, identifies the shadowy trout with himself. He admires how steady it is in the current, a current so strong he thinks of it twice as a "vortex" (117, 118). As André Bleikasten explains it, Quentin admires the trout for its "balance in the vortex" (101), its complete control of itself even in an environment it has no control over. Daniel Singal agrees: the trout represents "perfect control over the terms of its existence" (120). If only Quentin might be a fish. If only Nick might be as well. If only both could establish enough psychological control to hold themselves steady!

III. Why Control

Quentin's evident longing to reverse his father's teaching, heal his wound, and establish a measure of certitude and order may be a tacit, perhaps unrecognized, attempt to avoid his pending suicide. As he has traveled into and through the countryside, he has, after all, left behind not just Cambridge and Harvard but more particularly the bridge from which he intends to jump and the "two six-pound flat-irons" he intends to hold him on the bottom of the Charles River (90). Yet he has not been able to leave behind his father's words, which continue falling upon him like the bombs and mortars that fell on Nick when he was at war, and none of the shadowy sundials provide either certitude or order. Nor has he been able to become the source of order for the little Italian girl. Ironically, in fact, Quentin has become the cause and focus of disorder, dragged to the local squire and accused of "meditated criminal assault" (140), accompanied by an incensed, shouting brother, by the little girl he tried to protect who is "howl[ing] steadily" (139), and by, as Polk observes, a whole "network of characters who represent the array of his pathologies" (*Faulkner* 23). Finally, Quentin proves himself an utter failure at controlling both himself and his environment when he assaults Gerald Bland only to be mercilessly bloodied by him. Rather than leaving behind all that has wounded him, Quentin finds himself wounded anew. If his excursion offered a chance to gain control and avoid his planned suicide, it has failed so completely that it can only confirm Quentin's intent to end his life. Perhaps Quentin even sensed before he set out that his excursion would fail, that it would be what Kartiganer calls an empty gesture, a failure that he had "no hope of altering" (55). Perhaps he even sought that failure in order to confirm his plan.

Could Faulkner have sensed that not only a war wound but also a resulting impulse toward self-destruction could be in the submerged part of the iceberg in Nick's story? The answer may well be yes if Fruscione is right that Faulkner regularly "enhanced his creativity by reshaping others' stories" and that, in particular, "collaborative . . . intertextuality" marked his writing relationship with Hemingway as he "read, remade, and transformed some of Hemingway's work while trying to outduel him" (31, 32). Quentin, who cannot leave behind what haunts him, who finds no restorative retreat, commits the suicide that Nick Adams may have been struggling against in his retreat, a retreat through which Nick can delay returning to civilian life in hopes of restoring the control a soldier needs once he is home. In short, Faulkner may well have read Nick as a suicidal victim of PTSD long before readers and critics began realizing that possibility. After all, by the time he wrote *The Sound and the Fury*, Faulkner had already created two characters with major war wounds—Donald Mahon of *Soldiers' Pay* (1926) and Bayard Sartoris of *Sartoris* (1929), the former dying and the latter intent on self-destruction.

Nick is surely, as Ronald Smith argues, "a victim of PTSD" (40). Suffering from what this generation has come to call Post-Traumatic Stress Disorder, Nick needs to restore control over his primary issue, his war wound, because he can delay dealing with the secondary issues—the "other needs" and "everything" else he has left behind—only so long. He knows that dealing with them will be like fishing in the swamp, with "water deepening up under his arm-pits" and with only a little sun found "in patches" (211). He senses that even in peacetime the river of life creates not only free-flowing streams, in which he can exercise mastery and control, but also, inevitably and unavoidably, these dark and misty situations where control may be much more difficult, where he could be swamped in "a tragic adventure" if he attempts them too soon (211). Nick is using the trip as a means both to establish control and to delay deal-ing with issues which will demand a great deal of control if he is to handle them well. In creating a certain suicide in Quentin, Faulkner may have sensed the suicidal nature of the "tragic adventure" Nick would encounter if he fished the swamp—faced his complex sec-ondary issues—while his restoration is still underway, the weight of those issues being enough to send this victim of PTSD over the brink, so far over the brink that he might even end his own life.

If Nick is on his retreat primarily trying to handle an impulse toward suicide, he is in company with the numerous veterans suffer-ing from PTSD. The Department of Veterans Affairs reports that the suicide rate for male veterans is almost twice the rate of that for the general male population (Hudenko, Homaifar, and Wortzel par. 6), with "PTSD alone" being "significantly associated with suicidal ideation or attempts" even after "controlling for comorbid disorders" (par. 9). The Department also reports that "anger and impulsivity have also been shown to predict suicide risk in individuals with PTSD" (par. 10). Studies thus connect PTSD and potential sui-cide to Nick's need for control: Nick may sense that unless he is able to control emotions like anger and behaviors like impulsivity, he will face the direst of tragic experiences while tackling major issues awaiting him.

Contextual evidence in the whole of *In Our Time* could have convinced Faulkner that Nick is gaining control in order to stave off self-destruction. Nick witnesses a suicide as a child, as "Indian Camp," his first story in *In Our Time*, records. Then he "felt quite sure he would never die" (21). He must remember the surprise of that episode—the suicide of the Indian husband when his wife's suffering became too much to bear. Now he is an adult in the collection's closing story. Might he feel the attraction of death felt by that Indian man years ago, death feeling like a way out of a double load of pain—both the pain he witnessed during the war and still carries with him and the pain he will experience in dealing with "everything" that awaits him after his retreat?

Some critics have joined Faulkner and find a good bit of such contextual evidence in *In Our Time* indicating that Nick is staving off self-destruction. In a recent work, Lamb explores the unstated but implied suicide of the fishing guide in another story from that volume, "Out of Season," noting that Hemingway himself acknowledged the guide's implicit suicide in *A Moveable Feast* (*Art*, 46-47). In an earlier work, Lamb applies that same implication to "Big Two-Hearted River," seeing Hemingway's own "anxiety about non-being" in Nick ("Hemingway," 13). Kenneth Lynn agrees, also seeing Hemingway's "long debate with himself about self-destruction" implicit in the story's portrait of Nick (154). More generally, Flora implies that Nick is struggling with self-destruction when he posits that in this story Nick is "dealing, more meaningfully than he has ever done before, with issues of life and death" (147).

If the context of the story, critical insights, and an intertextual connection support the possibility that the tragedy represented by the swamp includes self-destruction, evidence within the story would also have fed Faulkner's early perception of Nick as a potential suicide. That evidence lies in the two creatures Nick identifies with—the grasshoppers and the trout. As we have already seen, the black grasshoppers have adapted in order to avoid predators, so when Nick wonders "how long they would stay that way" (181), he implicitly acknowledges that their black adaptation will be a death sentence when green returns to the countryside, perhaps as certain a death sentence as that executed upon Sam Cardinella in Chapter XV of *In Our Time*, the vignette between the two parts of "Big Two-Hearted River." Even more, the brown grasshoppers Nick collects as bait are all potentially under death sentences. Even the one that escapes, floating rapidly and kicking, quickly disappears: a "trout had taken him" as a satisfying breakfast (200). Many other hoppers will follow, first impaled on Nick's hook, then drowned, then snapped up by trout. Many of the grasshoppers that join Nick's retreat will die.

So will a number of the trout Nick admires. If grasshoppers die as they go into the water, the trout die as they come out of it. A fisherman, after all, is a predator. Certainly Nick is respectful of his prey, something of a conservationist, even—returning the small trout to the stream, hating to "come on dead trout, furry with white fungus" caused by other fishermen's carelessness (202), and satisfying himself with just two trout on his first day, unconcerned with "getting many trout" (207). Nevertheless, the point of fishing is to catch fish, to execute death sentences upon them, and Nick certainly does that. He lands two, breaks their necks, and guts them. Soon he will eat them as they have eaten the grasshoppers.

So Nick brings death to grasshoppers and trout alike. As his retreat continues over ensuing days, he will bring more death. Perhaps, then, the deaths Nick brings to the creatures he identifies with provide vicarious ways of enacting his own death and thus prevent an actual enactment—appropriately vicarious because if he were to die as these vicarious substitutes die, he would die in as careful, meticulous, and controlled a fashion as he brings to collecting grasshoppers at just the right time and place and to fishing the river in just the right spots. Thus he could take his own life in a fashion completely opposite from how it could have ended at war—randomly perhaps, at the hands of others, violently, bloodily, in the midst of the chaos of battle. He could take it quietly and cleanly, the cool stream washing over his lifeless form and cleansing his bones as Quentin imagines the water cleansing the tissue of a drowned leaf as it does of a drowned man (116), the "water peaceful" as the life of a man returned from war certainly is not (172). But having taken his life vicariously by taking the lives of the creatures he identifies with, Nick has lessened the pressure to carry out such a death. The Big Two-Hearted River where Nick fishes may be a river of life, but as Flora has noted, it is also a river of death (173). Life and death are its two hearts. Nick benefits from both.

Consciously or unconsciously, Nick knows he is not ready to face the great secondary issues before him, the "other needs" he has left behind (179). To do so now will rush his sensations and perhaps draw him closer to what may be his primary issue, an impulse toward self-destruction. First he must gain as full control as he can over his world and over himself. He is beginning to do so on this retreat. If he can thus restore himself, he will be strong enough to face life's swamps in due course. Once restored, in the "days coming," Nick will be ready to "fish the swamp" (212), facing his remaining trauma from the past tragedy of the war as well as new difficulties and issues, both with as much self-control as he can muster, even like the trout "keeping themselves steady" in the torrent of the stream under the Seney bridge (177), even with grace under pressure. Nick seems to know that he needs more than an hour or a day to recover from trauma, particularly the trauma of war, before he can finally reach the "far-off hills of the height of land" (180).

IV. Faulkner's Last Word

Faulkner repeatedly acknowledged that he was a literary thief. Critics now include him "among the reivers" that populate the literary world from the Greeks to our own time (Urgo 13). So it is never surprising to find Faulkner's thefts popping up. I have wondered, for example, whether the Popeye-Temple-Red triangle in *Sanctuary* (1931) is a dark parody of the Jake Barnes-Lady Brett-Romero triangle in *The Sun Also Rises* (1926), both triangles featuring an impotent male, a sexually charged female, and a surrogate for the impotent male. Other critics have long seen the "Wild Palms" section of *If I Forget Thee, Jerusalem* (1938) as Faulkner's response to *A Farewell to Arms* (1929), turning the Henry-Catherine love story into his Harry-Charlotte love story and in the process "correcting" Hemingway. William Van O'Connor, for example, argues that Faulkner's novel suggests that Faulkner disagrees with Hemingway's implicit premise that "society destroys love" and claims instead that "love is itself destructive" (214). I argue that Faulkner did not wait until that point to reive Hemingway's work. His earlier, perhaps his first, argument with Hemingway is in the Quentin section of *The Sound and the Fury,* and it is not about love but about the past. If Hemingway seems confident that Nick can leave behind all that wounded him, regain the control he lost in the war, and "move on with his life," as modern pop-counseling advises, Faulkner is not so sure Nick or anyone else can do so. Faulkner sees the past as far too permanent to be simply left behind, far too powerful. When Bleikasten writes that Faulkner sees the past as a "torture chamber" where memories are "recollected in fever and pain" rather than "in tranquility" (53), he could have used Quentin and Nick to embody those opposite poles. By 1929, Faulkner would be as familiar with Fitzgerald's 1925 volume as he was with Hemingway's, and he would agree with the assertion Fitzgerald ends *The Great Gatsby* with: that though we may beat on against the current aiming at the green light of the future, we are nevertheless "borne back ceaselessly into the past" (121). Faulkner put that truth into his own words in 1951 when he had Gavin Stevens assure Temple that the "past is never dead. It's not even past" (*Requiem* 92). In creating Quentin, then, not only may Faulkner have recognized the suicidal element in Nick that other readers took decades to recognize, but he may also have been correcting Hemingway's simple vision of a very complex human issue, our personal and social traumas and their persistence through time.

Works Cited

Benson, Jackson J. "Quentin Compson: Self-Portrait of a Young Artist's Emotions." *Critical Essays on William Faulkner: The Compson Family*, edited by Arthur F. Kinney, G.K. Hall, 1982, pp. 214-30.

Bleikasten, André. *The Ink of Melancholy: Faulkner's Novels from* The Sound and the Fury *to* Light in August. Indiana UP, 1990.

Brogger, Fredrik. "Whose Nature?: Differing Narrative Perspectives in 'Big Two-Hearted River.'" *Hemingway and the Natural World*, edited by Robert E. Fleming, U of Idaho P, 1999, pp. 19-30.

Cirino, Mark. "Hemingway's 'Big Two-Hearted River': Nick's Strategy and the Psychology of Mental Control." *Papers on Language and Literature: A Journal for Scholars and Critics of Language and Literature*, vol. 47, no. 2, Spring 2011, pp. 115-40.

Faulkner, William. *Requiem for a Nun*. Random House, 1951.

—. *The Sound and the Fury*. 1929. Vintage, 1990.

Fitzgerald, F. Scott. *The Great Gatsby*. Scribner's, 1925.

Flora, Joseph. *Hemingway's Nick Adams*. Louisiana State UP, 1982.

Fowler, Doreen. "Revising *The Sound and the Fury: Absalom, Absalom!* and Faulkner's Postmodern Turn." *Faulkner and Postmodernism: Faulkner and Yoknapatawpha 1999*, edited by John N. Duvall and Ann J. Abadie, UP of Mississippi, 2002, pp. 95-108.

Fruscione, Joseph. *Faulkner and Hemingway: Biography of a Literary Rivalry*. Ohio State UP, 2012.

Hagood, Taylor. *Faulkner's Imperialism: Space, Place, and the Materiality of Myth*. Louisiana State UP, 2008.

Hemingway, Ernest. "Big Two-Hearted River." 1925. *In Our Time*, Scribner's, 1955, pp. 177-212.

Hudenko, William, Beeta Homaifar, and Hal Wortzel. "The Relationship between PTSD and Suicide." United States Department of Veterans Affairs. PTSD: National Center for PTSD. 13 July 2015 http://www.ptsd.va.gov/professional/co-occurring/ptsd-suicide.asp.

Kartiganer, Donald. "'Getting Good at Doing Nothing': Faulkner, Hemingway, and the Fiction of Gesture." *Faulkner and His Contemporaries: Faulkner and Yoknapatawpha 2002*, edited by Joseph R. Urgo and Ann J. Abadie, UP of Mississippi, 2004. 54-73.

Lamb, Robert Paul. *Art Matters: Hemingway, Craft, and the Creation of the Modern Short Story*. Louisiana State UP, 2010.

—. "The Currents of Memory: Hemingway's 'Big Two-Hearted River' as Metafiction." *Ernest Hemingway and the Geography of Memory*, edited by Mark Cirino and Mark Ott, Kent State UP, 2010, pp. 166-85.

—. *The Hemingway Short Story: A Study in Craft for Writers and Readers*. Louisiana State UP, 2013.

Lynn, Kenneth. "The Troubled Fisherman." *New Critical Approaches to the Short Stories of Ernest Hemingway*, edited by Jackson J. Benson, Duke UP, 1990, pp. 149-55.

Moddelmog, Debra. "The Unifying Consciousness of a Divided Conscience: Nick Adams as Author of *In Our Time*." *American Literature*, vol. 60, no. 4, Dec. 1988, pp. 591-610.

O'Connor, William Van. "Faulkner's One-Sided 'Dialogue' with Hemingway." *College English*, vol. 24, Dec. 1962, pp. 208-15.

Polk, Noel. *Children of the Dark House: Text and Context in Faulkner.* UP of Mississippi, 1996.

—. *Faulkner and Welty and the Southern Literary Tradition.* UP of Mississippi, 2008.

Reynolds, Michael. *Hemingway: The Paris Years.* Basil Blackwell, 1989.

Ross, Stephen M. and Noel Polk. *Reading Faulkner*: The Sound and the Fury. UP of Mississippi, 1996.

Sensibar, Judith. *Faulkner and Love.* Yale UP, 2009.

Singal, Daniel. *William Faulkner: The Making of a Modernist.* U of North Carolina P, 1997.

Smith, Ronald. "Nick Adams and Post-Traumatic Stress Disorder." *War, Literature, and the Arts: An International Journal of the Humanities*, vol. 9, no. 1, Spring/Summer 1997, pp. 39-48.

Tebbetts, Terrell. "Postmodern Criticism." *A Companion to Faulkner Studies*, edited by Charles A. Peek and Robert W. Hamblin, Greenwood, 2004, pp. 125-61.

Urgo, Joseph. "Introduction: Reiving and Writing." *The Faulkner Journal*, vol. 13 no. 1-2, 1997/98, pp. 3-14.

Yuko Yamamoto

From Hemingway to Faulkner via Evans: "One Trip Across," "Sepulture South," and the Visual Aesthetics of Writing

We talk about Faulkner and Hemingway as Modernist contemporaries but seldom if ever consider their relationship in tandem with the photographer Walker Evans. Despite the continuing interest in the visual aesthetics of both writers, the influence of photography on their artistic development is rarely explored. Compared to the relatively well-documented impact of modern paintings on Faulkner and Hemingway, the influence of photography on their works and lives remains obscure at best, and thus calls for further investigation.[1] Just as Lincoln Kirstein says, "Walker Evans' eye . . . finds corroboration in the poet's voice" (194); Evans' photographs were given an afterlife in the works of Hemingway and Faulkner, in 1934 and 1954 respectively. With a keepsake of forty-six photographs taken by Evans in Havana, Hemingway wrote his first Cuban story "One Trip Across" (1934). Twenty years later, given a black-and-white photograph made by Evans, Faulkner wrote the short story "Sepulture South: Gaslight" (1954).

Taking these little-known instances as its point of departure, this essay attempts to explore the visual-verbal interplay that manifests itself in the works of Hemingway and Faulkner through the lens of Evans' photographs. An analysis of verbal-visual dialectics in their works yields an unexpected, though mediated, dialogue between Hemingway and Faulkner. Written at crucial junctures in their careers, Hemingway's "One Trip Across" and Faulkner's "Sepulture South" demonstrate each author's common aesthetic experiment in documentary. Moreover, from the analysis emerges the dynamics of print culture that prompted indirect collaboration among Modernists within the publishing industry.

I. The Documentary Style of Hemingway via Evans: Havana, 1933

Hemingway biographers tend to regard the spring of 1933 as uneventful in Hemingway's life. Hemingway stayed in Havana from April 13 to July 20 (Baker 244). They do not record much of his activity during this time, other than his girlfriend Jane Mason's car accident on May 24 and her subsequent attempted suicide in early June.[2] Even the first book-length study on Hemingway and Cuba, Grimes and Sylvester's *Hemingway, Cuba, and the Cuban Works* (2014), otherwise very informative and innovative, does not reference Hemingway's encounter with Evans in Cuba in late May and early June.

Walker Evans, then a 29-year-old budding photographer, who provided in 1930 three illustrative photographs for Hart Crane's *The Bridge* (1930) published by the Black Sun Press, was in Cuba at this time because he had been appointed to provide photographs to accompany Carleton Beals' *The Crime of Cuba* (1933), a political exposé of the Machado administration. Evans arrived in Havana in late May, and soon met Hemingway, who was sojourning in Havana, working, drinking, and fishing.[3]

Their stay overlapped for three weeks, and they never met again. Yet, in later years, they both recalled each other fondly. Evans, whose first ambition was to be a writer and who was a great admirer of Hemingway, reminisced about their shared experience almost forty years later in 1971: "I had a wonderful time with Hemingway. Drinking every night. He was at loose ends . . . and he needed a drinking companion, and I filled that role for two weeks" (qtd. in Mellow, *Walker Evans* 179). Hemingway's recollection of Evans is a bit more specific. In his letters to Harvey Breit, dated July 4 and 20, 1952, Hemingway wrote: "I remember clearest what a nice kid he was and takeing [sic] his pictures, or copies of them, across in the old Anita to Key West; We were both working against Machado at the time."[4] The meaning of Hemingway's cryptic remark became apparent in 2002, when the forty-six photographs were identified as authentic Walker Evans prints. They were among the miscellaneous items left in the storage room of the famous bar that Hemingway frequented in Key West, Sloppy Joe's.[5]

As Hemingway's memory attests, in 1933, Evans entrusted Hemingway with the task of bringing his forty-six photographic prints safely back to the United States, probably out of fear of their being confiscated in politically turbulent Cuba. His fear proved unfounded, and Evans never claimed his prints. He might have considered the prints to be the security for the twenty-five dollars he borrowed from Hemingway in order to stay longer in Cuba.[6] In any case, with those visual images in his grasp, Hemingway wrote his first Harry Morgan story, "One Trip Across," which would appear in the April 1934 issue of *Cosmopolitan*.

Given the fact that Hemingway could replenish his memory with concrete and precise visual images while writing his first Cuban story, it comes as no surprise that the whole passage of "One Trip Across" is dominated by visual imagery. In the opening paragraph, the camera eye of the first-person narrator records his vision in "cinematic objectivity," switching his focus from the dock, to the fountain in the square, to the surrounding buildings, and to the café (Kurt 86); the story begins with a cinematic scene as if captured by a panning camera. As if to indicate the direct influence of Evans' photographs on Hemingway's writings of Cuba, the famous opening line, "You know how it is there early in the morning in Havana with the bums still asleep against the walls of the buildings," perfectly describes Evans' photograph of a sleeping beggar (Figure 1). The unpublished portfolio created by Evans not only inspired Hemingway's "One Trip Across," but it also left a lasting impression on Hemingway in the way that it spurred the "shift" or "conversion" many detect in Hemingway's writing of the 1930s.[7] To Hemingway, searching for a new direction, Evans' aesthetic approach to political matters was quite an inspiration.

The subjects of the forty-six photographs are what Evans thought of as typically Cuban: street vendors, beggars, people taking a *siesta*, outdoor kitchens, the city crowds, palm trees, and the harbor. To accentuate the poverty and political unrest of Cuba, Evans inserted pictures of distressed families, shanties, people on the breadline, patrolling policemen, and newsboys. Probably to amuse Hemingway the *aficionado*, he even included a folk mural picture of a picador and a matador.[8] Added to these vernacular Cuban scenes, however, is a series of "appropriated" newspaper photographs which Evans, using his own camera, photographically copied from the Havana press archive.[9] These recycled documentary photographs, "traumatic photographs" or "shock photos" (Bear 233), disrupt the cohesive sequence of Evans' original photographs that capture the liveliness of everyday Cuba.

Figure 1 Walker Evans, A Sleeping Beggar. Image copyright © The Metropolitan Museum of Art. Image courtesy of the Betty and Toby Bruce Archive.

It is exactly the point of Evans' portfolio, of course, to show that the fatal violence inflicted upon the youth under the Machado regime suddenly destroys the normal pace of ordinary lives.[10] Hemingway seems to have taken heed of the shock effects of the portfolio, as "One Trip Across" also features such instances of violent disruption, where dead, mutilated bodies abruptly surface in the storyline. The two overwhelmingly violent incidents in the story, the shooting of the three young resistance group members and the controversial murder of the Chinese broker by the protagonist, Harry,[11] stand out in the narrative to the extent that they were illustrated in the frontispiece of "One Trip Across" in *Cosmopolitan*, by Rockwell Kent and Harold von Schmidt (20-21). Indeed, the shadow of the newspaper photographs haunts the narrative of "One Trip Across."

Among the twelve newspaper photographs that Evans "appropriated" in the unpublished portfolio, one especially attests to the fact that Hemingway himself appropriated the Evans portfolio in his story. The exchange between Pancho and Harry regarding "a long tongue"—"You're not a *lengua larga*, are you?" and "I'm sure you've cut plenty people's throats" (*The Complete Short Stories of Ernest Hemingway* 382)—evoke Evans' photocopied newspaper photograph of a man with a stitched-throat (Figure 2). Here the sign in Spanish reads, "the ABC will give this death to those who talk" (Estrada 195). This haunting image even takes a material shape in the story in the form of a fictional photograph which Harry receives as a death threat: "It was a close-up picture of the head and chest of a dead nigger with his throat cut clear across from ear to ear and then stitched up neat and a card on his chest saying in Spanish: "This is what we do to lenguas largas" (*The Complete Short Stories of Ernest Hemingway* 399). The passage reveals the direct influence of Evans' "appropriated" press photographs as well as Hemingway's "documentary impulse to picture the environment in whole."[12]

Hemingway's experiment in the documentary mode attains a heightened visibility during his career in the 1930s, which is also considered to be the time of his political phase.[13] Already in 1932, Hemingway himself had made his own portfolio of one-hundred and twelve black-and-white photographs that he carefully selected and sequenced for the nonfiction book, *Death in the Afternoon* (Trogdon 110). He also provided photographs for his articles in *Esquire* and *Ken* and participated in the documentary propaganda film *The Spanish Earth* (1937), where the war footage was interwoven into rural scenes of the Spanish countryside. Probably, the most direct influence of Evans' portfolio is felt in his appropriation of atrocity photography to alarm the reader in his article on the Spanish Civil War, "Dying, Well or Badly," for the April 21, 1938 issue of *Ken*. Hemingway provided six graphic photographs of dead soldiers, which he acquired and sent from Spain "to accompany" the text (Rodenberg 81). Hemingway warns the reader: "those pictures are what you will look like if we let the next war come" (qtd. in Rodenberg 83). The juxtaposition of the text and the photographs designates a mixture of Modernist aesthetic and documentary reportage. Hemingway's underestimated works of the 1930s can best be understood from the vantage point of "documentary modernism," where "formally

innovative experimentalism and naturalistic explorations of everyday life" converge (Miller 226). It was this converging of stylistic
experimentation and documentary representation that characterized
both Hemingway and Evans in Havana in 1933.

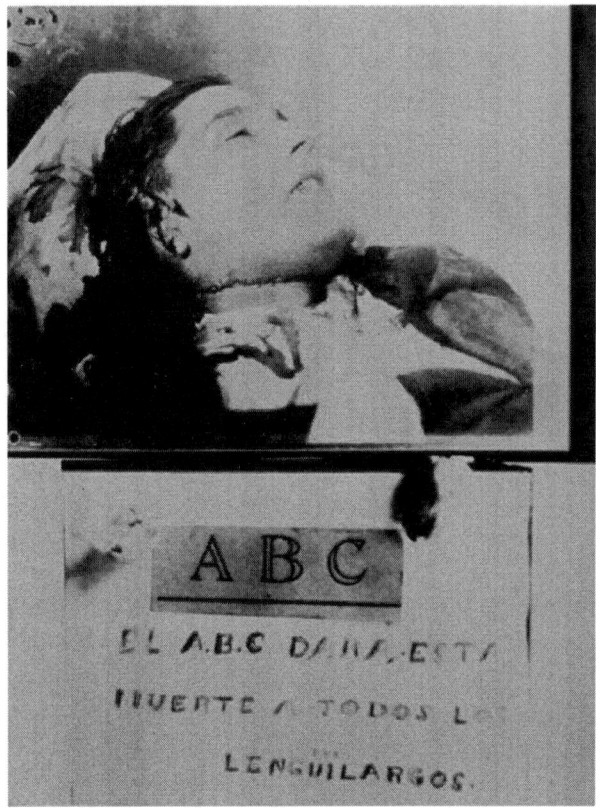

Figure 2 Walker Evans, The Newspaper Photograph of a Man with a Stitched-throat.
Image copyright © The Metropolitan Museum of Art. Image courtesy of Toby and Betty
Bruce Archive.

Oftentimes, Hemingway ostensibly enforced the boundary that
critics have delineated between his fictional stories as "high" literature and nonfictional articles as "base" journalism;[14] however, his
works in the 1930s show his attempt to bridge the link between art
and politics in a mixed-media format of text and photographs. Just as
Evans' "appropriated" press photographs disrupt the sequence of the
Cuban vernacular scenes and testify to the "terrors of horror" that

Cuban citizens faced daily, Hemingway's overwhelmingly violent scenes disturb the narrative cohesion and bring the Cuban political context to the fore. Over the dead bodies lies Hemingway's attempt to combine politics and art in aesthetic form. The dead, mutilated bodies in Hemingway's works in the thirties not only carry a political message, but also embody Hemingway's experiment in aesthetic documentary. Thus, what Hemingway appropriated from Evans was not just the visual images that he was able to transcribe verbally, but Evans' aesthetic approach to the overtly political assignment. The chance encounter with Evans in 1933 determined the course of Hemingway's new direction in the thirties.

II. The Documentary Style of Faulkner via Evans: The South Revisited

Faulkner and Evans are both renowned for their takes on the American South in the thirties. Faulkner is best remembered for his fictional portrayals of southern families in *The Sound and the Fury* (1929), *As I Lay Dying* (1930), *Light in August* (1932), and *Absalom, Absalom!* (1936) and Evans for his depression-era portraits of Alabama sharecropper families taken as part of the *Fortune* assignment with James Agee in 1936, many of which would later be included in the portfolio of *Let Us Now Praise Famous Men* (1941). Evans and Agee acknowledge, in the Notes to *Let Us Now Praise Famous Men*, the work of Faulkner as its foremost source of inspiration: "Suggested: Detail of gesture, landscape, costume, air, action, mystery, and incident throughout the writings of William Faulkner" (449). Thirteen years later, it was Faulkner's turn to be inspired by an Evans' work, a less well-known interaction between Faulkner and Evans that occurred at a time of historic developments in print culture in the fifties.

In the spring of 1954, Faulkner was given an Evans photograph by the literary critic and writer Anthony West. When Faulkner's semi-autographical story "Sepulture South" appeared in the December 1954 issue of *Harper's Bazaar*, it was accompanied by a full-page plate of a black-and-white photograph by Evans, which had inspired the story.[15] The picture that Faulkner biographers never attempted to identify was one of the four variants of the "Wooldridge Family Monument, Mayfield, Kentucky," completed in 1947 at Maplewood

Cemetery (Figure 3).[16] It captures a collection of eighteen life-sized statues of humans and animals, at the center of which is Colonel Henry G. Wooldridge's marble monument atop a pedestal. The accompanying photograph attests to the fact that the work of Evans had once prompted Faulkner to write a story and, to whatever extent, affected its production: "'Sepulture South' is a documented case of Faulkner's being influenced by photography, more specifically, by a work by Walker Evans" (Keller 335). Indeed, the accompanying Evans photograph defines both the form and the content of Faulkner's magazine story.

Figure 3 Walker Evans, Wooldridge Family Monument, Mayfield, Kentucky. Image copyright © The Metropolitan Museum of Art. Image source: Art Resource, NY.

The juxtaposition of Faulkner's text and Evans' photograph on the pages of a women's magazine is indicative of Faulkner's experiment in mixed-media format documentary in the fifties. Faulkner's experiment in the interplay of visual and verbal started very early in his career, in 1920, with the one-act play, *The Marionettes* (1975), where he illustrated ten images to accompany the text. Faulkner even considered adopting this technique more elaborately later in his career. In a letter to Robert Haas, Faulkner explains his idea about writing his memoirs as "half-fiction" with the aid of the visual:

> I am thinking about writing my memoirs. That is, it will be a book in the shape of a biography but actually about half fiction, chapters resembling essays about dogs and horses and family niggers and kin, chapters based on actual happenings but "improved" where fiction would help, which will probably be short stories. *I would like to use some photographs. Maybe some of my own drawings.* It would probably run about novel length, it will ramble some but will mostly be confined between Rowan Oak, my home in town here, and the farm, Greenfield. What do you think of the idea? (Blotner, *Selected Letters of William Faulkner* 320-21; my italics)

Faulkner never wrote a memoir. It was only in his later years that the concept was reshaped in the semi-autobiographical stories "Mississippi" (*Holiday*, April 1954), "Sepulture South: Gaslight" (*Harper's Bazaar*, December 1954), and his last work, *The Reivers* (1962). Only in "Sepulture South" does a photograph accompany his text as he wished. The Evans plate in *Harper's Bazaar* is a proof that Faulkner in the fifties, a time when many considered his writings were on the decline, was indeed still experimenting with an aesthetic style that combined the verbal and the visual, the style he first tested in *The Marionettes*. "Sepulture South," the last-published short story, is an experimental work that demonstrates Faulkner's documentary style of the fifties.

Not only is the Evans photograph integral to the article's mixed-media format, but it also resonates with the story's theme of the endurance of the Southern tradition. As the title "Sepulture South" ostensibly denotes, the documentary fiction elaborates, or "improves" in a Faulknerian sense, the traditional Southern cemetery featured in the Evans photograph. This "semi-autobiographical" (Brodsky 65) story is based on the funeral of Faulkner's grandfather, John Wesley

Thompson Falkner, in March of 1922. Yet, the scene at St. Peter's Cemetery is "improved" by the fictional details corresponding to those in the scene captured in the black-and-white photograph by Evans:

> And now we could already see them, gigantic and white, taller on their marble pedestals than the rose-and-honeysuckle-choked fence, looming into the very trees themselves, the magnolias and cedars and elms, gazing forever eastward with their empty marble eyes—not symbols: not angels of mercy or winged seraphim or lambs or shepherds, but effigies of the actual people themselves as they had been in life, in marble now, durable, impervious, heroic in size, towering above their dust in the implacable tradition of our strong, uncompromising, grimly ebullient Baptist-Methodist Protestantism, carved in Italian stone by expensive Italian craftsmen and shipped the long costly way by sea back to become one more among the invincible sentinels guarding the temple of our Southern mores. (Faulkner, *Uncollected Stories* 453-54)

This passage is surely a tribute to Evans whose photograph became the germ of the story and accompanies the text, but Faulkner's visual imagery embellishes Evans' photographic scene by adding more details to it. The fence is now adorned with rose and honeysuckle, the trees grow taller and of more various kinds from magnolias and cedars, to elms, and the material from which all the effigies are made is upgraded from local sandstone to Italian marble. Faulkner superimposes his own vision onto the Evans photograph. Faulkner's visual imagination, evoked by the photograph, further expounds on its subject matter: the commemoration of the dead patriarch.

The focal point of the photograph as well as that of the story is the monument, the figure of patriarchy placed at the center of the plot. However, Faulkner's description of the central statue does not correspond to the details captured in Evans' photograph. The statue of Colonel Wooldridge riding on the horse is transformed into the familiar figure of Faulkner's great-grandfather:

> Grandfather too on his pedestal beside her, not as the soldier which he had been and as I wanted him, but—in the old hard unalterable tradition of apotheosis' apogee—the lawyer, parliamentarian, the orator which he was not: in frock coat, the bare head thrown back, the carven tome carved open in one carven hand and the other extended in the immemorial gesture of declamation. (Faulkner, *Uncollected Stories* 454-55)

This passage, of course, is a verbalized vision of the monument of William Clark Falkner at Ripley Cemetery. Interestingly, Faulkner was not composing this passage from his memory but revising a passage from *Sartoris* (1929), the first Yoknapatawpha book that Faulkner called his starting point:

> He stood on a stone pedestal, in his frock coat and bare-headed, one leg slightly advanced and one hand resting lightly on the stone pylon beside him. His head was lifted a little in that gesture of haughty pride which repeated itself generation after generation with a fateful fidelity, his back to the world and his carven eyes gazing out across the valley where his railroad ran, and the blue changeless hills beyond, and beyond that, the ramparts of infinity itself. (375)

In the 1956 *Paris Review* interview, he famously declared: "Beginning with *Sartoris* I discovered that my own little postage stamp of native soil was worth writing about and that I would never live long enough to exhaust it, and by sublimating the actual into apocryphal I would have complete liberty to use whatever talent I might have to its absolute top" (255). Thus, in the process of "sublimating the actual into apocryphal," of transforming Evans' photographic vision into his literary poetics, Faulkner was re-discovering his native South and his youthful self through the lens of Evans.

In 1954, Evans' photograph gave shape to Faulkner's experiment in documentary fiction, a fictional memoir that combines stylistic experimentation and documentary representation. Blending the Southern past with his own genealogy, coloring the documentary with the personal tint, Faulkner appropriated Evans' aesthetic method of adding lyric quality to "straight" documentary photographs. Gilles Mora notes that, after the post-WWII era, Evans, "who so hated nostalgia, now found himself in a situation where he had to look with a nostalgic eye on a disappearing world" (259). The same was true with Faulkner. According to James Ferguson, "'Sepulture South' conveys with warm nostalgia but without sentimentality the atmosphere and tonality of the distant past, of a childhood in the Deep South" (48). Faulkner and Evans, both firmly established as High Modernists after the war, in their attempts to frame the Southern patriarch, found themselves nostalgically gesturing toward the South of their youth. What Faulkner appropriated from Evans, then, was not just the visual image that he could freely adapt and embellish upon, but Evans' aesthetic style of lyric documentary. The chance encounter with the Evans photograph spurred Faulkner's experiment of "memoirs" in his later years.

What is more, the indirect collaboration of Faulkner and Evans on the pages of *Harper's Bazaar* is a perfect example of print culture's popularization of Modernism at the mid-century. Six years prior to "Sepulture South," Evans had taken a photograph of Colonel Falkner's Monument for a *Vogue* assignment (Figure 4). Evans' photo-essay "Faulkner's Mississippi" appeared in the October 1948 issue of *Vogue*, with his fourteen photographs accompanying a text that extensively quotes from Faulkner's fiction. The *Vogue* essay was intended to support Random House by promoting Faulkner's latest novel, *Intruder in the Dust* (1948). The indirect collaborations between Faulkner and Evans on the pages of women's magazines in 1948 and 1954 were made possible by the integrated marketing strategy of the publishing industry that aimed to promote High Modernists in America and around the world.[17] The photographs of the two colonels' monuments that appeared in *Vogue* and *Harper's Bazaar* respectively, taken a year apart in Kentucky and in Mississippi, commemorate the intersection of Faulkner and Evans as well-established Modernists. The fifties saw the paths of these Modernists converging in the mainstream.

Figure 4 Walker Evans, William Clark Falkner's Monument, Ripley, Mississippi. Image copyright © The Metropolitan Museum of Art. Image source: Art Resource, NY.

On a final note, the Evans photograph that inspired "Sepulture South" also took its own course, as if to show Evans himself was not immune to Faulkner's influence. The plate used in *Harper's Bazaar* was a negative image, a reversed image, of the Evans photograph. The change might have been made intentionally to conform with Faulkner's description of the effigies as having their eyes "forever gazing eastward."[18]

III. Conclusion: Hemingway, Faulkner, and the Visual Aesthetics of Writing

In terms of prose style, Hemingway and Faulkner go in opposite directions. Donald M. Kartiganer has succinctly opposed Hemingway's "art of exclusion" to Faulkner's "art of inclusion" (54). From early in their careers, as has been shown in studies on their rivalry[19] Hemingway and Faulkner themselves were conscious of their contrasting styles. However, their common exploration of documentary aesthetics in a mixed-media format sheds new light on their kinship. Indeed, in terms of the visual aesthetics of their writing, Hemingway and Faulkner, often believed to possess very opposite literary sensibilities, were kindred spirits.

Late in their careers, Faulkner and Hemingway arrived at a surprisingly similar conclusion as to a writer's mission and motivation. In interviews with *The Paris Review*, they both expressed what might be called their visual aesthetics of writing. Hemingway, in a 1958 interview with George Plimpton, stated of the fundamental aesthetics of his writing that "you make something through your invention that is not a representation but a whole new thing truer than anything true and alive, and you make it alive, and if you make it well enough, you give it immortality" (239). Hemingway's claim to be inventing something truer than real life was, in fact, anticipated by Faulkner two years earlier, in a 1956 interview with Jean Stein: "the aim of every artist is to arrest motion, which is life, by artificial means and hold it fixed so that a hundred years later, when a stranger looks at it, it moves again since it is life. Since man is mortal, the only immortality possible for him is to leave something behind him that is immortal since it will always move" (253). Both claim that they create their art in permanent life-like resemblance. Their diction—"you make something through your invention not a representation but a whole new thing truer than anything true and alive"; "the aim of every artist is to arrest motion . . . by artificial means and hold it fixed"—reveals that their common goal was to transcend what a modern optical invention, the camera, can do. Only Hemingway's aesthetics of writing is more akin to the visual aesthetics of motion pictures and Faulkner's to that of still photography.

Furthermore, Faulkner and Hemingway's visual aesthetics found a kindred spirit in a 1964 lecture delivered by Evans at Yale on his visual aesthetics that he termed "lyric documentary." According to Evans, lyric documentary can be found in certain painters, engravers, and writers. Among them, James Joyce, James Agee, and Vladimir Nabokov, all had the quality of lyric documentary, of "purity and a certain severity, rigor, simplicity, directness, clarity" ("Lyric Documentary" 106). Also, Evans once said of Henry James and James Joyce that they were "unconscious photographers."[20] He could have added the names of Hemingway and Faulkner to his list of visual writers. As early as 1938, Lincoln Kirstein foresaw this affinity between Evans and literary authors: "Walker Evans' eye is a poet's eye. It finds corroboration in the poet's voice" (194). An avid reader of Modernist writers, Evans found an affinity with the photographic eyes of the writers. In 1933 and 1952 respectively, Hemingway and Faulkner verbally endorsed Evans' photography.

The two Modernists' previously little-known indirect collaborations with Walker Evans, in Havana and in the American South, encapsulate the similar, if not identical, aesthetic concerns of Hemingway and Faulkner in their combination of stylistic experimentation and documentary representation. Just as the passage of "One Trip Across" is dominated by visual imagery, so, too, is "Sepulture South." Their visual aesthetics of writing was very much represented in "One Trip Across" and "Sepulture South," as it can be said that Hemingway's adaptation of Evans' photographs was cinematic and Faulkner's photographic. Here lies the difference between their visual aesthetics: Hemingway arranges several visual descriptions in cinematic sequence; Faulkner frames the story on one photographic still image. Both "One Trip Across" and "Sepulture South" show that Hemingway in the thirties and Faulkner in the fifties were attempting to bridge the gap between art and documentary. While Hemingway's formalistic experiment in the thirties was characterized by his political inclination, Faulkner's was more self-reflexive and retrospective. Much of the difference, however, reflects the spirit of the times rather than their artistic sensibilities, as Hemingway's writings in the fifties, published posthumously, were also heavily self-reflexive and retrospective while Faulkner's writings around 1930, in their economic and racial concerns, were arguably more politically engaged than they have traditionally been considered. Reflecting the cultural milieu of the periods in which they were written, Hemingway's "One Trip Across" shows his preemptive attempt to combine politics and art in a mixed-media format of text and photographs, which was the dominant form of expression of the thirties,[21] whereas Faulkner's "Sepulture South," in conjunction with his memoir project that was never fully realized in his lifetime, demonstrates his willingness to innovate in a mixed-media format documentary style that recycles his early works, at a time when the print industry was "re-discovering" High Modernists of the early twentieth century. Just as Hemingway's experiment in documentary art in the thirties was spurred on by the rise of graphic magazines, Faulkner's in the fifties was sponsored by the publishing industry. The works "One Trip Across" and "Sepulture South" evince the common documentary aesthetics of Hemingway and Faulkner, and, at the same time, bear witness to a historic moment in the development of Modernism in print culture from the thirties to the fifties.

After all, all three of them—Hemingway, Faulkner, and Evans—were contemporaries working loosely together in the same publishing industry. They themselves were a historical product of the print culture of their time. Yet, to quote Faulkner's famous words from *The Paris Review*, each of the three had his own way of "sublimating the actual into the apocryphal" (255).

Acknowledgements

This article simply would not have been possible without the generous assistance of several individuals and institutions. I wish to express my most sincere gratitude to Benjamin "Dink" Bruce, who has so generously allowed the two photographs (Figure 1 and 2) from the Toby and Betty Bruce Archive to be reproduced in this article; to Scott DeWolfe, DeWolfe & Wood Rare Books, who has kindly and patiently answered my email inquiries, arranged everything for me in the best possible way, and generously sent me a copy of the unpublished catalogue of the Evans-Hemingway photographs; and to Michael Brown, Michael Brown Rare Books, who has promptly sent me the two digitized photographic images from the Toby and Betty Bruce Archive to be reproduced in this article. I am also indebted to Cori Convertito, Curator at Key West Museum of Art and History, who kindly referred me to Scott DeWolfe; and to Meredith Reiss, Collections Manager of the Department of Photography at the Metropolitan Museum of Art, who provided valuable assistance in the course of my research on the interaction between Evans and Faulkner. I also thank the Metropolitan Museum of Art for permission to reproduce Walker Evans images in this article and Art Resource for providing the two high-resolution images (Figure

3 and 4). This work was supported by JSPS Grant-in-Aid for Scientific Research (KAKENHI), Grant Numbers 15K02346 and 15K02368.

Notes

1. Faulkner and the visual, though far from neglected, has attracted a relatively small number of scholars, who focus on drawings, paintings, and film: for book-length studies, see Hönnighausen, Waid, and Lurie; for articles, among others, see Adams, Broughton, Wilhelm, and those edited in Fowler and Abadie, in Kartiganer and Abadie, and in Murphet and Solomon. On Faulkner and photography, see Henninger, Sensibar, and elsewhere in Watson. Hemingway and the visual arts is a well-explored topic, as he famously declared his indebtedness to painters, especially to Paul Cézanne; see Watts, Narbeshuber, Hegemann. On the topic of Hemingway and photography, an insightful observation, particularly relevant to this paper, is made by Zoe Trodd: "across Hemingway's work are the threads of both a one-shot photograph aesthetic and a multi-shot film aesthetic" (13).

2. Meyers 245-46. All biographers of Hemingway, except James R. Mellow, omit or overlook the 1933 encounter of Hemingway and Evans in Cuba.

3. So far the most extensive accounts of Hemingway and Evans meeting in Cuba are found in Mellow, *Hemingway* 425-26, Mellow, *Walker Evans* 179-83, and Estrada 193-95. A reference to the encounter can be found in Chamberlin 126 and Paul 130-31.

4. Breit, Harvey; 1950-1958; Carlos Baker Collection of Ernest Hemingway, Box 1 Folder 20-21; Manuscripts Division, Department of Rare Books and Special Collections, Princeton University Library.

5. See Carlson.

6. Hemingway "loaned $25.00" to Evans in Cuba; see "Ernest Hemingway and Walker Evans: Three Weeks in Cuba, 1933."

7. For the stylistic changes in Hemingway's writing of the 1930s, see

Ott, Shiflet and Curnutt, and Fenstermaker.

8. From the unpublished catalog, *Walker Evans: Ernest Hemingway, Havana, 1933*, Michael Brown Rare Books and De Wolfe and Wood, 2016.

9. See Mora 16-18. For insightful analyses of these "appropriated" photographs, see Bear, Tagg, and Kent.

10. Evans ascribed supreme importance to the sequence of his portfolios. He chose 64 from the 442 photographs he took in Cuba for the portfolio of *The Crime of Cuba* and requested the publisher "to leave the pictures in [his] order" (qtd. in Tagg 81).

11. Harry's murder of Mr. Sing has perplexed many critics, and many would agree with Stephen Cooper: "He turns to crime a little too quickly to make his claims of economic necessity completely convincing" (77).

12. Ott 147. Ott's study on the Anita fish log demonstrates that Hemingway "recycled" (152) his own visual description of the Gulf Stream in "One Trip Across." Also, according to Richard Grimes, in writing *To Have and Have Not*, "Hemingway asked journalist Richard Armstrong to provide him with a summary of detailed newspaper accounts of the uprising" and appropriated Armstrong's letter "sometimes almost verbatim" (75). Those findings prove Hemingway's documentary impulse in the thirties. However, one can only speculate as to why Hemingway changed the racial identity of the dead Evans photographed with the ABC sign. He may have conflated this image with another photograph that features a close-up of a bandaged face of a black man. Of the twelve "appropriated" newspaper photographs, eight images have the postmortem body as their subjects and three prints feature that of a black person.

13. For Hemingway's contested political views, see Cooper, Fleming, Kinnamon, and Rodenberg. Although Jeffrey Meyers states that "[t]he Spanish Civil War intensified his political convictions and led to a gesture of social commitment in *To Have and Have Not*" (267) and that "[a]fter several unsuccessful works in the 1930s,

the war in Spain turned him toward a truer source of inspiration" (296-97), I maintain that the true inspiration that later merged to Hemingway's compassion for Spain was Cuba, where he lived for over twenty years.

14. For example, J. F. Kobler states that "unquestionably Hemingway always rated journalism as a less significant, more facile kind of writing than fiction" (2).

15. See page 85. The most extensive accounts of the Evans photograph being the source of Faulkner's "Sepulture South" are those of Keller (334-35), Mellow *Walker Evans* (515-16), and Blotner (1516-17).

16. James R. Mellow claims that the Wooldridge photographs, presumed circa 1945, were made in 1947 (*Walker Evans* 509-10). Detailed accounts of the Wooldridge family monument can be found in Reigler.

17. For the elevation of Faulkner's status in post-war print culture, see Schwartz.

18. Faulkner, *Uncollected Stories* 455. For other possible interpretations of the reversal, see Keller 337.

19. On the Faulkner-Hemingway rivalry, see Monteiro, Fruscione, and Rovit and Waldhorn.

20. Interview of Walker Evans conducted by Paul Cummings for the Archives of American Art, Smithsonian Institution, on Oct. 13-Dec. 23, 1971.

21. See Allred.

Works Cited

Adams, Richard P. "The Apprenticeship of William Faulkner." *William Faulkner: Four Decades of Criticism*, edited by Linda Welshimer Wagner, Michigan State UP, 1973, pp. 7-44.

Agee, James, and Walker Evans. *Let Us Now Praise Famous Men: Three Tenant Families.* 1941. Houghton Mifflin, 2001.

Allred, Jeff. *American Modernism and Depression Documentary.* Oxford UP, 2010.

Baker, Carlos. *Ernest Hemingway: A Life Story.* Charles Scribner's Sons, 1969.

Beals, Carleton. *The Crime of Cuba: with 31 Aquatone Illustrations from Photographs by Walker Evans.* J. B. Lippincott Company, 1933.

Bear, Jordan. "In the Morgue: Censorship, Taste and the Politics of Visual Circulation in Walker Evans's Cuba Portfolio." *Visual Resources*, vol. 23, no. 3, 2007, pp. 221-43.

Blotner, Joseph. *Faulkner: A Biography.* Vol. 2, Random House, 1974.

—, editor. *Selected Letters of William Faulkner.* Random House, 1977.

Brodsky, Louis Daniel. "Faulkner's Wounded Art: The Aftermath of Hollywood and World War II." *Faulkner Journal*, vol. 2, no. 2, 1987, pp. 55-66.

Broughton, Panthea Reid. "Faulkner's Cubist Novels." *"A Cosmos of My Own": Faulkner and Yoknapatawpha, 1980*, edited by Doreen Fowler and Ann J. Abadie, UP of Mississippi, 1981, pp. 59–94.

Carlson, Coralie. "When the Have Met the Have-Not." *Washington Post*, 9 May 2004, p. D01.

Chamberlin, Brewster. *The Hemingway Log: A Chronology of His Life and Times.* UP of Kansas, 2015.

Cooper, Stephen. *The Politics of Ernest Hemingway.* U of Michigan Research P, 1987.

Curnutt, Kirk and Gail D. Sinclair, editors. *Key West Hemingway: A Reassessment.* UP of Florida, 2009.

"Ernest Hemingway and Walker Evans: Three Weeks in Cuba, 1933." Resource Library, Traditional Fine Arts Organization, www.tfaoi.com/aa/7aa/7aa121.htm. Accessed 28 July 2015.

Estrada, Alfredo Jose. *Havana. Autobiography of a City.* Palgrave Macmillan, 2007.

Evans, Walker. "Faulkner's Mississippi." *Vogue,* Oct. 1948, pp. 144-49.

—. "'Lyric Documentary': An Illustrated Transcript of a Lecture by Walker Evans Presented at Yale University, March 11, 1964." *Walker Evans and the Picture Postcard.* Edited by Jeff L. Rosenheim, Steidl/Metropolitan Museum of Art, 2009, pp. 103-24.

—. "Oral history interview with Walker Evans, 1971 Oct. 13-Dec. 23." Archives of American Art, Smithsonian Institution, www.aaa.si.edu/collections/interviews/oral-history-interview-walker-evans-11721. Accessed 26 April 2016.

—. *Walker Evans: Ernest Hemingway, Havana, 1933.* Michael Brown Rare Books and De Wolfe and Wood, 2016.

Faulkner, William. "Interview with Jean Stein vanden Heuvel [*The Paris Review* Interview]." *Lion in the Garden: Interviews with William Faulkner, 1926–1962.* Edited by James B. Meriwether and Michael Millgate, Random, 1968, pp. 237-56.

—. *Sartoris.* Harcourt, 1929.

—. "Sepulture South: Gaslight." *Uncollected Stories of William Faulkner.* Edited by Joseph Blotner, Vintage, 1981, pp. 449-55.

—. "Sepulture South: Gaslight." *Harper's Bazaar,* Dec. 1954, pp. 84-85, 140-41.

—. *The Marionettes.* UP of Virginia for the Bibliographical Society of the U of Virginia, 1977.

Fenstermaker, John J. "Why *Esquire*?: The Multiple Voices of Hemingway's Complex Public Persona." Curnutt and Sinclair, pp. 206-19.

Ferguson, James. *Faulkner's Short Fiction.* U of Tennessee P, 1991.

Fleming, Robert E. "Politics." Moddelmog and Gizzo, pp. 287-96.

Fowler, Doreen and Ann J. Abadie, editors. *Faulkner, Modernism, and Film: Faulkner and Yoknapatawpha, 1978.* UP of Mississippi, 1979.

Fruscione, Joseph. *Faulkner and Hemingway: Biography of a Literary Rivalry*. Ohio State UP, 2015.

Grimes, Larry. "Introduction to The State of Things in Cuba: A Letter to Hemingway." Grimes and Sylvester, pp.75-76.

Grimes, Larry and Bickford Sylvester, editors. *Hemingway, Cuba, and the Cuban Works*. Kent State UP, 2014.

Hegemann, Meyly Chin. "Hemingway's Secret: Visual to Verbal Art." *Journal of Modern Literature*, vol. 7, no. 1, 1979, pp. 87-112.

Hemingway, Ernest. "Interview with Ernest Hemingway by George Plimpton." *Writers at Work: The Paris Review Interviews, Second Series*, edited by George Plimpton, Viking, 1963, pp. 215-40.

—. "One Trip Across." *The Complete Short Stories of Ernest Hemingway: The Finca Vigía Edition*. Charles Scribner's Sons, 1987, pp. 381-409.

—. "One Trip Across: A Complete Short Novel by Ernest Hemingway." *Cosmopolitan*, April 1934, pp. 20-23, 108-22.

Henninger, Katherine R. "Faulkner, Photography, and a Regional Ethics of Form." *Faulkner and Material Culture: Faulkner and Yoknapatawpha, 2004*, edited by Joseph R. Urgo and Ann J. Abadie, UP of Mississippi, 2007, pp. 121-38.

Hönnighausen, Lothar. *Faulkner: Masks and Metaphors*. UP of Mississippi, 1997.

Kartiganer, Donald M. "'Getting Good at Doing Nothing': Faulkner, Hemingway, and the Fiction of Gesture." *Faulkner and His Contemporaries: Faulkner and Yoknapatawpha, 2002*, edited by Joseph R. Urgo and Ann J. Abadie, UP of Mississippi, pp. 54-73.

Kartiganer, Donald M. and Ann J. Abadie, editors. *Faulkner and the Artist: Faulkner and Yoknapatawpha, 1993*, UP of Mississippi, 1996.

Keller, Judith. "Faulkner Country." *Walker Evans: The Getty Museum Collection*. J. Paul Getty Museum, 1995, pp. 329-337.

Kent, James Clifford. "Walker Evans's Psychogeographic Mapping of Havana, 1933." *History of Photography*, vol. 37, no. 3, 2013, pp. 326-40.

Kinnamon, Keneth. "Hemingway and Politics." *The Cambridge Companion to Ernest Hemingway*, edited by Scott Donaldson, Cambridge UP, 1996, pp. 149-69.

Kirstein, Lincoln. "Photographs of America: Walker Evans." *American Photographs*, by Walker Evans, The Museum of Modern Art, 1938, pp. 189–98.

Kobler, J. F. *Ernest Hemingway: Journalist and Artist*. UMI Research P, 1985.

Kurt, Maria. "Selection from 'It is hard for you to tell,' Chapter Three of Cuba y Hemingway en el gran río azul (Cuba and Hemingway on the Great Blue River)." Translated by Mary Delpino, Grimes and Sylvester, pp. 84-101.

Lurie, Peter. *Vision's Immanence: Faulkner, Film, and the Popular Imagination*. Johns Hopkins UP, 2004.

Mellow, James R. *Hemingway: A Life without Consequences*. Houghton Mifflin, 1992.

—. *Walker Evans*. Basic, 1999.

Meyers, Jeffrey. *Hemingway: A Biography*. Harper and Row, 1985.

Miller, Tyrus. "Documentary/Modernism: Convergence and Complementarity in the 1930s." *Modernism/modernity*, vol. 9, no. 2, 2002, pp. 226-41.

Moddelmog, Debra A. and Suzanne del Gizzo, editors. *Ernest Hemingway in Context*. Cambridge UP, 2013.

Monteiro, George. "The Faulkner-Hemingway Rivalry." *Faulkner and His Contemporaries: Faulkner and Yoknapatawpha, 2002*, edited by Joseph R. Urgo and Ann Abadie, UP of Mississippi, 2004, pp. 74-92.

Mora, Gilles. "Havana, 1933: A Seminal Work." Translated by

Christie McDonald. *Walker Evans: Havana 1933*, by Walker Evans, edited by Gilles Mora and sequenced by John T. Hill, Pantheon, 1989, pp. 8-24.

Murphet, Julian and Stefan Solomon, editors. *William Faulkner in the Media Ecology*. Louisiana State UP, 2015.

Narbeshuber, Lisa. "Visual Arts." Moddelmog and Gizzo, pp. 183-92.

Ott, Mark. "The Anita logs and *To Have and Have Not*: The Gulf Stream as Transcribed Experience." Curnutt and Sinclair, pp. 143-57.

Paul, Steve. "Tropical Iceberg: Cuban Turmoil in the 1930s and Hemingway's *To Have and Have Not*." Curnutt and Sinclair, pp. 129-42.

Reigler, Susan. "Mayfield: Remarkable monuments." *Courier-Journal* [Louisville, KY], 9 April 2006, p. L4.

Rodenberg, Hans-Peter. *The Making of Ernest Hemingway: Celebrity, Photojournalism and the Emergence of the Modern Lifestyle Media*. LIT Verlag, 2014.

Rovit, Earl and Arthur Waldhorn, editors. *Hemingway and Faulkner in Their Time*. Continuum, 2005.

Schwartz, Lawrence H. *Creating Faulkner's Reputation: The Politics of Modern Literary Criticism*. U of Tennessee P, 1988.

Sensibar, Judith L. "Faulkner's Fictional Photographs: Beyond Patriarchy?" *Out of Bounds: Male Writers and Feminist Inquiry*, edited by Laura Claridge and Elizabeth Langland, U of Massachusetts P, 1990, pp. 290-315.

Shiflet, E. Stone and Kirk Curnutt. "Letters and Literary Tourism: Hemingway as Your Key West Correspondent in 'The Sights of Whitehead Street.'" Curnutt and Sinclair, pp. 220-40.

Tagg, John. "Crime Story." *Photographies*, vol. 2, no. 1, 2009, pp. 79-102.

Trodd, Zoe. "Hemingway's Camera Eye: The Problem of Language and an Interwar Politics of Form." *The Hemingway*

Review, vol. 26, no. 2, 2007, pp. 7-21.

Trogdon, Robert W. *The Lousy Racket: Hemingway, Scribners, and the Business of Literature*. Kent State UP, 2007.

Wilhelm, Randall. "Pictures and Words in Faulkner's Early Graphic Work." *Fifty Years after Faulkner: Faulkner and Yoknapatawpha, 2012*, edited by Jay Watson and Ann J. Abadie, UP of Mississippi, 2016, pp. 107-21.

Waid, Candace. *The Signifying Eye: Seeing Faulkner's Art*. U of Georgia P, 2013.

Watson, James G. *William Faulkner: Self-Presentation and Performance*. U of Texas P, 2000.

Watts, Emily Stipes. *Ernest Hemingway and the Arts*. U of Illinois P, 1971.

Michael Wainwright

Authorial Irresponsibility: Hemingway's "The Battler" and Faulkner's "Barn Burning"[1]

This double function, this simultaneous proclamation and concealment, will be a principal theme of what follows, for I shall concern myself with the radiant obscurity of narratives.

> Frank Kermode, *The Genesis of Secrecy: On the Interpretation of Narrative* (47).

It is impossible to dissociate the greatest profit and the greatest privation.

> Jacques Derrida, *On the Name* (13).

Generally speaking, as interpolated from the debate concerning authorial influence and intertextuality, the terms "omission" and "inclusion" can be usefully applied to the respective compositional techniques of Ernest Hemingway (1899–1961) and William Faulkner (1897–1962). Three statements that span Hemingway's career establish, describe, and recapitulate his technique of omission. "You could omit anything," recalls Hemingway in *A Moveable Feast* (1964) of his literary practice in the 1920s, "if you knew that you omitted and the omitted part would strengthen the story and make people feel something more than they understood" (74). The iceberg analogy from *Death in the Afternoon* (1932) expanded on this definition. "If a writer of prose knows enough about what he is writing about," states Hemingway, "he may omit things that he knows[,] and the reader, if the writer is writing truly enough, will have a feeling of those things as strongly as though the writer had stated them. The dignity of movement of an iceberg is due to only one-eighth of it being above water" (192). Hemingway's technical recapitulation appears in the unpublished "The Art of the Short Story" (1959). "A few things I have found to be true," he avers. "If you leave out important things or events that you know about, the story is strengthened. If you leave out or skip something because you do not know it, the story will be worthless. The test of any story is how very good the stuff is that you, not your editors, omit."

Faulkner's technique of inclusion, which earns that description from juxtaposition with Hemingway's technique of omission, rather than from Faulkner himself, partially stems from his own advice. "Read, read, read," he asserted during his "Classroom Statements at the University of Mississippi" in 1947: "Read everything—trash, classics, good and bad, and see how they do it. Just like a carpenter who works as an apprentice and studies the master. Read! You'll absorb it. Then write. If it is good, you'll find out. If it's not, throw it out the window" (55). Faulkner was selective, as this quotation suggests, but inclusion rather than exclusion often prefigured his thoughts, and Hemingway certainly associated his contemporary with an unguardedly inclusive style. "My operatives tell me," he declares in *Death in the Afternoon*, "that through the fine work of Mr. William Faulkner publishers now will publish anything" (173). Often, as Joseph Fruscione documents, Hemingway's criticism of his coeval focused on Faulkner's "verbose, ornate style, and (over) productivity" (82). If Hemingway's technique produced the tip of the iceberg, with seven-eighths of his material a subliminal mass, then Faulkner's technique inverted the iceberg, with a supraliminal mass atop a submerged point.

Particularly speaking, however, as interpolated from the two authors' close but distinct reformulation of symbolist poetics, the economy of secrecy offers an alternative focus on their respective compositional techniques, an interpretive perspective that the debate concerning authorial influence and intertextuality has somewhat overlooked. In *Given Time* (1992), Jacques Derrida (1930–2004) not only discusses the socioeconomic prescience of Charles Baudelaire's (1821–67) "La fausse monnaie" ("Counterfeit Money") from *Le Spleen de Paris* (or *Petits poèmes en prose*) (1869), but also anticipates his own poststructuralist thoughts in *On the Name* (1995) concerning the relationship between the economy of secrecy and authorial irresponsibility. Retrospectively applying these contemplations to Baudelaire's prose poem—an exercise that Derrida does not undertake—at once invests in the speculation engendered by "La fausse monnaie" and recommends that analeptic application to texts with comparable *avant-la-lettre* tendencies, such as Hemingway's "The Battler" from *In Our Time* (1925), and Faulkner's "Barn Burning," which was originally published by *Harper's Magazine* (June 1939).

Critics agree that Baudelaire's prose poetry influenced both Hemingway and Faulkner. Baudelaire, as James D. Brasch outlines, was among the "19th Century poets with whom Hemingway was most seriously involved" (29), and "Faulkner's reading of Baudelaire," as Scott G. Williams traces, "influenced his writing" (72). Baudelaire's renown stems in part from *Les Fleurs du mal* (1857), with its foundation of literary symbolism. Hemingway, as Brasch and Joseph Sigman's manifest of his library shows (25), would eventually own four copies of this work. He probably acquired his earliest edition (Lévy's 1894 imprint) in Paris during the 1920s. "Faulkner," as Williams traces, "gorged himself on Baudelaire" (69) during his European sojourn of 1925. Most obviously, Faulkner would rework "La chambre double" from *Le Spleen de Paris* into "A Rose for Emily" (1930). Less obviously, as Michel Gresset remarks, Faulkner "absorbed" (51) stylistic nuances from Baudelaire's prose poetry.

Against common expectation, Jean Moréas's *Le Symbolisme* (1886), which codified the guidelines developed from Baudelaire's groundwork into a manifesto, preferences expression for the sake of expression, evocation rather than description, social detachment instead of social involvement, and the efficacy of economy before the effects of symbolism. The resultant indeterminate complex, which promotes what Richard Rorty would have called a poststructural "lubriciousness of the tangled" (126), and which characterizes both *Les Fleurs du mal* and *Le Spleen de Paris* throughout, requires a surrender of authorial control, and that submission necessarily partakes of the relationship between inviolable (or absolute) and revealable (or conditional) secrecy. Derrida's analysis of this relationship offers a means of gauging and interrogating the irresponsibility displayed by writers in surrendering authorial control. This irresponsibility, this willful submission to freedom of expression upholds at once the democratic rights of literature and the literary rights of democracy, withholding no subject from the author, but paradoxically and necessarily seeding lucidity with ambiguity—and this irresponsibility, this occlusion of transparency, this letting go before the reader is what guarantees Hemingway's works their place in (to appropriate Frank Kermode) "the secular canon"; that is, his writing is "of such value that every effort of exegesis is justified without argument, as it is in the cases of, say, Joyce and Faulkner" (5). A Derridean approach to the economy of secrecy and authorial irresponsibility, therefore, recommends itself to an interpretation of the manner in which Hemingway and Faulkner surrender control, as each author considers his protagonist's rite of passage, or movement toward the responsibility of self-authorship through the revelation of conditional secrets, in "The Battler" and "Barn Burning," respectively.

The inviolable secret connotes an open rather than a hidden truth and is, therefore, a paradoxical secret without secret. This obvious enigma, as Derrida expounds in *On the Name*, fills the reader with desire:

> When all hypotheses are permitted, groundless and *ad infinitum*, about the meaning of a text, or the final intentions of an author, whose person is no more represented than nonrepresented by a character or by a narrator, by a poetic or fictional sentence, which detaches itself from its presumed source and thus remains *locked away* [*au secret*], when there is no longer even any sense in making decisions about some secret behind the surface of a textual manifestation (and it is this situation which I would call text or trace), when it is the call [*appel*] of this secret, however, which points back to the other or to something else, when it is this itself which keeps our passion aroused, and holds us to the other, then the secret impassions us. (29)

The absolute secret, like an unbreakable code, encourages endless hypotheses of impassioned interpretation. Literary worth is the open secret of absolute secrecy against and allied to which the conditional secret inscribes a marked contrast. The condition of linguistic secrecy ensures that the revelation of a conditional secret cannot help but retain an inviolable level of secrecy: profit from exposure pointing toward privation from inviolability.

This curious relationship has political ramifications for Derrida. While absolute secrecy arises from a reserve of unfathomable information, conditional secrecy depends on a store of potential knowledge.[2] Proprietorship of a revealable secret privileges its owner with a power over others, and this surplus potential can support interpersonal structures of an undemocratic nature. Inviolable secrecy, however, as its openness suggests, cannot fall foul of individual speculation. "Through its aporetic structure," writes Alex Segal, absolute secrecy "displaces the use of (conditional) secrecy to attain power and is thereby tied to democracy" (190). This displacement makes literature a democratic form of expression: at one level, as explicitly promoted by *Le Symbolisme*, social detachment tends toward impersonality; at another level, as implicitly engaged with by all literature, the aporia of the inviolable secret, which connotes the gap between the actually communicated and the intended but inexpressible communication, separates a writer from his work. An author cannot decrypt the absolute mysteries of his texts anymore than a reader of those texts can. This absolute secrecy, as *On the Name* makes plain, is that "something *about*" literature that Derrida admires: "There is no passion without secret, this very secret, indeed no secret without this passion" (28). Breaking the power of mastery, breaking the obsession over personal identity, the inviolable secret offers literature as a form of gift, where gifting implies benevolence without return. Literature is an absolutely secret donation that thanks, or another form of payment, cannot repay.

Responsibly speaking, the essential affinity between the aporetic essences of literature and the gift both identifies a literary work with, and frees that work from, its author. In giving his name to a text, an author appears to feed his narcissism, but that appetite remains insatiable because that author is not his name. "Suppose that X, something or someone (a trace, a work, an institution, a child), bears your name, that is to say, your title," posits Derrida in *On the Name*. "The naive rendering or common illusion [*fantasme courant*] is that you have given your name to X, thus all that returns to X, in a direct or indirect way, in a straight or oblique line, *returns* to you, as a profit for your narcissism." But, cautions Derrida, "as you *are* not your name, nor your title, and given that, as the name or the title, X does very well without you or your life, that is, without the place toward which something could *return*—just as that is the definition and the very possibility of every trace, and of all names and all titles, so your narcissism is frustrated a priori by that from which it profits or hopes to profit" (12).

Both Hemingway and Faulkner experienced the narcissistic dilemma of authorship. Each man would win notable literary awards; each man would suffer mental privations. Summing up the psychological perspective, Christopher D. Martin posits Hemingway's "narcissistic personality traits" (351), while Michael Grimwood proffers Faulkner's life as "ample evidence of his narcissistic tendencies" (52). Faulkner would win the 1949 Nobel Prize for Literature; Hemingway would win the 1954 Nobel Prize for Literature; but both men would have recourse to electroconvulsive therapy (ECT) to expunge, rather than simply secrete, certain aspects of the psychological states that had earned them their laureateships.

Frighteningly for such psyches, which require, yet also fear, reception and recognition, literature can survive without authorship. Indeed, the unattributed work of logographers (or ghostwriters) and the secrecy of anonymous authors (or "anon") instantiate the durability of autonomous texts. "The ability to disappear *in your name*," maintains Derrida in *On the Name*, is what "returns to your name." The absolute secrecy that frees a text from its authorial seal is at the same time the condition that augments that authorial self. "In the two cases of this same divided passion," as Derrida maintains, as if describing the creative struggles of either Hemingway or Faulkner, "it is impossible to dissociate the greatest profit and the greatest privation" (13). Although the author can disappear into the inviolable privacy of literary ownership, the greater the autonomy of a text, the greater the possibility that intentionality lurks behind that supposed independence.

"For Derrida," as Segal stresses, "attention to authorial intention is a fundamental guardrail in the interpretation of texts" (191), with the relationship opened between text and author by absolute secrecy (in allying the aporias of literature and the gift) exhibiting paradoxical degrees of authorial responsibility. At one extreme, authorship is an irresponsible activity: the inviolable secrets of literature leave the field of expression unrestricted; secrecy hereby ties the destiny of literature, as Derrida argues in *On the Name*, "to a certain noncensure, to the space of democratic freedom (freedom of the press, freedom of speech, etc.)" (28). From this perspective, as Derrida contends in "Before the Law" (1991), the literary domain "is not only that of an instituted *fiction* but also a *fictive institution* which in principle allows one to say everything." To say all is "to totalize by formalizing, but to say everything is also to break out of [*franchir*] prohibitions"; that is, "to *affranchise oneself* [*s'affranchir*]—in every field where law can lay down the law" (36). At the other extreme, authorship is a responsible activity: the propositional nature of a work is an authorial duty. Unscrupulous literature, whether perfunctorily penned or knowingly produced, can spread unethical or politically fallacious messages through the accepted protocols of semiotics and the traditional meanings of (Saussurean) signs. Thus, the Derridean focus on authorial intention, as Segal insists, "no more consigns literary interpretation to unbridled subjectivism and pure arbitrariness than [it] severs literature from ethical or political accountability" (206 n5).

Literature is at once the complete responsibility of an author and an appeal to impersonal democratism. Although usually a singular creation of an individual, which no one can gainsay, and so a secret matter of inviolable control, a literary work nevertheless leaves the propositional intent of that absolute accountability open to public scrutiny. "Responsibility must be infinite. That's why I always feel not responsible enough" (48–49), explains Derrida in "following theory" (2003): "because I'm finite and because there are an infinite number of others to whom or for whom or from whom I should be responsible. I'm always not responsible enough, and responsibility is infinite or it *is* not, but I cannot be responsible *to some extent* in the strict sense of 'responsibility.'" That is why, he concedes, "I always feel guilty" (49). The double bind of textual accountability, as pursued by Derrida in "Remarks on Deconstruction and Pragmatism" (1996), can thereby challenge the standard yet ironic concept of "politics and democracy as openness—where all are equal and where the public realm is open to all—which tends to deny, efface or prohibit the secret" (83). In another way, this double bind makes the responsible writer feel irresponsible, inscribing the impossible dissociation between authorial profit and privation more deeply into that author's psyche.

***

After this typically Derridean introduction, as though the boundaries of *Given Time* testify to the central relevance of the works of that author, works that lie just beyond its margins, the approach to Hemingway's "The Battler" and Faulkner's "Barn Burning" begins somewhat more earnestly with Derrida's typically elliptical approach to the textual accountability of Baudelaire's "La fausse monnaie." "The referential structure of a title," states Derrida, "is always very tricky" (84)—and "La fausse monnaie" is no exception. This heading refers not only to the phenomenon of counterfeit money, "a sign without value, if not without meaning," but also to the subsequent narrative, "this text *here*, this story of counterfeit money" (85). "The title of a text," observes Segal, "would seem to be connected to its demarcation, its identity. Yet Derrida argues that in so far as counterfeit money is illegal, the title of 'Counterfeit Money' is without title" (194). Ordinarily, an introductory heading both identifies and begins a text; yet, according to Derrida's thesis in "Before the Law," "the power and import of a title have an essential relationship with something like the law" (188–89). The illegality of forged currency means that "La fausse monnaie" displays at once a valid and an invalid heading.

While "The Battler," as the title of an episode from Hemingway's *In Our Time*, engenders a similar sense of titular invalidity, seemingly announcing a particular individual's cognomen, but ultimately spilling over its definite article by referencing at least four agents, "Barn Burning," as the title of Faulkner's short story, engenders a stronger sense of dehiscence, referring not only to a transgressive activity that courts a break with lawful power, but also to the narrative that follows. As with "La fausse monnaie," yet to differing degrees, "The Battler" and "Barn Burning" are invalid headings—or titles without title.

Opening from its titular framework to reveal two friends emerging from another frame, a Parisian shop doorway, Baudelaire's prose poem immediately arouses speculation with the behavior of the narrator's colleague. "As we were walking from a tobacconist's," recalls the narrator, "my friend carefully sorted out his change: into the left pocket of his waistcoat he slipped the small gold coins, into the right, the small silver coins; into the left pocket of his breeches, a mass of large copper coins, and finally, into the right, a two-franc silver piece he had examined with noticeable attention" (48–49). The two men shortly encounter a beggar; each man hands over a coin; "my friend's offering," admits the narrator, "was much larger than mine." Embarrassed, the narrator points out this discrepancy, but his friend dismisses the issue nonchalantly: "it was the counterfeit coin" (49). This rejoinder about the two-franc piece that had caught its possessor's attention only minutes earlier perplexes the narrator. Moreover, as Derrida explains in *Given Time*, "the narration is framed in such a way that, like the narrator, we are the friend's debtors, but to the paradoxical extent that we live on the very credit *we are obliged to extend to him*. Whether or not we take him at his word, we have only his word. We are at once his debtor and his creditor" (151). The reader partakes of the narrator's viewpoint and must ask, as the narrator does, why his colleague made his admission about the two-franc coin. Credence, as a matter of speculation, and credit, as the issue of accreditation, are suddenly at stake.[3]

In "The Battler," the unnamed, heterodiegetic, and inviolably secret narrator immediately arouses speculation by introducing both the protagonist Nick Adams, as he watches a "caboose" (97) disappear into the distance, and a series of short, puzzling details that concern Nick's physical and sartorial states. The reader, as Hemingway surely intends, must speculate; he must live on the credit he is obliged to extend to the narrator. This accreditation, which invests in the conditional secret of the narrator's disjunction between fabula and sjuzhet, immediately pays dividends. A form of lawful process has in fact been enacted on the train, as an analepsis reveals in expressing Nick's impotent rage at the brakeman who threw him off the caboose. The feigned sincerity of the man's interest in Nick— a ruse in which the brakeman, as a type of battler, retained the conditional secret of his actual hostility—had disarmed the naïve Adams. "He had fallen for it," concedes Nick. "What a lousy kid thing to have done" (97). That concession signifies an early step on Nick's rite of passage. While the caboose, as a car attached to the rear of a freight train and dedicated to the occupancy of railroad workers (a group to which Nick does not belong), falls under the brakeman's authority on the tracks, the caboose, as a site in which the brakeman exercises that authority, represents a jail from which a chastised offender has been evicted.

In "Barn Burning," a similarly constituted narrator—unnamed, heterodiegetic, and inviolably secret—immediately arouses speculation by introducing both "the Justice of the Peace's court" and the seemingly inconsistent detail that this room "smelled of cheese" (3). The reader, as Faulkner surely intends, must speculate; he must live on the credit he is obliged to extend to the narrator. Again, this investment immediately pays dividends, with the revelation that due lawful process has in fact seconded a general store. Thus, Nick's rude awakening in "The Battler" to the excesses of seconding responsibility in a practically unlimited or undemocratic fashion finds a parallel in Colonel Sartoris (or Sarty) Snopes's growing awareness of the incongruity of a lawful hearing in an incommensurate setting. The differing potential of the two characters as bearers of conditional secrecy—their potential to fight undemocratic power with undemocratic power—lies within this parallel: Nick, who has already renounced his father, as textual interpolation from the other episodes of *In Our Time* suggests in positing the absolute secret of a silent paratext, should be capable of accepting the demands of conditional secrecy; Sarty, who attends his father Abner's appearance before the justice, and is both young enough and too young for the defendant to trust, is a potential revealer of conditional secrets. In each case, privileged knowledge slowly announces itself as a significant narratological detail within a peculiar ambiance of law, law enforcement, and the economics of exchange.

After his rough lesson at the hands of the brakeman, Nick's continued journey (or rite of passage) repeatedly promises a relatively easy prospect: the track "was well ballasted and made easy walking, sand and gravel packed between the ties, solid walking" (97).

Nick spots a fire below the railway embankment, but he heeds the brakeman's lesson, his cautious approach retaining the secrecy of his presence: "Nick dropped carefully down the embankment and cut into the woods" and "waited behind the tree and watched" (98). Finally, he "walk[s] into the firelight" (98), approaching what (in effect) is another source of enlightenment, another (titular) battler, "the former champion fighter" (101), or no longer titled titleholder, Ad Francis.

Ad and Nick appear to hit it off. Ad admits to being "crazy" (99), but the extent of his aberration is left as a conditional yet seemingly unimportant secret. In response, revealing his latent desire to shirk the demands of conditional secrecy, Nick recounts his treatment at the hands of the brakeman to this startlingly improbable imago. Nick's willingness to drop his guard reveals a cordiality that the unexpected appearance of Ad's companion, the African American Bugs, seems to confirm. Ironically, however, the accustomed protocols of that geniality lull Bugs into a false sense of serenity; as a result, in forbidding Nick from lending Ad his knife, Bugs openly retains the conditional secret about Ad's craziness while accepting Nick's presence.

In the peculiar smelling courtroom of "Barn Burning," a local landowner, Mr. Harris, recalls the events that culminated in these proceedings against his tenant Abner Snopes. Snopes's "hog got into my corn," he tells the court. "I caught it up and sent it back to him. He had no fence that would hold it. I told him so, warned him. The next time I put the hog in my pen. When he came to get it," continues Harris, "I gave him enough wire to patch up his pen. The next time I put the hog up and kept it. I rode down to his house and saw the wire I gave him still rolled on to the spool in his yard," maintains Snopes's landlord. "I told him he could have the hog when he paid me a dollar pound fee" (3–4). That evening, relates Harris, "a strange nigger" came to collect Snopes's pig. Having paid the fine, and with the pig in tow, this intermediary then delivered a message: "He say to tell you wood and hay kin burn." Rather at a loss, Harris asked this strange African American, this secret agent, to repeat himself, but the tenor of the message remained the same. "That whut he say to tell you," the man replied. "Wood and hay kin burn." The transitive relations that marked this communication—the human links in its chain—simultaneously indict Abner for and absolve him from responsibility for the message. Harris being the origin of this evidence, rather than the unknown messenger, further weakens its legitimacy before the law. The justice's repeated call to produce the African American in person testifies to this flaw in Harris's suit against Snopes. Notwithstanding these legal considerations, complains Harris, "that night my barn burned. I got the stock out but I lost the barn" (4).

Harris's strange interlocutor has been the subject of much critical speculation. John Duvall, in particular, has invested himself in unmasking the (supposed) blackface of Abner Snopes. "As [Richard] Godden has pointed out," and as Duvall appreciates, "everything about Abner is associated with blackness—his black hat and frock-coat, but most particularly his relationship with fire. Faulkner's repeated use of the term 'niggard' to describe the fire that Abner burns for his family," notes Duvall, "serves as wordplay that both points toward, even as its etymological difference deflects attention away from, 'nigger.'" Duvall, however, takes Godden's argument further. "I wish to suggest that the story's 'strange nigger,' is actually in the store where the hearing takes place and is the very figure of the man in black, Abner Snopes. Since almost the only person Abner would trust with a dollar is himself (or close kin)," contends Duvall, "it seems plausible that Abner (or perhaps his eldest son) blackened up in order to collect his hog and deliver his warning in person without being recognized" (115).

Duvall immediately acknowledges "one logical and one textual" weakness to his proposal of a blacked up Abner: "Harris would recognize such a ruse and would be immediately able to distinguish an artificial from an authentic black" (115). Moreover, and perhaps because the cultural mediation of race is his focus, Duvall misses the logical *and* textual objection to his thesis, the obvious reason why a blackened face would not have fooled Harris: that something other, that sign divorced from race, that Achilles' heel in terms of mimicry: Abner's "stiff and ruthless limp" (8). This alternative reasoning leaves Abner's secretive eldest son—presumably the Flem of Faulkner's subsequent fiction, but in "Barn Burning" the absolutely secret offspring who goes unnamed—as the sole candidate for the unknown African American (other than an unknown African American). What Faulkner no doubt intended, however, is the implantation of a fact that complicates racial issues by partaking of both conditional and absolute secrecy. From within the narrative, Abner inverts the structures of social power by withholding the truth behind this revealable secret. From outside the narrative, this retention becomes an absolute secret that displaces the use of conditional secrecy to attain such power—a displacement that reveals the reader's conditioning toward racial issues.

A tellingly empty communication, one that presages a dangerous change in attitudes, also comes into play in "The Battler." Bugs offers Ad some food, but "Ad did not answer. He was looking at Nick." Bugs repeats the offer—"I spoke to you, Mister Francis"— but "Ad kept on looking at Nick." Only now, within this insistent silence, does Nick feel "nervous." Ad now accuses Nick of abusing the economics of exchange. "Who the hell do you think you are?" he rails. "You're a snotty bastard. You come in here where nobody asks you and eat a man's food and when he asks to borrow a knife you get snotty" (101). In inviting Nick to join the camp, Ad had gifted him an entrance to conviviality, yet the prizefighter, who spent his professional career in the so-called "noble art" of exchanging blows for money, cannot help but confuse gifting, or benevolence without return, with the redemption of extended credit. Self-interest has precipitously undercut altruism. One genuine attitude has destabilized another. This confusing excess of motivational forces, which secrete as much as they reveal of Ad's mental state, leaves Nick as dumbfounded as Faulkner's similarly shaken Harris. Only after Bugs has revealed the conditional secret of "the cloth-wrapped blackjack" (102) in knocking out Ad without warning does he explain Ad's discreditable behavior.

A conditional secret from Ad's past continues to influence his actions. Ad's supposed "sister" (102), who "looked enough like him to be twins" (103), had managed his career. During this period, however, the pair had married. Physical resemblance had supposedly precluded this alliance, and while the dubiousness of the relationship presumably contributed to the couple's eventual estrangement,

Ad remains indebted to her financial management of his winnings. Bugs's revelation of this unresolved mystery complicates the economy of race that would normally have dominated his violent quieting of Ad. Bugs has revealed himself as not only the fourth battler in the story (after Nick, the brakeman, and Ad), but also Ad's partner in the economics of exchange. In benefitting from Ad's financial indebtedness, Bugs is his economic debtor, but in slaking Ad's annoyance, Bugs is his creditor—that credit prevents severer damage, either physical or lawful, to Ad than the future otherwise portends.

From Harris's point of view in "Barn Burning," Abner Snopes has slaked his annoyance through the impropriety of barn burning, an act of dissent Abner hopes to cloud in conditional secrecy; yet, without further personal evidence to offer the court, Harris must produce another witness. Harris hopes Sarty is still innocent enough to respect the name of truth and so reveal his father's conditional secret. When called to testify, Sarty wrestles with his conscience, but says nothing other than his whispered name. Faced with an otherwise silent, or secretive, minor in his court, the justice asks Harris incredulously, "Do you want me to question this boy?" Harris's conflict of responsibilities to the law, which he recognizes with a "violently, explosively" stated acquiescence to the justice's implicit expectation, falls in Abner's favor. Without an independent witness, the justice dismisses the case; nevertheless, he orders Abner to take his "wagon and get out of this country before dark" (5). The expectancy induced by the title of Faulkner's story is maintained, and the reader is free to speculate whether "Barn Burning" will reveal the currently inviolable secret about Harris's strange interlocutor, which the Snopeses hold in conditional secrecy. The tale immediately repays this speculation in kind. Displaced by the judge's sentence, Abner finds himself the tenant of Major de Spain, with whom he soon clashes. Unsatisfied by a judgment against this landowner, Abner risks no gratuitous communication, whether in blackface or not, before taking his revenge. Worried about Sarty's conscience, Abner devises a safeguard against the boy's revelation of his father's plan to raze the major's barn, telling his wife to confine Sarty to their cabin. She does as ordered, but with his hopes for a settled life again disrupted, Sarty now accepts the role of messenger. Escaping his mother, he freely delivers (or gifts), in the name of "truth, justice" (8), a warning to the major.

Like "La fausse monnaie," therefore, a supposedly revealable secret empowers its holders in both "The Battler" and "Barn Burning," with each author's readers indebted to an equivocal sort of messenger. Unlike "La fausse monnaie," however, both Hemingway and Faulkner deepen this equivocation by investing their authorial gifts in the economics of alterity. Duvall argues that Faulkner's deployment of "figurative blackness is literally productive because it allows him a way to map imbricated relations between one form of otherness (racial) and other forms of otherness (gender/sexuality and class)." Figurative blackness, maintains Duvall, "allows Faulkner's readers to see that, whatever the residual racism of William Faulkner, his narratives negotiate racial struggle even when race seems absent from their field of vision; these narratives are, in other words, racialized in a way that enables a critical purchase on whiteness" (108). More fundamentally, however, the economy of secrecy rather than of race enables both Hemingway in "The Battler" and Faulkner in "Barn Burning" to map imbricated relations between multifarious forms of otherness.

Hemingway does so with Bugs's final openness, his revelation of conditional secrets, blossoming into his temporary acceptance of the role of narrator: asking Nick questions and responding to Nick's unreported answers, Bugs temporarily erases not only Nick (in repeatedly referencing Hemingway's protagonist and assuming that character's unreported answers), but also the unnamed, heterodiegetic, and inviolably secret narrator:

> I can wake him up any time now, Mister Adams. If you don't mind I wish you'd sort of pull out. I don't like to not be hospitable, but it might disturb him back again to see you. I hate to have to thump him and it's the only thing to do when he gets started. I have to sort of keep him away from people. You don't mind, do you, Mister Adams? No, don't thank me, Mister Adams. I'd have warned

you about him but he seemed to have taken such a liking to you and I thought things were going to be all right. You'll hit a town about two miles up the track. Mancelona they call it. Good-bye. I wish we could ask you to stay the night but it's just out of the question. Would you like to take some of that ham and some bread with you? No? You better take a sandwich. (103)

Faulkner does so with a combination of the permanently unrevealable secret of Harris's strange messenger and Sarty's revelation of related but conditional secrecy. At once the strange man's debtor and creditor, was Harris (and, in turn, the reader) to have taken the relayed message as a warning or as an expression of inevitable intention? The secretive traces interwoven throughout the textual surface of "Barn Burning" pose this question and also imply that whatever the answer, the message from this stranger was a curious form of gift. Sarty's revelation of a conditional secret, which structural and narratological analogies place alongside Bugs's rather than Nick's similar form of revelation, subtly intensifies the subtle differences between "The Battler" and "Barn Burning." Comparing the closing sentence of each story, sentences that bespeak the breaking of prohibitions through the affranchisement of the self, confirms this slight but significant separation.

Nick, who "climbed the embankment and started up the track," cannot help "looking back from the mounting grade before the track curved into the hills," as he somewhat elliptically exits the narrative, to "see the firelight in the clearing" (104). Having seen the blaze of his father's revenge burst against the night sky, with Abner's arson "blotting the stars," Sarty is "running again before he knew he had begun to run, stumbling, tripping over something and scrabbling up again without ceasing to run, looking backward over his shoulder at the glare as he got up, running on among the invisible trees" (24). His consternation spent, however, Sarty heads down into the enveloping prospect of "dark woods" (24) and the stark conclusion to his story: "he did not look back" (25). Firelight has enacted a double function in each tale—at once a beacon of enlightenment for the protagonist and a radiant signal of obscurity for the reader—but Hemingway supplements that enactment, so while the futures for Nick and Sarty project beyond and through the frame of their respective stories, these two projections diverge. On the one hand, "The Battler" segues, almost without interruption, into the vignette of Chapter VI from *In Our Time*. This "is the only place in the book," as Philip Young observes, "where the interchapter material meets with the stories, and this crossing unmistakably signals the climax of *In Our Time*: X marks the spot, as a short paragraph reveals that Nick is in the war, tells us that he has been hit in the spine, and that he has made a 'separate peace' with the enemy, [and] is no longer fighting the war for democracy" (14). Seen in retrospect, "the fire-light in the clearing" (104) at the end of "The Battler" illuminates the narrative route into Nick's wartime experiences of shooting (or firing), with the vignette revealing his physical trauma, his psychological scarring, and the culminating enlightenment of his rite of passage. Only now, with his survival of adolescent death, can Nick look "*straight ahead brilliantly*" (105). Nick's journey in "The Battler" continues into Hemingway's canon. On the other hand, Sarty's future after "Barn Burning" remains untold; Abner's "niggard blaze[s]" during the Civil War were "the living fruit of nights passed during those four years in the woods hiding from all men, blue or gray, with his strings of horses (captured horses, he called them)" (7); but the postbellum fires of the mercenary Abner offer no narrative illumination for his son; and Sarty appears nowhere else in Faulkner's canon, because (presumably) Faulkner can learn nothing of that future. The profit of "Barn Burning" and the privation of Sarty Snopes are indissoluble. This difference between potentially revealable and absolute secrecy returns the critical focus to the inspiration provided by Baudelaire.

While the explicit narrative of Baudelaire's "La fausse monnaie" reveals a mendicant and the gifts of two benefactors, the implicit composition of his prose poem concerns receptive expectation and authorial responsibility. The reader is the author's other; textual expectancy inscribes that reader; and the author's gift confronts that expectation. Like Baudelaire's beggar, a credulous reader will accept any offering, but like Baudelaire's narrator, a scrupulous critic never dismisses all doubt. Alterity inscribes the downtrodden and the oppressed. Just as the imposition of alterity inscribed French beggars, so the enforcement of otherness inscribed African Americans, and while the prodigal gift presented in "La fausse monnaie" remains in doubt, the gifts of Baudelaire, Faulkner, and Hemingway remain no secret. These responsible authors, as their irresponsible art attests, never took their readers for granted. What remains in doubt (or somewhat secretive) are the specifics that differentiate between these authors' perspectives on otherness, authorial responsibility, and revealable and absolute secrecy.

Derrida's thoughts concerning messianicism (or the messianism of theology) and the messianic proper (or the messianism of atheology) help to articulate these distinctions. Messianicism, as Derrida elucidates in "Faith and Knowledge" (1998), looks forward to the messiah's advent as a foreseeable occurrence. In contrast, remaining inviolably secret in its irreducibility to actual presence, the messianic proper is "without horizon of expectation and without prophetic prefiguration" (17). The secrets of Colonel Sartoris Snopes, as absolute and conditional secrets that authorize and censure a democracy to come, propel this figure beyond the frame of his particular tale and toward an infinitely unrealizable hope, a future without horizon, as his canonical non-reappearance silently implies. "Breaking with the present," explains Segal, "the secret (and with it the gift and literature) testifies to such a radical future, as do the groundless and ad infinitum hypotheses to which the secret gives rise about the literary text, hypotheses never to be verified or falsified in any present" (193). Segal turns to John Caputo to corroborate this interpretation of Derridean thinking: "The 'messianic secret' is, there is no secret and the Messiah is never going to show up. Derrida's secret is not some hyperousiological high he has had and that he now whispers in our ear. Far from it. To be 'in on the secret' does not mean you know anything, that you are 'in the know'—but rather in the 'no,' *non-savoir*" (102).

The profound emanations of literature, which paradoxically lie on the surface of its texture, are depthless arrivals that gesture toward an unrealizable future. Baudelaire's "La fausse monnaie," which overtly considers secrecy and voluntary donation, is noticeably immanent, with the messianic proper, the ever-presently democratic, as a necessity of its own critical standing. "The Battler" and "Barn Burning" testify to comparable considerations of secrecy and voluntary donation by two of Baudelaire's keenest American admirers, but while the messianicism of the omissive Hemingway echoes that of the influential Baudelaire, the messianic proper of the inclusive Faulkner echoes that influence more distantly. In continuing Baudelaire's legacy, each author employs conditional secrets to fight the power of conditional secrecy, but the Faulkner of "Barn Burning" is more responsible than the Hemingway of "The Battler" is in handling the irresponsibility of authorship, more democratic in his call on inviolable secrecy to displace the use of revealable secrecy to command interpretation.

Notes

1. This paper has evolved from "A Stiff Man-Child Walking: Derrida's Economy of Secrecy and Faulkner's 'Barn Burning,'" which the *European Journal of American Studies* published in 2016, and whose editors I thank for granting permission to use this earlier material.

2. Inviolable and revealable secrets litter the works of Hemingway and Faulkner. Two instances of each, one from each author, appear below.

Faulkner's "A Bear Hunt" (1934) presents an inviolable secret in linking the former violation of Native Indians to an unbridgeable gap between their descendants and those of their oppressors. History, historiography, postcolonialism, and (especially) popular culture will never reveal the inviolable secrets of the Chickasaw past to majoritarians. The narrator's comments about the Indian mound, or barrow, reveal the two perspectives contesting for authority: "Aboriginal, it rises profoundly and darkly enigmatic, the only elevation of any kind in the wild, flat jungle of river bottom. Even to some of us—children though we were, yet we were descended of literate, town-bred people—it possessed inferences of secret and violent blood, of savage and sudden destruction, as though the yells and hatchets which we associated with Indians through the hidden and secret dime novels which we passed among ourselves were but trivial and momentary manifestations of what dark power still dwelled or lurked there" (65).

The spasmodic and unpredictable events of the Greco-Turkish War that contextualize Hemingway's "On the Quai at Smyrna"—a story first published in *Scribner's* 1930 edition of *In Our Time*—are predicated on an inviolable secret: "because they never knew about the Turk. They never knew what the old Turk would do" (64). As Matthew Stewart observes, "'On the Quai at Smyrna' provides a fitting and *typically indirect* introduction to the stories of Nick Adams's boyhood" (35; emphasis added).

In Faulkner's "There Was a Queen" (1933), Narcissa Benbow reveals a succession of secrets to Miss Jenny (Virginia Du Pre), the first of which she has been harboring for thirteen years when she admitted to receiving an indecent letter. "Don't you remember?" Narcissa asks Miss Jenny. "You wanted to give it to Colonel Sartoris and let him find out who sent it and I wouldn't do it and you said that no lady would permit herself to receive anonymous love letters, no matter how badly she wanted to." Miss Jenny remembers: "Yes. I said it was better for the world to know that a lady had received a letter like that, than to have one man in secret thinking such things about her, unpunished. You told me you burned it." Narcissa had lied. "I kept it," she admits. "And I got ten more of them. I didn't tell you because of what you said about a lady" (739). What is more, not only were the letters subsequently stolen, but Narcissa was also forced into a compromising position with the Federal agent who eventually rediscovered them. This cascade of revelations triggers the death of the heretofore-indomitable Miss Jenny.

In Hemingway's "The End of Something," from the original edition of *In Our Time*, Nick finally tells Marjorie that their relationship "isn't fun any more" (81). This revelation causes Marjorie's abrupt departure. The subsequent revelation of Bill's hitherto secret presence confirms that Nick and Marjorie's relationship is over.

3. "Here," argues Derrida in *Given Time*, "we can speculate and extend credit." In doing so, "at least three hypotheses, but in fact a series of innumerable prognostications," arise (149). According to one premise, as the narrator in "La fausse monnaie" opines to himself, his colleague has lied "to justify his own largesse" in donating an amount that "might serve as the germ for several day's capital, in the hands of a poor, small-time speculator" (49). Putting this reasoning another way, his friend is not only modest, but

also sensitive to the narrator's self-reflective qualms concerning his own meanness. Into the narrator's "miserable brain" (49), however, comes another thought. Did his colleague merely wish to enjoy the possible consequences of giving a mendicant counterfeit money? On the one hand, the beggar might not recognize the forgery; as a result, he might be arrested when trying to spend it. On the other hand, the next recipient of the coin might not recognize it as counterfeit, and the beggar might prosper. Just as the narrator reaches this seemingly unjust conclusion about his friend's motive, his colleague "brusquely breaks into his reverie," repeating the narrator's contention. "Yes, you are right," he confesses, "there is no sweeter pleasure than surprising a man by giving him more than his hopes allowed" (50). In the light of this admittance, the colleague's declaration signifies what Derrida calls "a surplus of naïve triumph and boastfulness close to cynicism;" as a corollary, the narrator's friend has gratuitously accredited himself through secretive reckoning, which (for Derrida) amounts to this: "So, you recognize how good I am at treating myself to the greatest pleasure; well, I am even sharper than that: I bought myself the greatest pleasure at the lowest price: you give me credit, but I speculate even better than you think" (149). Crucially, these two conjectures, the first concerning self-effacing altruism, the second concerning self-interested arrogance, exhibit a relationship that classical dialectics cannot resolve; "on the contrary," as Derrida expounds, "they superimpose themselves on each other, they accumulate like a capital of true or (perhaps) counterfeit money that may produce interest; they overdetermine each other in the ellipsis of the declaration." Each conjecture "is justifiable and each has a certain right to be credited, accredited. This is the phenomenon without phenomenality of counterfeit money" (149), concludes Derrida, and the third of his immediate prognostications.

Works Cited

Baudelaire, Charles. "La fausse monnaie." 1869. *Le Spleen de Paris*, translated by Wainwright, edited by Melvin Zimmerman, Manchester UP, 1968, pp. 48-50.

Brasch, James D. *That Other Hemingway: The Master Inventor*. Trafford, 2009.

Brasch, James D., and Joseph Sigman. *Hemingway's Library: A Composite Record*. Garland, 1981.

Caputo, John D. *The Prayers and Tears of Jacques Derrida: Religion without Religion*. Indiana UP, 1997.

Derrida, Jacques. "Before the Law." *Acts of Literature*, edited by Derek Attridge, Routledge, 1991, pp. 181-220.

—. "Faith and Knowledge: The Two Sources of 'Religion' at the Limits of Reason Alone." *Religion: Cultural Memory in the Present*, translated by Samuel Weber, edited by Jacques Derrida and Gianni Vattimo, Stanford UP, 1998, pp. 1-78.

—. "following theory / Jacques Derrida." *life.after.theory*, edited by Michael Payne and John Schad, Continuum, 2003, pp. 1-51.

—. *Given Time: I. Counterfeit Money*, translated by Peggy Kamuf. U of Chicago P, 1992.

—. *On the Name*, edited by Thomas Dutoit. Stanford UP, 1995.

—. "Remarks on Deconstruction and Pragmatism." *Deconstruction and Pragmatism*, edited by Chantal Mouffe, Routledge, 1996, pp. 77-88.

Duvall, John N. "'A Strange Nigger': Faulkner and the Minstrel Performance of Whiteness." *The Faulkner Journal*, vol. 22, nos. 1/2, Fall 2006/Spring 2007, pp. 106-19.

Faulkner, William. "Barn Burning." 1939. *Collected Stories of William Faulkner*. Vintage, 1995, pp. 3-25.

—. "A Bear Hunt." 1934. *Collected Stories of William Faulkner*. Vintage, 1995, pp. 63-79.

—. "Classroom Statements at the University of Mississippi." 1947. *Lion in the Garden: Interviews with William Faulkner 1926– 1962*, edited by James B. Meriwether and Michael Millgate, Random House, 1968, pp. 52-58.

—. "There Was a Queen." 1933. *Collected Stories of William Faulkner*, Vintage. 1995, pp. 727-44.

Fruscione, Joseph. "Rivalry and Influence in the Afternoon: Faulkner, Hemingway, and *If I Forget Thee, Jerusalem*." *South Atlantic Review*, vol. 71, no. 4, Fall 2006, pp. 78-98.

Godden, Richard. *Fictions of Labor: William Faulkner and the South's Long Revolution.* Cambridge UP, 1997.

Gresset, Michel. *Fascination: Faulkner's Fiction, 1919-1936.* Duke UP, 1989.

Grimwood, Michael. *Heart in Conflict: Faulkner's Struggles with Vocation.* 1987. U of Georgia P, 2009.

Hemingway, Ernest. "The Art of the Short Story." 1959. Unpublished typescript, 251. Kennedy Library.

—. "The Battler." 1925. *The Complete Short Stories of Ernest Hemingway.* 1987. Scribner, 2003, pp. 97-104.

—. *Death in the Afternoon.* Cape, 1932.

—. "The End of Something." 1925. *The Complete Short Stories of Ernest Hemingway.* 1987. Scribner, 2003, pp. 79-82.

—. *A Moveable Feast.* Cape, 1964.

—. "On the Quai at Smyrna." 1930. *The Complete Short Stories of Ernest Hemingway.* 1987. Scribner, 2003, pp. 63-64.

Kermode, Frank. *The Genesis of Secrecy: On the Interpretation of Narrative.* Harvard UP, 1979.

Martin, Christopher D. "Ernest Hemingway: A Psychological Autopsy of a Suicide." *Psychiatry: Interpersonal and Biological Processes*, vol. 69, no. 4, Winter 2006, pp. 351-61.

Rorty, Richard. *Contingency, Irony, and Solidarity.* 1989. Cambridge UP, 2005.

Segal, Alex. "Deconstruction, Radical Secrecy, and *The Secret Agent.*" *Modern Fiction Studies*, vol. 54, no. 2, Summer 2008, pp. 189-208.

Stewart, Matthew. *Modernism and Tradition in Ernest Hemingway's* In Our Time*: A Guide for Students and Readers.* Camden House, 2001.

Williams, Scott G. "Eating Faulkner Eating Baudelaire: Multiple Rewritings and Cultural Cannibalism." *The Faulkner Journal*, vol. 25, no. 1, Fall 2009, pp. 65–84.

Young, Philip. "Adventures of Nick Adams." *Nick Adams*, edited by Harold Bloom, Chelsea House, 2004, pp. 7-25.

Carl Rollyson

Faulkner's Shadow: Hollywood, Hemingway, and *Pylon*

If *Absalom* proves to be about the sins of the father, lines of descent, a society's decline, and the burden of the Southern past, *Pylon* takes up the irrelevance of sin (not to mention fathers), lines of ascent, a society's transformation, and a weightless future.

John T. Matthews (61)

Published before *Absalom, Absalom!* (1936), and seemingly a deviation from the Yoknapatawpha saga, *Pylon* (1935), usually considered a minor work, nevertheless has more in common with its esteemed successor than has been commonly supposed. Both novels are about deracination and displacement. Like Thomas Sutpen, *Pylon*'s rootless flyers swoop down on land that has been converted into property, into the possession of one man, the not so fine Colonel Feinman. *Pylon* has its Judith Sutpen in the figure of Laverne Shumann, who contends with love and power and holds her own in a male-dominated world, as does Ann, played by Joan Crawford in *Today We Live* (1933), the screen adaptation of Faulkner's World War I story "Turnabout" (1932). Crawford, understanding perfectly the demands of her role, insisted on dialogue that was as clipped as that delivered by her male counterparts. She realized that she had to adopt the same taciturn style of the males who understate their emotions and prove themselves in action. Even on the ground, women such as those whom Crawford embodies, are with their men in the air.[1] They are aerial bodies and, like their lovers, are alienated from their terrestrial contemporaries and the conventional obligations that women are supposed to fulfill.[2] Laverne is the most extreme example of these daring women, especially when she taunts her own son with "who's your father?"[3] That the boy can take his pick of two men, and that Laverne cannot assure her husband's father, Dr. Shumann, that the boy is Roger's, is far from the boundaries of Yoknapatawpha. Or is it? What do Charles Bon and Judith Sutpen ever really know about their consanguinity?

Laverne Shumann is not the nymph pursued in Faulkner's early poetry but is rather full-bodied—part of a life intensely lived, which means risking death. She is a woman possessed, the cynosure of male society, but also her own woman, dogged by a reporter, who is a descendent of Keats's frail knight, "alone and palely loitering"—in effect, a knight manqué (Yonce 206). The war is mentioned only once in *Pylon*, when Jiggs, the air crew's mechanic, buys "one of the pulp magazines of war stories in the air," which will give Laverne and her male companions "something to do on the train" that takes them to the air shows in which they will duel with their competitors (273). If this is not the world of gentleman flyers, it remains, nevertheless, a kind of chivalric endeavor involving sacrifice and heroes, however corrupted for popular entertainment and profit.

By 1935, in several short stories, film scripts, and novels, Faulkner had already connected the world of Yoknapatawpha to the high flyers of World War I and the barnstormers of the postwar period in the figure of young Bayard Sartoris, bereft of his place in traditional Southern culture and willing to risk all in the test piloting that results in his death. Young Bayard and his twin, John, belong to that reckless crew of aviators in "Death Drag" (1932), "Honor" (1930), and other short stories. They live in the moment, unsure of the future, even as they continue to engage in "mock heroic" actions (Paddock 111). On what terms, if any, can the world of the gentlemanly ideal, still in the sway of the Faulkner family and their community, prevail in the modern world of airports and circuses of the air? It is a question posed by Faulkner's own actions when he encouraged all of his brothers to fly and to put on air shows. In New Orleans in 1925, he accompanied Hamilton Basso who was writing a feature story about "The Gates Flying Circus." Basso recalled that Faulkner seemed to relish the frightening flights in a rickety Wright Whirlwind two-seater: "Nobody *else* in our crowd had gone looping-the-loop in a bucket seat and open cockpit over the Mississippi River" (Blotner, *Biography* 419).

Faulkner's daredevil testing of himself is reminiscent of the Hemingway credo of grace under pressure. While Faulkner did not come under fire, as Hemingway did during the First World War, Faulkner nevertheless tested himself again and again, not only in the very airplane in which his brother Dean crashed and died but much later in his persistent efforts to take his horses on jumps that resulted in repeated agonizing injuries and broken bones. Called Pappy by his family, Faulkner's hazarding of life-threatening situations places him closer to the bull-fighting, safari-hunting Papa than has been previously supposed. *Pylon*, an underappreciated novel, is at the nexus of major aspects of Faulkner's fiction and life including Hollywood, flight, and craft. The novel is also part of an important intersection with Hemingway in terms of the fiction Hemingway wanted to write while he felt forced to pursue a secondary publishing milieu (journalism) even as Faulkner bound himself to Hollywood scriptwriting.

Faulkner was writing in the era of Governor Huey Long, whose administration promoted the construction of high visibility projects that enhanced the profile of Louisiana and his own reputation as a politician who put people to work during the Depression while contributing to the progress that made modern life comfortable. Faulkner had little interest in Long and thought that the governor's life could not be the basis of a great novel (Blotner, *Selected Letters* 239). But the consequences of a regime that conjoined commerce and politics and cut corrupt deals, afterwards staging celebrations purported to be for the public good, agitated an author who had become part of a Hollywood no less self-promoting and venal than Long's Louisiana.

The Shushan Airport layout may have reminded Faulkner of a movie set. The airport had two large hangars not so different from sound stages and a tower with murals commemorating the history of flight in high relief depictions of airplanes and their daring pilots. And like a Hollywood studio emblazoning its logo, the airport had Shushan's name or his initials inserted in every available spot. In short, if you wanted to see the show, you had to put up with the advertising. And Faulkner was there for the show, indulging his keen interest in barnstorming pilots who had already appeared in

"Death Drag" and "Honor." He had organized his own local air shows, and flying was a Faulkner business, taken up by his brothers Murry, John, and Dean. The very idea of flight had captivated all of them since the day Faulkner had convinced them they could make their own air machine. That their dreams had crashed into a ditch did not dissuade the boys from pursuing the lift that flying always offered. And crashing, after all, was part of the excitement.

The Shushan show did not disappoint. Milo Burcham defied the rainy weather and demonstrated why he was the world champion at upside-down flying. The famous Michel de Troyat, on a calmer day, performed his air acrobatics, as did Clem Sohn, jumping from 10,000 feet with a flour sack he emptied to mark his descent. After some near miss collisions and a forced landing, a pilot and parachute jumper plunged to their deaths in Lake Ponchartrain. In one case, the body could not be found; in another, no relatives could be located for the nomadic airman.[4]

Faulkner first thought the show could be the basis for a popular story, "This Kind of Courage," which his agent, Morton Goldman, submitted to *Scribner's* on May 10, 1934. But by mid-October, Faulkner asked Goldman to send the story back to him because "I'm now writing a novel out of it" (Blotner, *Selected Letters* 85). Why not publish the story and write the novel? Faulkner did not say. It never troubled him to reuse and adapt published material, but perhaps he had no other copy to work with. At any rate, he had discovered more in the story and wrote it just about as quickly—in about two months—as *As I Lay Dying*. Why the urgency when he was already hard at work on *Absalom, Absalom!*?

Faulkner's own explanation is that *Absalom, Absalom!* had stalled, and he needed the relief that writing a different kind of novel provided (Gwynn and Blotner 36). But as Robert W. Hamblin suggests: "It seems significant that the novel Faulkner wrote 'to get away from' the high modernist *Absalom, Absalom!* is a book patterned to a degree after Hollywood criteria" (19-20). In fact, in July 1934, Howard Hawks suggested to the stalled novelist that he should write about flyers, and Faulkner told him about "This Kind of Courage," which Hawks liked, saying, "That sounds good" (McBride 57). By October, Faulkner had begun work on the novel, finishing a first draft on November 25 and sending a revised version to the publisher in mid-December.

With *Pylon*, he could dispense with the genealogy of his characters fraught with the intricacies of a narrative overwhelmed by the eruption of the past in the present. Faulkner's flyers—Roger, Laverne, and Jack—have, for most of the novel, no past. Their lives seem the work of happenstance. Their mechanic, Jiggs, is an unreliable alcoholic who is nevertheless devoted to them, which is all they seem to require. The novel's center of consciousness—always referred to as "the Reporter"—is not even given a name. He is drawn to the aviators because they are so alive in the air. On the ground, their lives seem rootless and sordid. Roger and Jack share Laverne, who is married to Roger because he won the roll of the dice with Jack. Laverne is, as Tom Dardis observes, like the tough talking women—Hildy Johnson in *His Girl Friday* (1940) and "Feathers" in *Rio Bravo* (1959)—that populate Howard Hawks's later films. She is also like Joan Crawford's character, Ann, in *Today We Live*, the female fulcrum of male triangles—first of a brother and a lover, then of two lovers, involved with her brother in the terse tension of war and romance.

Faulkner's treatment of the Reporter is original and yet probably based on Hermann Deutsch, a thin, tall journalist with a shambling gait that Faulkner transformed into his shambolic, skeletal character. The two men first met in 1925 in New Orleans and were impressed with one another. Deutsch remembered Faulkner saying to him, "If somebody in the Yale Bowl was going to be shot, you'd be standing next to him." It was a line Faulkner would elaborate on in *Pylon* when the editor says as much to the Reporter (Blotner, "Deutsch").

At the air show, the novelist spent a good deal of time in Deutsch's company, watching the journalist carry around on his shoulders a little boy who belonged to one of the aviators. Out of this meager material, Faulkner conceived of the Reporter who becomes increasingly involved in the lives of the flyers he comes almost to worship because they seem solely intent on their air missions, so to speak. They are, in Cleanth Brooks's words, "hooked on speed" (Brooks 183).[5] They are adventurers and likened to "immigrants walking down the steerage gangplank of a ship" (Faulkner 79). They are refugees hazarding a trip into what was still then the new world of flight. They no longer have a secure place, a home to which they could return "even if it's just only to hate the damn place good and comfortable for a day or two"—as Faulkner seemed to do when he arrived in Oxford after his days in Hollywood (46).

It also looks as though Faulkner patterned the besotted, drunken Reporter on himself, according to Howard Hawks. Faulkner could become voluble when it came to talking about flying, one of his friends told biographer Carvel Collins (Collins, "Spain"). When Faulkner turned up in New Orleans after the air show, he looked as if he had slept in the gutter, according to one witness who said so to him. "Yes, ma'am, I have," he assured writer Roark Bradford's wife. Faulkner claimed to have become involved with the flyers, sleeping and fighting. It was a "disjointed, confused, nightmarish tale of having been offered a ride by a man and woman riding a motorcycle, or perhaps riding two motorcycles, with stops to visit bootleggers," said Roark Bradford's son, who also remembered that Faulkner never forsook his "elaborately polite and chivalrous" manners: "He was the only person over the age of twenty-one who was allowed to call my mother 'ma'am'" (Blotner, "Bradford"). Faulkner had not eaten for several days. He certainly acted like the starved Reporter when he devoured three eggs and bacon she made for him. He talked about two women and three men living together indiscriminately (Collins, "Bradford"), which he compacted into the one woman and two flyers who become the Reporter's obsession. At the same time, this was a Faulkner who was a kind of hanger-on in this world of high flyers. To Vernon Omlie's wife, Phoebe, he was very much like the reticent Reporter who goes along for the ride and puts himself at the service of the flyers. She said Faulkner had "no real desire . . . to be a precision flyer" or make flying a business. It became, instead, "a mental and emotional release," as it does for the Reporter who liberates himself from the grimy and gloomy environs of the newspaper office. Phoebe observed a "rather shy man who wanted to be left alone." In a "pair of old coveralls," he would lose himself in a "group of mechanics, and help out by washing parts or doing what he would around the general aircraft operation rather than be out where people could see him and lionize him" (Collins, "Omlie"). In short, Faulkner craved the anonymity he confers on his Reporter.

The Reporter appears like an allegorical figure, almost like a ghost in a medieval mystery play. In the popular imagination, especially as it was fed by movies like *I Cover the Waterfront* (1933), the journalist is usually self-sufficient and cynical, manipulating the woman he loves and willing to do whatever it takes to get the story, which often involves corruption and solving a crime or a criminal conspiracy. The journalist is like H. Joseph Miller (Ben Lyon) in *I Cover the Waterfront* or Hildy Johnson (Pat O'Brien) in *The Front Page* (1931). Both journalists are humanized and redeemed by beautiful women, who bring out the reporter's qualms about newspaper work. In fact, in Miller's case, he is a budding novelist—a sure sign that morally he is better than most crass reporters.

Faulkner forgoes the Hollywood sin-and-redemption scenario with characters who never do follow a conventional moral compass and are not bound by any community's standards of propriety. This air crew belongs nowhere and everywhere. It does not matter where they go so long as they can perform their show. By one definition, these are free spirits, not bound by any rules except those of the air races funded by capitalists like Colonel H. I. Feinman, Faulkner's version of Colonel A. L. Shushan. To emphasize the impurity of Feinman's power, he is identified as chairman of the Sewage Board. He is, in effect, the lord of a landfill since the airport rests on reclaimed lake bottom. Ironically, the press treats Roger, Laverne, and Jack with fascination and scorn while spending not a moment inquiring into how the airport got built or what purpose the air race show fulfills in Feinman's master plan that includes stamping "F" all over his property.

Only the Reporter believes the story is the air crew itself, not just their antics in the air. He is fascinated with how they live apart from the society they entertain. They seem to find it enough to be with one another. They work together as one unit, although Jack has a temper he expresses by kicking Jiggs, and Roger—even more than the others—lives to fly. Even as he expects to survive, he never discounts the risks of death. The Reporter alone sees these characters as admirable—in part because he is a Prufrock, afraid to bring the moment to its crisis, to confess his love for Laverne and for what the flyers represent to him. As the Reporter, he is a passive observer. He is repeatedly described as a scarecrow and a cadaver, one of the walking dead in T. S. Eliot's unreal wasteland city, one of the poet's impotent hollow men. Using journalistic jargon like "dogwatches" evokes the environs of journalism, but the novelist's compounded neologisms like "typesplattered" create a vocabulary that vitiates the Reporter's profession. The stories journalists tell are a sensationalistic mess.

The factitious Feinman Airport opening, set in New Valois (New Orleans), is presided over by a disembodied amplified voice, "apocryphal, sourceless, inhuman" (Faulkner 39). The newspaper office is similarly disquieting, a room right out of a film noir, with "downfunneled light" from the editor's desk lamp (41). Journalism would not be depicted in such dim surroundings until the release of *Citizen Kane* (1941). In the hermetic "dusty gloom," the editor expresses a frustration with the Reporter that many readers of the novel have also experienced:

> You have an instinct for events .... If you were turned into a room with a hundred people you never saw before and two of them were destined to enact a homicide, you would go straight to them as crow to carrion; you would be there from the very first: you would be the one to run out and borrow a pistol from the nearest policeman for them to use. Yet you never seem to bring back anything but information. Oh you have that, all right, because we seem to get everything that the other papers do and we haven't been sued yet and so doubtless it's all that anyone should expect for five cents and doubtless more than they deserve. But it's not the living breath of news. It's just information. It's dead before you even get back here with it. (42)

Like the new journalists Tom Wolfe first touted in the 1960s, the Reporter becomes part of the events and people he covers, latching on to just those characters that appeal to newspaper readers. But then he is unable to go beyond recording what they say to him. He cannot, in other words, turn his reports into stories, the "living breath of the news." But what the Reporter wants to do cannot be contained within a newspaper article, any more than Faulkner felt his talent could be fully articulated in movie scripts or stories for popular magazines. As Jay Parini points out, Faulkner's "anxieties about his place in the world—as an artist and reporter on life, as a man subjected to the wiles of larger economic forces, as a frustrated novelist unable to focus entirely on his major vision—seem reflected in the figure of the Reporter, who tellingly has no name. He is, in a sense, Faulkner's shadow" (191). In his psychological reading of the novel, Frederick Karl detects an inner disturbance: "The entire fantasy world Faulkner had created about himself from the war divides him here" (529).

Faulkner's anomie is akin to the flyers who are confined to stunts and have neither the equipment nor the venue to show just how good they are. Journalism is a dead end for the Reporter, and the editor explains, "patiently, almost kindly," why:

> The people who own this paper or who direct its policies or anyway who pay the salaries, fortunately or unfortunately I shant attempt to say, have no Lewises or Hemingways or even Tchekovs on the staff: one very good reason doubtless being that they do not want them, since what they want is not fiction, not even Nobel Prize fiction, but news. (50)

Hemingway, like the other writers the editor names, ultimately worked for himself, for the cause of literature alone, which can never be the province of newspapers. As Joseph Fruscione observes, both Faulkner and Hemingway wanted to be "*the* author of their milieu" (15). The Reporter, on the other hand, can never own his story, or root himself, as Hemingway and Faulkner did, in their work. The flyers, in other words, seek fulfillment only in flight, but are bound, nevertheless, to paymasters who determine when they can fly. Hemingway, fully established as a novelist by 1935, when *Pylon* was published, might continue to write for the newspapers but only as their special correspondent, hired precisely because of his name. And of course he never did have to work a day in Hollywood.

Nevertheless, both Faulkner and Hemingway, for all their independence, did write to suit the deadlines of employers. Well into his career, after the great successes and sales of *The Sun Also Rises* (1926) and especially *A Farewell to Arms* (1929), Hemingway became a hired hand of a press syndicate covering the Spanish Civil War. Faulkner in this same period (the mid to late 1930s) had to take scriptwriting assignments of all kinds and also accept his removal from films like *Banjo on my Knee* (1936), which dealt with the Mississippi River denizens he knew well. For the newspapers, Hemingway did not write prose like Chekhov, even if he was not the anonymous reporter of Faulkner's *Pylon*, which is perhaps why Hemingway singled out *Pylon* for praise. He recognized himself in Faulkner's treatment of journalism and the subordination of the writer to "news." Both writers, in effect, did not want to report the news but to create it. The Reporter, for all his failings, however, wants to write literature, and thus he speaks to the ambition that Faulkner and Hemingway shared: to adapt these secondary publication milieus, journalism and scriptwriting, to their overarching imaginations. The Reporter's struggle against his editor, in other words, cuts close to the psyches of these two great novelists.

In the popular imagination, as depicted in *The Front Page* and *I Cover the Waterfront*, the conflict is between the wayward reporter and his disciplinarian editor. Seldom, until *Meet John Doe* (1941), did Hollywood take on newspaper owners. But in *Pylon*, the editor could just as well be a Hollywood producer advising Faulkner to stay within the conventional boundaries of a script. And the Reporter's reaction, like Faulkner's, is to drink and subside into silence rather than engage any more deeply in the corporate culture that enmeshes him. The editor is like Monroe Stahr in *The Last Tycoon* (1941) lecturing the recalcitrant writer about how to make movies. News, the editor implies, is not a narrative of lives and events per se but an account of a certain set of circumstances:

> [W]hat I am paying you to bring back here is not
> what you think about somebody out there nor what
> you heard about somebody out there nor even what
> you saw: I expect you to come in here tomorrow
> night with an accurate account of everything that

occurs out there tomorrow that creates any reaction
excitement or irritation on any human retina; if you
have to be twins or triplets or even a regiment to do
this, be so. (51)

The newspaper reader has to get it all in one gulp, one documented day, in a "you-are-there drama" or movie.

Of course, the repressed Reporter romanticizes the flyers, who fascinate him because of their uninhibited sex lives, which the reporter as voyeur watches—but not with the journalist's practiced passivity. He yearns to be one of them, just as Faulkner coveted the role of war pilot, which his Hollywood buddy, Laurence Stallings, accorded him in a review of *Pylon* (Bassett 178). Hemingway liked this novel, probably because, as one reviewer put it, "these reckless nomads of the air are not essentially different from the graceful toreadors that court death so beautifully in the pages of Hemingway" (Bassett 180). Hemingway may also have been intrigued by one of the novel's closing scenes, in which we learn that Roger Shumann is the son of a small town Ohio doctor who lived the kind of predictable, risk-averse life that Hemingway's father pursued. The Reporter, emanating from that dim newspaper office and the grind of a reporter's routines, gravitates to the open spaces that the deracinated Roger, Laverne, and Jack navigate with aplomb. The air is their world elsewhere come to grief on the wasted ground of New Valois.

Like Hemingway's doomed heroes and heroines, the flyers forsake bourgeois values and live for their own sakes. They are willing to risk everything to pursue a society of their own. Faulkner, no less than Hemingway, realizes that such an uncompromising sense of self results in tragedy because of their human fallibility which is caught up in modern mechanisms over which they cannot exert complete control. Even in the air, this liberated trio is fixated on those pylons that enforce the boundaries of the racers' route. Roger, flying first an inferior plane, bests his competitors but crashes because the drunken Jiggs has not performed all of the necessary maintenance. Then in a dangerously experimental plane, he plunges to his death. This flawed teamwork contributes to the flyers' fates as much as Feinman's machinations. *Pylon* is not a parable of economic determinism. Faulkner's characters are too implicated in their own destiny to attribute their actions to forces outside themselves. Faulkner might rail against Hollywood, but he never forgot he chose to be there to pick up the check.

In the novel's closing chapters, the journalists cluster together to chew over the crash story, just like they do in countless newspaper movies—most memorably in *Citizen Kane*, a film *Pylon* anticipates by layering together reporters, editors, and their corporate masters. Unlike the star reporters in Hollywood dramas, Faulkner's reporter is hardly a hero. What he discovers makes him ill. "I could vomit too," one of the journalists says to the Reporter, "But what the hell? He aint our brother" (238). The irony, of course, is that the Reporter wants to write about his brotherly feeling for Roger. When the Reporter says, "you dont understand" (239), he might as well quote Prufrock's lament that it is impossible to say just what he means.

The Reporter's final effort to tell the story ends up in fragments the copyboy picks out of a wastebasket. Like an embryonic editor or budding scholar experiencing his first joy in deciphering an unpublished manuscript, the copyboy—bright, ambitious, and with a literary sensibility—pastes together the fragments which "he believed to be not only news but the beginning of literature" (314). After a bald summary of Roger's crash, the Reporter observes that the pilot's "competitor was Death" (314). Acknowledging Roger's honorable end—he deliberately steered his plummeting plane away from the people below—his two rivals circle the spot where he disappeared: "Two friends, yet two competitors too, whom he had met in fair contest and conquered it the lonely sky from which he fell, dropping a simple wreath to mark his Last Pylon" (314). Less florid than the narrator of *Flags in the Dust*, the Reporter nevertheless ennobles the aviators as knights of the air in a scene reminiscent of the romantic salute to war pilots in *Wings* (1927)—and also in the florid prose of Hermann Deutsch, who wrote about the dead aviator as "a gay cavalier of the skies" whose ashes are scattered from "scudding clouds," the remains of a man with "pulsing tissues" that had "once formed a living part" that had "clouded in the fine tingle of zestful living" (Brooks 402). It is not hard to imagine Faulkner's scorn, and yet affection, for such romantic literary effects.

Reporters in Hollywood films—like H. Joseph Miller in *I Cover the Waterfront*—are often aspiring novelists, chafing at the constraints of journalism, or playwrights like Stu Smith in *Platinum Blonde* (1931) seeking to evade the daily grind of the news. That they overcome the limitations of the trade and also, of course, win their lady loves, is precisely what Faulkner's novel contradicts as it shows how deeply mired the Reporter is in events that he cannot surmount through literature. Thus the copyboy spots another draft on the editor's desk, a draft that is factual, detailed, specifying time, place, and outcome, but not the Reporter's personal response:

> At midnight last night the search for the body of Roger Shumann, racing pilot who plunged into the lake Saturday p.m. was finally abandoned by a threeplace biplane of about eighty horsepower which managed to fly out over the water and return without falling to pieces and dropping a wreath of flowers into the water approximately three quarters of a mile away from where Shumann's body is generally supposed to be since they were precision pilots and so did not miss the entire lake. (315)

Of this version, the Reporter comments in a penciled note to the editor: "I guess this is what you want you bastard" (315). The Reporter's last words are directions to where he will be getting drunk and where the editor can come with cash to pay for the drinks. This disgust with the higher-ups is typical of movie journalists who delight in charging whatever they can to their bosses, and it is also, of course, the Reporter's declaration of independence. His behavior is not so different from Faulkner's conflicted relationship with Hollywood producers.

It is not surprising that Faulkner wanted to sell the novel to Howard Hawks.[6] It contains crucial elements of their earlier collaborations: a love triangle in the fraught world of flyers. Tom Dardis goes so far as to argue that *Pylon* is an homage to Hawks (Dardis 99). It is an action story resembling the director's *Ceiling Zero* (1936) and *Only Angels Have Wings* (1939). Faulkner's characters exhibit,

Dardis notes, "all of the typical Hawksian virtues of professional competence before danger, combined with stoical endurance, qualities equally esteemed by Faulkner" (100). That the Reporter can only observe these taciturn figures from the outside is, of course, consonant with what the camera can capture. The Reporter is, so to speak, the camera eye.

Peter Lurie calls the novel's basic elements—"the courageous pilots, the love triangle, and the boldface 'headlines'" used in Faulkner's own screenplays—"Hollywood fodder" (Lurie 16). The absence of other salable features, however, argues for a more ambitious novel-cum-film. "*Pylon* evokes Wiene's classic German Expressionist film *The Cabinet of Dr. Caligari*," Susie Paul Johnson observes: "As the reporter appears for the first time, the narrator describes the way the other characters 'were now looking at something which had apparently crept from a doctor's cupboard and, in the snatched garments of an etherized patient in a charity ward, escaped into the living world'" (Lurie 181). Faulkner's anti-realism in such passages countermands the journalistic imperative to record and document. So often in *Pylon,* journalists resort to their lurid imaginations when they are stymied by what they cannot see, when Roger, Laverne, and Jack are offscreen, so to speak. As Bruce Kawin concludes, the novel is "a story trying to tell a story" (Kawin 47), and such films are rare in Hollywood and evoke the kind of hostile reactions Orson Welles had to confront after the release of *Citizen Kane.* The Reporter himself pivots between elite and popular culture. He is the "sensitive go-between . . . alternately the tough, alert reporter of the American newspaper tradition or his more detached, urbane, Eliotic contemporary" (Torchiana 307). That kind of oscillation has perplexed certain readers of a novel Hollywood would have been hard put to homogenize. Without a clear denouement separating fact from fantasy, the novel-cum-film founders. Even the ambiguous *Citizen Kane* required an RKO resolution, a Rosebud.

And yet in 1957, Universal International released *The Tarnished Angels*, a film directed by Douglas Sirk and starring Robert Stack as Roger Shumann, Jack Carson as Jiggs, Dorothy Malone as Laverne, and Rock Hudson as the Reporter. Bruce Kawin scorns the adaptation—as did most reviewers—calling it "sentimental garbage," although he observes that Hudson is "more complex and interesting than the part as written." He also praises Malone, but deplores Carson's role as an "impossible combination of Jiggs and Jack" (Kawin 50). Kawin does not argue that casting a movie star like Hudson destroys the very conception of Faulkner's frail Reporter, who has no name and looks nothing like the handsome Hudson. "Sirk has no choice," it has been argued,

> but to glamorize Faulkner's pathetic trio, whereas in the novel, the glamour, invisible to all under the tawdry exterior, emerged only through the newspaperman's insight into the characters' lives. These limitations, however, are only the medium's limitations. They do not prevent the film from succeeding on its own terms, or, for that matter, from being by far the best screen version of a Faulkner novel. (Coursodon and Sauvage 288).

Robert Stack is so convincing as the tough—even menacing—Roger, who pushes around the hunky yet sensitive Jack Carson—that Hudson's yearning, tentative pursuit of Malone is persuasive. Hudson is grounded by doubts that never bother Shumann, and wisely the film does not allow Hudson to fly with Shumann, as he does in the novel. Carson's character is the perfect, economical solution to a film that cannot risk taking on extra scenes that would include Jack. Carson becomes, as he so often was in decades of film, the wisecracking, worldly, but also, sometimes, the empathetic complement to the hero. Jiggs fixes airplanes and, broadly speaking, fixes things between Roger and Laverne. He is their go-between, which is to say the film develops its own emotional logic and truth, even if Roger and Laverne talk too much about their feelings, as they never do in *Pylon*, and even if Laverne, at the Reporter's urging, returns to her Midwest home with not a hint that she will relinquish her child to Roger's father.

Since its release, *The Tarnished Angels* has steadily risen in the estimation of critics and has even been regarded as one of Sirk's "masterworks."[7] Sirk himself called it "perhaps, after all . . . my best film" (French). He had wanted to adapt Faulkner's novel since his early years in the German film industry. Sirk, born Hans Detlef Sierck just three years after Faulkner, arrived in the United States in 1939 and experienced the Depression firsthand, making it the subject of one of Stack's terse speeches when he upbraids Carson for buying an expensive pair of boots when they do not even have a place to stay. Hudson immediately offers his apartment to these refugees, whose homelessness obviously spoke directly to the deracinated Sirk. Faulkner's fiction is full of wanderers from Quentin Compson, Joe Christmas, and Lena Grove to Lucius Priest and Ned McCaslin— all of whom experience disequilibrium and discomposure that so often dogged Faulkner away from home. They are his emigrés.

James Harvey observes that *The Tarnished Angels* is the "closest thing to an art movie he [Sirk] ever got to make at Universal," a studio better known for its horror and science fiction films (Harvey 382). Next to Howard Hawks, no director in Hollywood had a greater reverence for Faulkner's work or a sensibility receptive to what many of Faulkner's American critics consider one of his weakest works. Sirk does not seem to have consulted Faulkner, and there is no record of contact between them, but Faulkner recognized their affinity when he called *The Tarnished Angels* "pretty good, quite honest" (Inge 162). Since he did not elaborate, a critic can only surmise what he meant. The film captures much of the novel's bleakness, especially in the way it intercuts the gawdy—even sinister—Mardi Gras scenes, emphasizing a society besotted with masking and dumb shows that make the heroism of Roger Shumann into just another carnival appearance. His World War I exploits are revered but also made into a poster, so that he becomes a prop of fandom, so to speak.

Not surprisingly though, Faulkner drew a line between the film and his book, saying of the former, "I'll have to admit I didn't recognize anything I put into it" (Inge 162). Sirk would not have objected, admitting that he had to "unFaulknerize" the film. Presumably, the director had in mind the requirement to make the characters explain themselves so that even the taciturn Stack tells Malone he loves her just before taking off in the plane that will crash and end his life. In *Pylon*, Roger and Laverne are unable or unwilling to express themselves because they are the antithesis of the world the Reporter wants to put into words. They elude the explicit.

After so much work in Hollywood, Faulkner understood the possibilities and limitations of popular cinema, just as he had mastered the art of writing popular magazine stories, conflating, as David M. Earle puts it, "modernism and pulpism" (Earle 194). Judging by Faulkner's response to *The Tarnished Angels*, he realized better than reviewers and academics how his work arose out of both elitist and popular sources. If he drew distinctions between his novels, screen work, and adaptations of his novels, he did not ignore their synchronicity. With *Pylon*, after all, he had Howard Hawks in mind. If the novel was not made to order for Hollywood, it had— as all critics agree—the basic elements, especially the love triangle he had worked out in earlier Hawks films. And Faulkner himself had done his share of Hollywood reductionism to suit the demands of the film medium, as he implied when mentioning, for example, his work on *To Have and Have Not* (1944), which Faulkner called Hemingway's worst novel.

If *Pylon* has not been deemed Faulkner's worst novel, it has certainly been ranked well below his greatest achievements. A far more confident man and writer than Hemingway, Faulkner does not seem to have been bothered by those who treated his work as a property to be exploited, or that he might exploit himself—for, yes, the money, but also, I think, out of a never explicitly expressed desire to impress his themes on the world at large using many different media and platforms. He might appear to be shy in public and reticent, speaking in that hushed soft patter, if he spoke at all, and yet he served in the role of writer-as-ambassador that Hemingway, for all his cultivation of a public image, did not. Those later diplomatic junkets to Japan and Greece, Faulkner holding court at the University of Virginia and West Point, were part of his work and became a part of his persona. Surely he did not have to go to work for Howard Hawks on *Land of the Pharaohs*. By 1955, his income was assured. He could say he was doing a favor for an old friend, but Hawks could not have been desperate for Faulkner's services. Hemingway, who never deigned to work for the Hollywood he disdained while cashing its checks, would surely have regarded working on a movie after the award of a Nobel Prize as demeaning. Howard Hawks said Hemingway told him "he didn't know whether he could be a good writer of movies" (Laurence 24-25). Although Hawks's testimony has been challenged, it seems reasonable to suppose that the highly competitive Hemingway would have been concerned about perceptions of him as a Hollywood hack—just one of those schmucks with typewriters that Jack Warner dismissed and humiliated as he did with Faulkner. In 1932, both writers were offered short-term contracts to write for the movies. Only Faulkner accepted. He did worry about Hollywood stunting his style, but never, it seems, about how others might devalue his work because he wrote for Hollywood. Faulkner, it appears, could look on his stints in Hollywood as just that—stints that could not bring down the house of Faulkner that even as early as 1932 had become impregnable. As Leonard Leff reminds us, Faulkner "threaded his way through the slicks" and even published in *The Woman's Home Companion* whereas Hemingway feared his appearance in such a magazine would be regarded as a sellout (Leff 33).

Faulkner was very much a part of the commercial world that his flyers have to navigate in *Pylon*. He cared about great writing just as they devoted themselves to great flying. He deplored his periods of indenture to Hollywood, but even hack work became a modest point of pride and even pleasure. "I had me some fun," he told an interviewer and even admitted to enjoying the "technical aspects of production" (Inge 14, 169). And he was not camera-shy, as is sometimes supposed when he is compared with the self-promoting Hemingway. Faulkner would say to his agent, "Don't tell the bastards anything" (Leff 112), but such a comment reflected a writer who wanted to be in charge of when and where he became a public spectacle whereas the bragging Hemingway liked to take on all comers. Faulkner's seeming imperviousness to the corruption that Hollywood and the slicks were supposed to exert on a writer's reputation dogged Hemingway like his own shadow and perhaps even infuriated him, which is perhaps why Hemingway implied that Faulkner did not know what was good for him.

I can imagine Howard Hawks saying, "Bill, I know you don't need the money now, but I'd appreciate your helping me out on this *Land of the Pharaohs*. And we might have us some fun." Was it for old time's sake? How could Faulkner resist making pharaohs talk like Southern plantation owners? This was, after all, a world-class novelist who said at MGM that he had an idea for a Mickey Mouse cartoon. That remark is sometimes brought up as a joke or to show how little Faulkner knew about who owned the rights to the rodent.[8] But ignorance or naïveté seem doubtful, since Walt Disney was already a highly celebrated Hollywood figure, and Faulkner did go to the movies and had his favorites like *Citizen Kane*, *The Magnificent Ambersons* (1942), and *High Noon* (1952) (Inge 162). Like the Reporter, Faulkner was fascinated by those ungrounded pilots who could seem like characters in a movie, unreal and yet palpably alive, figments of the imagination who remain, nevertheless, their own selves that neither the Reporter nor the novelist can quite fathom.

Notes

1. For the most detailed account of the short stories that culminate in *Pylon*, see MacMillan.

2. See Bradley, 19-20.

3. Laverne eschews the sentimentality of the wife in "Honor," who feels bound to tell her flyer-husband that she has fallen in love with his wing-walker partner.

4. For details about the Shushan air show, see Millgate, 140-41.

5. See also pp. 399, 402 for Brooks's identification of Deutsch as the model for the Reporter.

6. In December 1934, Faulkner wrote to his agent mentioning he had sent a copy of the novel to Hawks. See *Selected Letters*, 86.

7. See the entry on Sirk in Roud, 925-28.

8. Dardis believes that Faulkner was adopting a country bumpkin persona when he made the remark about Mickey Mouse.

Works Cited

Bassett, John, editor. *William Faulkner: The Critical Heritage*. Routledge & Kegan Paul, 1975.
Blotner, Joseph. *Faulkner: A Biography*. Vol. 1. Random House,

1977.

—. Interview with Hermann Deutsch. Louis Daniel Brodsky Collection of William Faulkner Materials, Center for Faulkner Studies, Southeast Missouri State University.

—. Interview with Richard Bradford. Louis Daniel Brodsky Collection of William Faulkner Materials, Center for Faulkner Studies, Southeast Missouri State University.

—, editor. *Selected Letters of William Faulkner*. Random House, 1977.

Bradley, Patricia L. "Angelic Acrobats and Fallen Southern Women: William Faulkner and Robert Penn Warren Go to the Circus." *Faulkner and Warren*, edited by Christopher Rieger and Robert W. Hamblin, Southeast Missouri State UP, 2015, pp. 19-30.

Brooks, Cleanth. *Toward Yoknapatawpha and Beyond*. Yale UP, 1978.

Collins, Carvel. Interview with Murray Spain. William Faulkner: An Inventory of His Collection at the Harry Ransom Center, Harry Ransom Center, University of Texas at Austin.

—. Interview with Mrs. Roark Bradford. William Faulkner: An Inventory of His Collection at the Harry Ransom Center, Harry Ransom Center, University of Texas at Austin.

—. Interview with Mrs. Vernon Omlie. William Faulkner: An Inventory of His Collection at the Harry Ransom Center, Harry Ransom Center, University of Texas at Austin.

Coursodon, Jean-Pierre and Pierre Sauvage. *American Directors: Volume 1*. McGraw-Hill, 1983.

Dardis, Tom. *Some Time in the Sun: The Hollywood Years of F. Scott Fitzgerald, William Faulkner, Nathanael West, Aldous Huxley, and James Agee*. Limelight Editions, 2004.

Earle, David M. *Re-Covering Modernism: Pulps, Paperbacks, and the Prejudice of Form*. Ashgate, 2009.

Faulkner, William. *Pylon*. 1935. Random House, 1962.

French, Philip. "The Tarnished Angels." *The Guardian*, 13 Sept. 2013. http://www.theguardian.com/film/2013/sep/15/tarnished-angels-douglas-sirk-dvd.

Fruscione, Joseph. *Faulkner and Hemingway: Biography of a Literary*

Rivalry. Ohio State UP, 2012.

Gwynn, Frederick L. and Joseph L. Blotner. *Faulkner in the University: Class Conferences at the University of Virginia 1957-1958*. UP of Virginia, 1959.

Hamblin, Robert W. "Faulkner and Hollywood: A Call for Reassessment." *Faulkner and Film*, edited by Peter Lurie and Ann J. Abadie, UP of Mississippi, 2014, pp. 19-20.

Harvey, James. *Movie Love in the Fifties*. Da Capo Press, 2002.

Inge, M. Thomas, editor. *Conversations with William Faulkner*. UP of Mississippi, 1999.

Karl, Frederick. *William Faulkner: American Writer*. Ballantine Books, 1989.

Kawin, Bruce F. *Faulkner and Film*. Frederick Ungar, 1977.

Laurence, Frank M. *Hemingway and the Movies*. Da Capo, 1981.

Leff, Leonard J. *Hemingway and His Conspirators: Hollywood, Scribner's, and the Making of American Celebrity Culture*. Rowman & Littlefield, 1997.

Lurie, Peter. *Vision's Immanence: Faulkner, Film, and the Popular Imagination*. Johns Hopkins UP, 2004.

MacMillan, Duane. "*Pylon:* From Short Stories to Major Work." *Mosaic*, vol. 7, no. 1, Fall 1973, pp. 186-212.

Matthews, John T. *William Faulkner: Seeing Through the South*. Wiley Blackwell, 2009.

McBride, Joseph, editor. *Hawks on Hawks*. U of California P, 1982.

Millgate, Michael. *The Achievement of William Faulkner*. U of Georgia P, 1989.

Paddock, Lisa. *Contrapuntal in Integration: A Study of Three Faulkner Short Story Volumes*. International Scholars Publications, 2000.

Roud, Richard. *Cinema: A Critical Dictionary*. Secker and Warburg, 1980.

Torchiana, Donald T. "Faulkner's *Pylon* and the Structure of Modernity." *Modern Fiction Studies*, Winter 1957, reprinted in *Faulkner and His Critics*, edited by John N. Duvall, Johns Hopkins UP, 2010, pp. 305-23.

Yonce, Margaret. "'Shot Down Last Spring': The Wounded Aviators of Faulkner's Wasteland." *Critical Essays on William Faulkner: The Sartoris Family*, edited by Arthur F. Kinney, G. K. Hall, 1985, pp. 204-11.

Andrew B. Leiter

Rotten Logs and Mud Holes: *Bildungsroman*, Sex, and the Other in Faulkner and Hemingway

In an odd scene from Faulkner's *Light in August* (1932), Joe Christmas flees Freedman Town and "the fecundmellow voices of negro women" that suggest to Joe the "lightless hot wet primogenitive Female" (115). Joe's flight from this racialized ur-Vagina encapsulates the conjoined racial and sexual anxieties that appear throughout Faulkner's fiction. The language also reflects Faulkner's ambiguous relationship to notions of racialized sexual primitivism that permeate modern American literature in supposedly positive contradistinction to Euro-American sexual repression. Likewise, we might understand how Mr. Compson of *Absalom, Absalom!* (1936) characterizes the female products of generations of interracial rape as informed by a white male perspective on sexual primitivism:

> He [the white man] planted the seed which brought her to flower—the white blood to give the shape and pigment of what the white man calls female beauty, to a female principle which existed, queenly and complete, in the hot equatorial groin of the world long before that white one of ours came down from trees and lost its hair and bleached out—a principle apt docile and instinct with strange and ancient curious pleasures of the flesh (which is all: there is nothing else) which her white sisters of a mushroom yesterday flee from in moral and outraged horror. (92)

In Mr. Compson's sexually defined characterization of mixed-race New Orleans women, the primitivism he associates with African ancestry complements the beauty he associates with white women. I do not want to conflate Faulkner with Joe Christmas or Mr. Compson; rather, I want to highlight the continuity of imagery featuring an original, primitive, racialized vagina that is metonymic for sexuality or "female principle" in two Faulkner texts thoroughly invested in the cultural pathologies associated with interracial sex.

Hemingway's work shares a similarly troubling fascination with gender and sex refracted through the lens of early twentieth-century concepts of racial primitivism. We might take, for example, the conclusion of *The Torrents of Spring* (1926), Hemingway's parody of the multicultural angst in Sherwood Anderson's *Dark Laughter* (1925), when a naked Indian woman walks into a restaurant and arouses a "vague primordial feeling" in Scripps O'Neil—a feeling that is fully realized in Yogi Johnson whose dormant sexual desires reawaken as "he silently strips off his garments" and walks off naked into the North with the still naked Indian woman (79, 87). This comic evocation of racialized primitivism in *Torrents* emerges in more serious fashion in other Hemingway texts such as *The Sun Also Rises* (1926) and *To Have and Have Not* (1937). In the latter novel, Marie, during sex with Harry Morgan, asks him, "did you ever do it with a nigger wench?" (113), while in the former novel, in a slightly subtler scene, Brett Ashley's relationships and sexual tensions with various characters play out in front of a "nigger drummer" who identifies suggestively with Brett while playing jazz and singing "you can't two time—" (69, 70). Such scenes establish racially defined sexual primitivism as basic fictive elements with which Hemingway contextualizes his exploration of "white" sexuality.

If Faulkner's and Hemingway's works reflect modern America's interest in racial primitivism, they also share a propensity to conflate concepts of the feminine with the natural world in a manner resonating with the tendency in American culture that Annette Kolodny outlines in her influential study, *The Lay of the Land*:

> America's oldest and most cherished fantasy: a
> daily reality of harmony between man and nature
> based on an experience of the land as essentially

feminine—that is not simply the land as mother, but the land as woman, the total female principle of gratification—enclosing the individual in an environment of receptivity, repose, and painless and integral satisfaction. (4)

Hemingway, in particular, idealizes the association between landscape and receptive female. In *For Whom the Bell Tolls* (1940), for example, Robert Jordan and Maria have intercourse in the heather of a mountainside, and the description of the natural world and the copulation are conjoined before the erotic culmination in which the "earth move[s]" (159). In his safari memoir *The Green Hills of Africa* (1935), Hemingway compares his love for the land to his love for a woman:

I loved the country so that I was happy as you are after you have been with a woman that you really love, when, empty, you feel it welling up again and there it is and you can never have it all and yet what there is, now, you can have, and you want more and more, to have, and be, and live in, to possess now again for always, for that long, sudden-ended always. (51)

In such instances, the feminine and nature become integrated objects of emotional and physical desire, an idealized state of connectedness—or, perhaps more accurately, possessiveness—that transcends temporality.

Faulkner's conflation of femininity and nature is arguably more widespread in his oeuvre and more multifaceted than Hemingway's association of sex and nature. Certainly, Faulkner at times concretely identifies the female form with nature or landscape, such as in *As I Lay Dying* (1930) when Darl considers his sister Dewey Dell in her wet dress and "those mammalian ludicrosities which are the horizons and the valleys of the earth" (164) or in *Light in August* as the pregnant Lena Grove walks across the Mississippi countryside. However, as André Bleikasten has argued relative to the latter example, Lena Grove embodies the "mythic space" of "primal mother or earth goddess" associated with generative feminine power and the cycles of the natural world (131), a space of feminized pastoral unity existing in sharp contrast to the story of Joe Christmas. In this sense, aspects of *Light in August* are predicated on Kolodny's notion of a male-imbued vision of harmonious feminized nature, but Faulkner's exploration of this idea is driven specifically by masculine alienation from the "environment of receptivity, repose, and painless and integral satisfaction." Faulkner's work is filled with similar, often critical, assessments of masculine struggles defined by, against, and within this fusion of the feminine and the natural world. Christopher Rieger, for example, argues convincingly that "*Go Down, Moses* reveals how the feminizing of nature helps to justify its exploitation" (154), and other critics have noted similarly gendered paradigms of nature in *As I Lay Dying*, *The Wild Palms* (1938), and *The Hamlet* (1940).[1]

This essay examines the intersection of Faulkner's and Hemingway's work in terms of their treatment of race, sexual initiation, and the natural world in stories of white male maturation. Concentrating on Faulkner's *The Reivers* (1962) and Hemingway's Nick Adams stories, I argue that both authors explore their characters' sexual anxieties and initiation from racialized perspectives and similarly suggest that coming of age necessitates, at best, a coming to terms with—and, at worst, the conquest of—the Other in terms of sexual maturation. Nick's retrospective consideration of his sexual experiences with Ojibway women reflects a simultaneous attraction and repulsion expressed in images of the natural landscape, such as muddy swamps and rotting logs. Likewise, Lucius Priest's retrospective tale of his rivalry with the mixed-race Boon Hogganbeck for the affection of a prostitute has similar racialized contours in which sex or "pugnuckling" is compared to immersion in a mud pit and fishing "Mary's hole" (140, 249). I contend that the two authors, in their prioritization of white male sexual initiation, objectify the female body by associating the female Other with the natural world as a primitive or primordial site of struggle for masculine growth. The similarities suggest that *The Reivers* might be a text demonstrating, as Joseph Fruscione argues in *Faulkner and Hemingway: Biography of a Literary Rivalry*, that Faulkner "had read, remade, and transformed some of Hemingway's work while trying to outduel him" (32). At the very least, the intersections illustrate a shared and troubling approach to modernist concepts of masculinity evident in Hemingway's and Faulkner's pervasive interests in the *Bildungsroman* genre. Despite these similarities in the construction of young white male identity, however, the authors offer distinct valuations of "primal" sexuality: Hemingway embraces that sexuality as a positive alternative to, or escape from, Victorian repression whereas Faulkner expresses more conservative reservations about the contingent social implications.

An experimental collection of stories and vignettes, *In Our Time* (1925) launched Hemingway's career, and he would return to the maturation of the protagonist Nick Adams in subsequent short stories, such as "Ten Indians" and "Fathers and Sons." The combined Nick Adams material, arranged by Philip Young and published posthumously in 1972 as *The Nick Adams Stories*, addresses a variety of initiation or maturation moments including knowledge of birth and death, sex and love, as well as a rivalry with the father. As numerous critics have argued, this development often takes place against a Native American backdrop and thus provides a distinctly racialized construction of white masculinity.[2] Considering the autobiographical roots of the Nick Adams stories, the Native American presence likely reflects to at least some extent the way the racial Other figured into Hemingway's concept of self and masculinity at both the self-consciously constructed and subconscious levels.

During Hemingway's youthful summers spent at the family cottage in Michigan, he became acquainted with the local Ojibway people and culture that would later filter into his fiction. Hemingway would remember, in particular, a young woman named Prudence Boulton whom he identified much later in life as his first sexual partner. Scholars agree that the Native American females of Hemingway's Nick Adams fiction were inspired by Prudence Boulton, but they disagree whether Hemingway ever consummated his relationship with the Ojibway adolescent. Carlos Baker has suggested that "Ernest's fictional accounts of sexual initiation with Prudy Boulton were more likely the product of wishful thinking than of fact" (26), while Jeffrey Meyers asserts flatly that there was "no sexual consummation" (502). Peter Griffin, on the other hand, asserts that it was "young Indian girls, some hardly into their teens, with whom he [Hemingway] discovered the pleasures of adolescent sex" (32). Ultimately, I am more interested in Hemingway's literary imagination and find myself in agreement with James R. Mellow, who takes no definitive stance on the biographical question of intercourse but argues, "Whether he had sex with Prudence in his budding adolescence matters little in terms of the persuasive power of her image in his fiction" (31).

Nick's moments of sexual initiation occur within a broader series of initiatory experiences related throughout the Nick Adams stories, but I am particularly interested here in those which feature the Ojibway people as measuring sticks of sorts for white masculinity. The most famous of these, "Indian Camp," offers Nick's simultaneous introduction to birth and death as he accompanies his father to deliver an Indian women's baby by Caesarian after two days of labor. Hemingway draws a pointed and, to some critics, crass distinction between Nick's father, a doctor who dismisses the woman's screams as "not important" in order to operate successfully, and the woman's husband who slices his own throat because, according to Nick's father, "He couldn't stand things, I guess" (18, 20).[3] Philip Young claims this first Nick Adams story establishes "what was to become the basic pattern of all his [Hemingway's] fiction, which is to expose a character to violence, to physical or psychological shock, or severe trial, and then to focus on the consequences" (32). More specific to *In Our Time*, Howard L. Hannum argues that the brutal operation and suicide establish the themes that unite the collection: "The Caesarian fixed Nick's association of blood and death with sex, and his obsession with the separation of body and soul" (93). Most importantly for this essay, Nick's traumatic introduction to these aspects of life is embodied by the objectified Native American female; meanwhile, Nick's father's masculinity or ability to "stand things" is more demonstrative in contrast to the Native American male's inability to do so.

Similarly, in "The Doctor and the Doctor's Wife," Dr. Adams's masculinity is measured against that of a Native American man when the mixed-race Ojibway Dick Boulton arrives to cut logs for

Nick's father. Reluctant to work off a debt (according to Dr. Adams), the Indian intentionally provokes the doctor into a potentially violent confrontation from which the doctor backs down. The story is riddled with phallic imagery of logs and guns that stress the masculine contest between Boulton and the doctor. Boulton arrives literally and metaphorically "to cut up logs for Nick's father" (22), and he warns the doctor not to "go off at half cock" before spitting "tobacco juice on the log" in question (24). The doctor in turn assuages his injured sense of masculinity by cleaning a shotgun on his knees and ejecting shells from the gun of which he is "very fond" (26).[4] "Indian Camp" and "The Doctor and the Doctor's Wife," Hemingway's first two Nick Adams Indian stories, thus explore the father's masculinity as an unstable identity that fluctuates in relationship to the Indian Other.

In the later Nick Adams stories, however, Hemingway moves beyond the father's masculinity relative to the Ojibway and turns to Nick's adolescent sexuality as it develops relative to Native American women in tandem with Hemingway's concepts of the primitive. Debra A. Moddelmog has contextualized Hemingway's primitivist notions within early twentieth-century Eurocentric understanding of non-Western sexuality. Specifically, she argues that Hemingway's attitude reflected the Freudian concept of non-Western cultures "as more in touch with their primal, sexually uninhibited selves" as opposed "to the repression, fast-pace, and over-civilization of the Western world" (361). In "Ten Indians" (published in the 1927 collection of stories *Men without Women*) and "Fathers and Sons" (published in the 1933 collection of stories *Winner Take Nothing*), Hemingway's sexualized Other highlights this cultural perspective as fundamental to Nick's maturation. Criticism of the two short stories has tended to focus on the prominent father-son relationship, but read in conjunction, the stories demonstrate a continuum of Hemingway's conflation of sexuality with the natural world as proving ground for white masculinity.[5]

"Ten Indians" relates Nick's return trip from a Fourth of July outing with the Garner family, during which they pass drunken Indians and discuss Nick's relationship with the Indian girl Prudence. The story contains stereotypical depictions of Indian drunkenness, odor, and promiscuity. Most notably, Prudence is compared to a skunk, yet, despite the unclean and degradingly animalistic association, Nick is proud "and happy inside himself to be teased about Prudence Mitchell" (29). Whether Nick and Prudence have had sex yet is unclear, and although Nick denies to the Garners that Prudence is his girlfriend, he clearly considers her to be so. "Ten Indians" offers an initial association between the Native American sexual object and the natural world that "Fathers and Sons" will later develop in full. Specifically, Nick's attraction to an "unclean" sexual object is reinforced by his barefoot walk home, which suggests a pleasurable descent into yonic filth: "The path was smooth and the dew was cool on his bare feet. He climbed a fence at the end of the meadow, went down through a ravine, his feet wet in the swamp mud, and then climbed up through the dry beech woods until he saw the lights at the cottage. He climbed over the fence and walked around to the front porch" (30). The fence Nick crosses might reasonably be understood as a demarcation between the sexualized natural world through which Nick has passed and the family space of the Adams cottage. This division between sexualized primitive space and non-primitive space is similar to Faulkner's aforementioned presentation in *Light in August* of Joe's passage through Freedman Town, his flight from the "fecundmellow voices of negro women," and his emergence into a white section of town and "the cold hard air of white people" (115). Unlike Joe, who at this stage is many years removed from his adoptive father's stern moralizing against fornication, the younger Nick still lives with his father who, although less physically abusive than McEachern, has a similarly corruptive influence on Nick's sexual psychology. When Nick enters their home, his pride in his relationship with Prudence is quickly shattered by his father's assertion that he saw Prudence "threshing around" in the woods with Frank Washburn (32). This revelation, while easily read as protective if somewhat cold, contains an inherent warning against associating with a promiscuous Native American woman, a warning that Christopher Schedler suggests may "reveal his [Nick's father's] own sexual repression and cultural biases" (72). Whether or not one reads Dr. Adams as sexually repressed in this instance, he is positioned antagonistically toward the racialized and sexualized natural world with which Nick happily identifies until informed of his sexual rival in the woods.

"Fathers and Sons" is the last of Hemingway's completed Nick Adams fiction, and the short story provides a culmination to Hemingway's construction of white masculinity through the objectification of the racial Other complete with sexual reservations expressed through images of the natural world. The story is framed by the adult Nick Adams travelling in a car with his son and thinking back to his youth and his relationship with his own father. Although Nick is appreciative of his father in some regards, he resents, as Paul Strong and Joseph Flora have argued, his father's Victorian sexual repression, which is more definitively established here than in "Ten Indians" and which Dr. Adams seeks to instill in his son with admonishments against buggery, masturbation, and prostitutes (Strong 53-54; Flora 240). Nick's resistance to his father's sexual repression is symbolized through a suit of hand-me-down underwear that Nick's father gives him but which Nick refuses to wear and hides under "two stones in the creek" (265). Nick's father whips him "for lying," and Nick fantasizes about murdering his father while sitting with his "shotgun loaded and cocked" and "feeling a little sick about it being the gun that his father had given him" (265). Against this phallus-heavy, father-son rivalry, Nick remembers his sexual "education … acquired in the hemlock woods behind the Indian camp" (260).

The hemlock woods feature prominently in the story as the old growth trees are under assault by Native American bark-peelers who supply the commercial market, "but there was still much forest then, virgin forest where the trees grew high" (261). The emphasis on deforestation has led to ecological readings of the story that address Hemingway's notions of the primitive. Robert W. Lewis, for example, ties the relatively unspoiled forest of Nick's youth to "chronological primitivism" through "language reminiscent of many other descriptions of a golden age or a sacred time and place" (205), and Susan F. Beegel analyzes the relationship of ecological loss, the father-son relationship, and the Indian content to contend that "the deliciousness of unbridled sexuality with his Ojibway lover becomes an erotic appreciation of nature itself, a kind of sensuous merging with the primeval forest … as though the earth itself and not earth's feminine emblem, Trudy, had received his seed" (96).[6] Hemingway and Nick certainly conflate the sexual with the natural world, and I agree with Beegel's assessment that the merger is "an erotic appreciation of nature." Furthermore, I would argue that both Hemingway and Nick intend to celebrate the Native American female in that merger:

> Could you say she did first what no one has ever done better and mention plump brown legs, flat belly, hard little breasts, well-holding arms, quick searching tongue, the flat eyes, the good taste of mouth, then uncomfortably, tightly, sweetly, moistly, lovely, tightly, achingly, fully, finally, unendingly, never-endingly, never-to-endingly, suddenly ended, the great bird flown like an owl in the twilight, only it daylight in the woods and hemlock needles stuck against your belly. (266)

The exultingly orgasmic language, however, is not only obviously problematic in its objectification of Trudy; it is also, within the fuller context of the story, revelatory as a celebration of white masculinity conquering the sexualized natural state of the primitive Other.

Trudy is one of the more debased sexual objects in Hemingway's oeuvre. She speaks pidgin English when she speaks at all, and her silence is indicative of her vacuity. She is indifferent to having sex in front of her brother, explaining: "I no mind Billy. He my brother" (261). She expresses an idle hope that they might have made a baby, which Nick dismisses with brusque and seemingly accurate authority as unlikely. The scene also makes it explicitly clear that the interracial sexual prerogative is not reciprocal in terms of gender and race. When Billy suggests that his half-brother plans on having sex with Nick's sister, Nick imagines annihilating the offending Indian by shooting him, scalping him, and feeding him to the dogs. The scene anticipates Faulkner's *The Sound and the Fury* (1929) and Quentin Compson's fantasy of shooting Caddy's fiancé Sydney Herbert Head as well as his confrontation with her lover

Dalton Ames at the bridge; however, Nick's "protective" rage has an additional interracial dynamic. Marc Dudley reads Nick's violent outburst as evidence of his racial anxieties at a time when "notions of assured racial dominance are fast becoming unraveled and, in some instances, altogether irrelevant" (64), while Richard McCann argues that Nick loses his idyllic connection to nature (and a corresponding distance from his father) by "casting for himself the role of white man defending the pure maid from the 'half-breed renegade'" (15). While it may be acceptable and even admirable in Hemingway's fictive world for the white male to embrace the primitive as a release from repressive Victorian norms, a further marker of Nick's burgeoning white, masculine identity is his desire to limit such seemingly liberating transgressions to the realm of white patriarchal power. Furthermore, the story suggests that, while the female Other represents a permissible, temporary sexual adventure for the white male, such a relationship remains relegated to the woods and unfit as a permanent, respectable relationship.

As with "Ten Indians," "Fathers and Sons" also—and with more extensive development—details Nick's barefoot walks, this time to his liaison with Trudy near the Indian camp, and again the descriptions imply a sordid femininity with Nick walking through "the black muck of the swamp" and "fresh warm manure" (260). This walk, however, is also littered with phallic images suggestive of endangered masculinity: "fallen logs crumbled into wood dust," "splintered pieces of wood [hanging] from the tree that was struck by lightning," "cat-tails ... that you soaked in kerosene to make jack-lights ... for spear fishing," and more logs "peeled ... huge ... and yellow ... left to rot" (260). These images resonate with the dangers of sex that Nick's father has warned him about in terms of disease and thus suggest that Trudy provides a primitive antidote and liberation from the father's Victorian repression. The imagery, however, also implies a broader danger to a masculine sense of sexual worth in the image of the cast aside, abandoned, valueless penis. In "Fathers and Sons," Hemingway alludes to and counteracts the sense of sexual inconsequentiality and betrayal implied in "Ten Indians" when Nick's father tells him about Prudence and Frank Washburn. Although "Fathers and Sons" does not relate the subsequent details of Nick and Trudy's relationship, the triumphal language—jointly sexual and natural—that Hemingway uses to describe their lovemaking anticipates his overt conjunction of sexual prowess and love for a particular landscape two years later in *Green Hills of Africa*. Moreover, Nick's reminiscence of Trudy years after their juvenile relationship suggests a possessiveness through memory that transcends temporality in similar fashion to the power of good lovemaking as described in *Green Hills of Africa* "to possess [the lover] now again for always." Having once possessed Trudy "fully" in a sexual sense, Nick may return to her in perpetuity as a seminal identifier for his masculinity.

Faulkner arrived at the *Bildungsroman* a little later in his career than Hemingway, and his first novelistic foray into the genre features a sort of anti-*Bildungsroman* in *Light in August* as Joe Christmas's childhood development reveals less of maturation than it does of psychological stagnation.[7] Joe's racial indeterminacy and corresponding masculine anxieties result in his repetitive cycle of violence against women. In later novels, including *The Unvanquished* (1938), *Go Down, Moses* (1942), *Intruder in the Dust* (1948), and *The Reivers* (1962), Faulkner explores the maturation of young white male protagonists as they grapple with, among other issues, Southern history, their fathers' and grandfathers' complicity in that problematic history, knowledge of class stratification, death, sex, and always race.

In comparison to Hemingway, Faulkner spent his childhood and youth in a more consistent relationship with a racial Other as he grew up with an African American "mammy," Caroline Barr, and in close proximity to other African American family employees and playmates. No evidence indicates that Faulkner had any African American sexual partners in his youth, yet his fiction suggests that the racially subordinate position of African Americans contributed to white males coming of age sexually with black women. For example, in *Absalom, Absalom!* (1936), Charles Bon introduces Henry Sutpen to the sensuous world of the New Orleans plaçage system in which wealthy young white men take light-skinned African American lovers as a routine part of coming of age in the antebellum world; furthermore, Mr. Compson imagines that Henry would have had no problem with miscegenation because he came from a world in which white women are sexually inaccessible until marriage, and white youths have access to "only the slave girls, the housemaids neated and cleaned by white mistresses or perhaps girls with sweating bodies out of the fields themselves" (87). Such sexual depredations were not limited, Faulkner indicates, to the antebellum world. In *Light in August*, Joe Christmas and a group of nearby farm youths "arranged" to lose their virginity to a young African American girl in a barn stall (156). It is unclear whether this encounter should be characterized as prostitution, a gang rape, or some other "arrangement," but the woman is thoroughly debased.[8]

Unlike Hemingway's "Fathers and Sons," Faulkner's *The Reivers* does not detail the white male's maturation as a specifically physical and sexual conquest of the racial Other, but rather, he frames the acquisition of sexual knowledge as a racialized experience which the youth must navigate and restructure from a white male perspective. It is a work whose racial implications, as Teresa Towner argues, have been largely ignored due to its comic format; however, Faulkner "situates virtually every question of self-representation squarely inside the contexts of individual identity and racial representativeness, and the resulting novel poses a thorough criticism of the ideology of whiteness" (4).[9] Faulkner described his final novel as "a sort of Huck Finn" in reference to the eleven-year-old Lucius Priest who absconds to Memphis with the new family car and two Priest family dependents, the part-Chickasaw Boon Hogganbeck and the African American Ned McCaslin. The interracial alliance follows a similar flight from societal norms as *Adventures of Huckleberry Finn*, but rather than a raft on the Mississippi, Faulkner presents a partial road novel that leads to the seedier elements of Memphis, including prostitutes, brutal cops, and horse racing. The novel highlights the transition into modernity with the juxtaposition of the automobile and the horse, both of which serve as emblems of masculine power that Lucius masters.[10] He first learns, in richly suggestive language, to drive with Boon's help: "So I moved under the wheel, and with Boon beside me, over me, across me, one hand on mine to shift the gears, one hand on mine to regulate the throttle, we moved back and forth across the vacant sun-glared waste, forward a while, backward a while, intent, timeless" (52). The sexually suggestive description of learning to drive is not coincidental, and we might read the passage as homoerotic in orientation and something akin to Leslie Fiedler's classic analysis of white heteronormative relationships being displaced by homoerotic attachments to the racial Other. Critics such as Anne Goodwyn Jones and Caroline Miles have convincingly identified homosexual tensions in the novel; however, I think that Faulkner is establishing within this scene, instead—or at least simultaneously—the role Boon has in Lucius's indoctrination into manhood that moves from the automotive to the sexual, two concepts with a long history of association in American literature and culture.[11]

The journey from Jefferson to Memphis on the dirt roads of 1905 is a difficult one, made particularly problematic by "Hell Creek Bottom," where a man has intentionally churned up a mud hole that is impassable for automobiles without the assistance of his ready-for-hire mules. Boon unsuccessfully attempts to drive through the mud hole, which is described as "a big receptacle of milk-infused coffee from which protruded here and there a few forlorn impotent odds and ends of sticks and brush and logs" (84). Similar to Nick traversing the swamp in "Fathers and Sons," Faulkner's mud hole evokes the image of a vagina with inconsequential phallic logs and sticks engulfed in mud. This phallic imagery is replaced by the equally impotent males who, as Lucius explains, descend into the mud to try to push the car through the mud hole: "I took off my pants and shoes and stepped down in to the mud. It felt good, cool. Maybe it felt that way to Boon too. Or maybe his—Ned's too—was just release, freedom from having to waste any time now trying not to get muddy" (86). Lucius goes on to describe the "almost primeval setting of ooze and slime and jungle growth and heat" in which "the three of us, three forked identical and now unrecognizable mud-colored creatures engaged in a life-and-death struggle with it" (87). Again, this scene might be read as homosexual in nature, but the subsequent contextualization of their struggle in the morass associates the mud hole with the image of a naturalized ur-Vagina present in Faulkner's earlier texts.[12]

The reduction of part-Indian, African American, and white youth to indistinguishable mud-coated entities resonates with the

Biblical Adam whom God created from clay and suggests an original and shared masculine identity that is helpless in the face of a primeval, elemental notion of the feminine that is in turn suggestive, perhaps, of stereotypical notions of Eve as seductress and source of original sin. If the males have been reduced symbolically to a pre-racial, original identity, the same may be said of the yonic imagery of "milk-infused coffee" that evokes a mixed-race or, more accurately in this context, a pre-racial vagina. It is of significance as well, however, that the males floundering in the muck have been darkened by the mud casting a racialized filter on their subsequent behavior in Memphis. The relationship of the mud hole to the brothel becomes more explicit when Boon, upon their arrival at Miss Reba's house, cautions Lucius that what happens in Memphis stays in Memphis while talking around the subject of sex: "think how much you have learned: how to drive a automobile ... even how to get out of a mud-hole." The two debate the value of knowing how to get out of a mud hole before Boon clarifies, "I aint talking about mudholes. I'm talking about the things a fellow—boy can learn that he never even thought about before, that forever afterward, when he needs them he will already have them" (104).

Although Boon avoids explaining the sex act to Lucius, the boy will learn about the act from Otis, a diminutive fifteen-year old who claims to be eleven and is visiting his aunt Corrie who works at Reba's. A thoroughly corrupt foil to Lucius, Otis is already a drunkard and thief whose largest regret at the moment is that he cannot drill a hole in the floor and charge people to watch the "pugnuckling" as he did when Corrie was prostituting back in Arkansas. Upon listening to Otis's explanation of "pugnuckling" and realizing what the other boy has been charging men to watch, Lucius goes berserk and begins pummeling Otis, who in turn draws a knife and slices Lucius's hand before Boon and Corrie can intervene. This entry into sexual knowledge through the utterly debased prism of incestuous voyeurism and prostitution serves as Lucius's welcome to the mud hole, an entrance which Boon succinctly summarizes with admiration: "Eleven years old ... and already knife-cut in a whorehouse brawl" (159). As the story proceeds, we witness Lucius's compatriots deep in the mud as well. Boon has a special interest in and jealousy over Corrie, which leads to repeated physical altercations with his sexual rival, the drunken and brutal Butch Lovemaiden, who uses his power as an officer of the law to extort sex from Corrie. Ned, meanwhile, relentlessly pursues the black help at Reba's, especially Minnie whose gold tooth is stolen by Otis and retrieved by Ned who hopes to parlay the recovery into a sexual conquest.

The adventures are comic but address serious questions about the commodification and objectification of women. Corrie, for example, was orphaned and forced into childhood prostitution. Boon's violence is not limited to his rival, and he beats Corrie because she had sex with Butch in order to get Boon and Ned out of jail. Ned, in turn, assures Lucius that hitting a woman is not problematic, "Because what better sign than a black eye or a cut mouf can a woman want from a man that he got her on his mind?" (263). Within this sexual cesspool and in contradiction to the mentoring of his black and part-Indian companions, the genteel and well-mannered Lucius seeks to redeem sexuality and women from their degradation with the chivalrous attitude he has already inculcated at eleven years old by being raised correctly, and in doing so, he seeks to redeem himself in light of his introduction to sexual knowledge. Although Boon admires Lucius's whorehouse altercation with Otis, which seems to mirror Boon's violent behavior, Corrie understands it quite differently: "You fought because of me. I've had people—drunks—fighting over me, but you're the first one ever fought for me" (159). The relationships of the novel from this point turn on the redemption of the prostitute whose full name turns out to be Corintha Everbe. The highlights of this redemption include Corrie renouncing sex much to Boon's dismay, Boon and Lucius's confrontations over her new celibacy, her extorted fall from grace at the hands of Butch, and her renewed efforts toward a different life.

During this restoration of a healthier and traditional relationship, Faulkner includes a scene that resonates with the earlier mud hole scene. It is a pastoral moment amidst the chaos in which Lucius fishes "Mary's hole," a fishing spot so named for the African American woman who usually fishes there (248). It is a scene of psychological struggle distinctly reminiscent of Nick's fishing trip in "Big Two-Hearted River" and his memories of fishing in "Now I Lay

Me" (1927), but Lucius's psychological concern is readily identifiable as his indoctrination into a new world of sexuality, about which—similar to Nick's attempts to control his thoughts—Lucius repeatedly asserts, "*I wont think*" (248). The return to nature here is a distinct juxtaposition to the commodified mud hole of Hell Creek Bottom, and although Lucius attempts to avoid thinking, the scene implies his struggle through the pointed phallic imagery of cane fishing poles, "a log to sit on," and, most importantly, "long frantic worms" which Lucius digs "out of the dirt" and which resonate with the three males wallowing in the mud earlier in the novel (248). Fishing Mary's hole suggests an alternative—less objectified, less commodified, less brutalized—female sexuality than Lucius encounters at Miss Reba's brothel. Moreover, Mary's hole alludes to either the Virgin Mary, the tradition of Mary Magdalene as a redeemed prostitute, or both. Mud hole and pristine fishing hole might suggest the dichotomy of virgin and whore, but the current of the novel, as seen in Lucius's developing knowledge of sexuality and Corrie's redemption, challenges the absolutism of such binaries. Lucius's awareness of debased sexuality and his refusal to adopt Boon's and Ned's eager validations of the debauchery should be read as a "white" rejection of sexual primitivism. Lucius's struggle to maintain a higher valuation of femininity plays out over the metaphoric pastoral vagina, and he continues to fight "for" Corrie as opposed to "over" her, an effort that ultimately brings Corrie back into the fold of respectable white womanhood with her marriage to Boon and the introduction of their baby named Lucius Priest Hogganbeck.

The conclusion of *The Reivers* represents a fitting culmination to Faulkner's literary career that addresses again and again the masculine effort to control or "protect"—with varying degrees of empathy, viciousness, and futility—women from their sexuality. Lucius's nearly ubiquitous predecessors range from the Compson brothers of *The Sound and the Fury* and Uncle Doc Hines of *Light in August* to Henry Sutpen of *Absalom, Absalom!* and Jody Varner of *The Hamlet*. Most significantly, *The Reivers* marks Faulkner's return to Quentin's psychological paralysis in the face of his sister's pregnancy, a return in which Lucius supersedes Quentin's failures to control or come to terms with Caddy's sexuality. Unlike his prior explorations of the male compulsion to exercise authority over femininity, Faulkner, in *The Reivers*, does not critique that compulsion so much as celebrate it through Lucius's gallant innocence. Rather than conceding to the examples of debased, guttural sexuality that mark his coming of age, Lucius redeems the fallen woman (Corrie) and elevates the racial Other (Boon) through his imposition of "white," genteel norms. This comic restoration of order in terms of sexuality and family, as it occurs against the background of racialized primitivism, might in this sense be best understood as Faulkner's late and even fantastical indulgence of a comforting white patriarchal order—an order that he elsewhere critiques as flawed and in collapse despite his characters' misguided and tragic efforts to preserve it.

Hemingway wrote "Fathers and Sons" in his thirties, and the story is certainly not a culmination of his literary engagement with sexuality as *The Reivers* was for Faulkner. It is the end, however, of his biographically infused *Bildungsroman* writing, and it represents a strain of Hemingway's thought on sexuality that endured through his life. Hemingway did not leave behind his notion of the "primitive" Other as an object for testing white virility and freedom from sexual repression. Most notably, he "went native" in 1953 while on safari and took an African "fiancée" named Debba. In a letter to Harvey Breit, Hemingway explained how he had shaved his head, begun carrying a spear, and taken a Masai fiancée: "My girl is completely impudent, her face is impudent in repose, but absolutely loving and delicate rough. I better quit writing about it because I want to write it really and I musn't spoil it. Anyway it gives me too bad a hardon [sic]" (*Selected Letters* 827). According to Jeffrey Meyers, Hemingway even compared Debba to Prudence Boulton of his youth (502), suggesting that the older Hemingway had—or wanted to have—much in common with his fictional Nick Adams and validate his masculinity through sex with the racial Other.

As the two most influential male fiction writers of American modernism, Hemingway and Faulkner significantly portray white masculinity as a constructed entity that develops against a conceptualization of the feminine in relation to the natural world, a relationship that establishes a primeval site for masculine sexual development and relies on notions of race and sexual primitivism.

In Hemingway's case, this involves the white male engaging in sex with a female Other whose promiscuous availability promises an escape from Victorian sexual repression, and despite the dangers and reservations Hemingway implies about unclean sex, he positions the debased and objectified female as the source of white male sexual liberation. Faulkner, however, presents the male maturation not as a sexual conquest, but rather as a contest between the racial Other (Boon and Ned) and the white male in terms of female sexual identity. In what may arguably be described relative to Hemingway as a more conservative text in terms of sexual attitudes relative to Victorian sexual norms and at the same time less misogynistic, *The Reivers* descends into a grotesque and racialized sexual swamp but emerges with a restored image of femininity that is determined by the white male coming of age.

Notes

1. See, among others, Shinya Matsuoka's "Faulkner's *As I Lay Dying* and Hurston's *Their Eyes Were Watching God*: An Ecofeminist Reading," Cynthia Dobbs's "Flooded: The Excesses of Geography, Gender, and Capitalism in Faulkner's *If I Forget Thee, Jerusalem*," Thomas L. McHaney's "Oversexing the Natural World: *Mosquitoes* and *If I Forget Thee, Jerusalem [The Wild Palms]*," Minrose C. Gwin's *The Feminine and Faulkner: Reading (Beyond) Sexual Difference*, and Lori Watkins Fulton's complication of this general paradigm in "He's a Bitch: Gender and Nature in *The Hamlet*."

2. See Linda Lizut Helstern's "Indians, Woodcraft, and the Construction of White Masculinity: The Boyhood of Nick Adams," Amy Strong's "Race and Ethnicity: American Indians," Paul Strong's "Gathering the Pieces and Filling in the Gaps: Hemingway's 'Fathers and Sons,'" Joseph DeFalco's "Initiation ('Indian Camp' and 'The Doctor and the Doctor's Wife')," Christopher Schedler's "The 'Tribal' Legacy of Hemingway's Nick Adams," and Joseph Flora's *Hemingway's Nick Adams*.

3. For concerns about the doctor's and/or Hemingway's treatment of

the pregnant woman and her husband, see among others, Christopher Schedler, "The 'Tribal' Legacy of Hemingway's Nick Adams" (67); Lisa Tyler, 'Dangerous Families' and 'Intimate Harm' in Hemingway's 'Indian Camp,'" *passim*; J. Andrew Wainwright, "The Far Shore: Gender Complexity in Hemingway's 'Indian Camp'" *passim*; and Judith Fetterley, *The Resisting Reader* (46).

4. This scene resonates with the closing scene of Faulkner's "The Bear" in *Go Down, Moses*, replete with similar phallic imagery as Boon Hogganbeck hammers at a broken shotgun in his lap.

5. For informative analyses of father-son relationships in "Ten Indians" and "Fathers and Sons," see, among others, Anne Edwards Boutelle's "Hemingway and 'Papa': Killing of the Father in the Nick Adams Fiction," Nancy R. Comley and Robert Scholes's *Hemingway's Genders: Rereading the Hemingway Text*, Joseph M. Flora's *Hemingway's Nick Adams*, Erik Nakjavani's "The Fantasies of Omnipotence and Powerlessness: Commemoration in Hemingway's 'Fathers and Sons,'" and Christopher Schedler's "The 'Tribal' Legacy of Hemingway's Nick Adams."

6. See also Marc K. Dudley who contends, "The Indian woods, stripped and gutted as they are, become an outward manifestation of Native moral decline" (59).

7. David L. Vanderwerken has argued in his essay, "Faulkner's Anti-*Bildungsromane*," that the anti-*bildungsroman* is the predominant pattern in Faulkner's presentations of childhood development: "The lessons they learn lead to confusion instead of insight, regression instead of growth, alienation instead of security" (56).

8. Eden Wales Freedman argues that the scene is a gang rape in her essay, "'You got tuh *go* there tuh *know* there': Reading Race, Gender, and the Womanshenegro' in the Novels of Faulkner and Hurston."

9. Most of the criticism regarding race in *The Reivers* concentrates

on Ned McCaslin, the most prominent African American character, with emphasis on how his presence forces a cultural reckoning of sorts on interdependent racial identities. In addition to Towner, see François Pitavy's "'You Can't Know. You're the Wrong Color': Faulkner's Copernican Revolution in *The Reivers*" and Walter Taylor's "Faulkner's *Reivers*: How to Change the Joke without Slipping the Yoke."

10. For informative cultural studies of the automobile and the horse relative to Faulkner and *The Reivers*, see, respectively, Deborah Clarke's "William Faulkner and Henry Ford: Cars, Men, Bodies, and History as Bunk" and Frank P. Fury's "Snaffles and Derbies: Horseracing and Southern Folk Culture in William Faulkner's *The Reivers*." For readings of the novel as a document of social change, see Richard C. Moreland's "Looking Back at Social Change in *The Reivers*" and Cheryl Lester's "'What the Future Will Now Bring Forth': Reminiscing for Posterity in *The Reivers*."

11. See Jones, "A Loving Gentleman and the Corncob Man: Faulkner, Gender, Sexuality, and *The Reivers*," and Miles, "Little Men in Faulkner's 'Barn Burning' and *The Reivers*." Other scenes with homosexual subtext include the mud hole at Hell Creek Bottom that might be suggestive of anal, as well as, vaginal imagery and Boon and Lucius's shared bed at the Memphis bordello.

12. Miles also reads the mud hole as vaginal in nature and this scene as the "total fusion of masculine and feminine [which] therefore points to the son's lack of a separate male identity when attached to the mother" (161).

Works Cited

Baker, Carlos. *Ernest Hemingway: A Life Story*. Charles Scribner's Sons, 1969.

Beegel, Susan F. "Second Growth: The Ecology of Loss in 'Fathers and Sons.'" *New Essays in Hemingway's Short Fiction*, edited by Paul Smith, Cambridge UP, 1998, pp, 75-110.

Bleikasten, André. "In Praise of Helen." *Faulkner and Women: Faulkner and Yoknapatawpha, 1985*, edited by Doreen Fowler and Ann J. Abadie, UP Mississippi, 1986, pp. 128-43.

Boutelle, Anne Edwards. "Hemingway and 'Papa': Killing of the Father in the Nick Adams Fiction." *Journal of Modern Literature*, vol. 9, no. 1, 1981, pp. 133-46.

Clarke, Deborah. "William Faulkner and Henry Ford: Cars, Men, Bodies, and History as Bunk." *Faulkner and His Contemporaries: Faulkner and Yoknapatawpha, 2002*, edited by Joseph R. Urgo and Ann J. Abadie, UP of Mississippi, 2004, pp. 93-112.

Comley, Nancy R. and Robert Scholes. *Hemingway's Genders: Rereading the Hemingway Text.* Yale UP, 1994.

DeFalco, Joseph. "Initiation ('Indian Camp' and 'The Doctor and the Doctor's Wife')." *The Short Stories of Ernest Hemingway: Critical Essays*, edited by Jackson J. Benson, Duke UP, 1975 pp. 159-67.

Dobbs, Cynthia. "Flooded: The Excesses of Geography, Gender, and Capitalism in Faulkner's *If I Forget Thee, Jerusalem*." *American Literature*, vol. 73, no. 4, 2001, pp. 811-35.

Dudley, Marc K. *Hemingway, Race, and Art: Bloodlines and the Color Line.* Kent State UP, 2012.

Faulkner, William. *Absalom, Absalom!* 1936. Vintage, 1990.

—. *As I Lay Dying.* 1930. Vintage, 1990.

—. *Light in August.* 1932. Vintage, 1990.

—. *The Reivers.* 1962. Vintage, 1992.

Fetterley, Judith. *The Resisting Reader: A Feminist Approach to American Fiction.* Indiana UP, 1978.

Fiedler, Leslie A. *Love and Death in the American Novel.* 1960, rev. ed., Stein and Day, 1966.

Flora, Joseph M. *Hemingway's Nick Adams.* Louisiana State UP, 1982.

Freedman, Eden Wales. "'You got tuh *go* there tuh *know* there': Reading Race, Gender, and the Womanshenegro' in the

Novels of Faulkner and Hurston." *Faulkner and Hurston*, edited by Christopher Rieger and Andrew B. Leiter, Southeast Missouri State UP, 2017, pp. 111-28.

Fruscione, Joseph. *Faulkner and Hemingway: Biography of a Literary Rivalry*. Ohio State UP, 2012.

Fulton, Lorie Watkins. "He's a Bitch: Gender and Nature in *The Hamlet.*" *Mississippi Quarterly*, vol. 58, no. 3-4, 2005, pp. 441-62.

Fury, Frank P. "Snaffles and Derbies: Horseracing and Southern Folk Culture in William Faulkner's *The Reivers.*" *Mississippi Quarterly*, vol. 59, no. 3-4, 2006, pp. 435-54.

Griffin, Peter. *Along with Youth: Hemingway, The Early Years.* Oxford UP, 1985.

Gwin, Minrose C. *The Feminine and Faulkner: Reading (Beyond) Sexual Difference.* U of Tennessee P, 1990.

Hannum, Howard L. "'Scared Sick Looking at It': A Reading of Nick Adams in the Published Stories." *Twentieth Century Literature*, vol. 47, no. 1, 2001, pp. 92-113.

Helstern, Linda Lizut. "Indians, Woodcraft, and the Construction of White Masculinity: The Boyhood of Nick Adams." *Hemingway Review*, vol. 20, no. 1, 2000, pp. 61-78.

Hemingway, Ernest. "The Doctor and the Doctor's Wife." *The Nick Adams Stories.* 1972. Scribner, 2003, pp. 22-26.

—. "Fathers and Sons." *The Nick Adams Stories.* 1972. Scribner, 2003, pp. 256-68.

—. *For Whom the Bell Tolls.* 1940. Scribner, 1987.

—. *Green Hills of Africa.* 1935. Scribner, 2016.

—. *In Our Time.* 1925. Scribner, 2003.

—. "Indian Camp." *The Nick Adams Stories.* 1972. Scribner, 2003, pp. 16-21.

—. *The Nick Adams Stories.* 1972. Scribner, 2003.

—. *Selected Letters: 1917-1961.* Edited by Carlos Baker, Charles Scribner's Sons, 1981.

—. *The Suns Also Rises.* 1926. Scribner, 2006.

—. "Ten Indians." *The Nick Adams Stories.* 1972. Scribner, 2003, pp.

27-33.

—. *To Have and Have Not*. 1937. Scribner, 2003.

—. *The Torrents of Spring*. 1926. Scribner, 2004.

Jones, Anne Goodwyn. "A Loving Gentleman and the Corncob Man: Faulkner, Gender, Sexuality, and *The Reivers*." *A Companion to William Faulkner*, edited by Richard C. Moreland, Blackwell, 2007, pp. 46-64.

Kolodny, Annette. *The Lay of the Land: Metaphor as Experience and History in American Life and Letters*. U of North Carolina P, 1975.

Lester, Cheryl. "'What the Future Will Now Bring Forth': Reminiscing for Posterity in *The Reivers*." *Fifty Years after Faulkner: Faulkner and Yoknapatawpha, 2012*, edited by Jay Watson and Ann J. Abadie, UP of Mississippi, 2016, pp. 254-67.

Lewis, Robert W. "'Long Time Ago Good, Now No Good': Hemingway's Indian Stories." *New Critical Approaches to the Short Stories of Ernest Hemingway*, edited by Jackson J. Benson, Duke UP, 1990, pp. 200-12.

Matsuoka, Shinya. "Faulkner's *As I Lay Dying* and Hurston's *Their Eyes Were Watching God*: An Ecofeminist Reading." *Faulkner and Hurston*, edited by Christopher Rieger and Andrew B. Leiter, Southeast Missouri State UP, 2017, pp. 168-82.

McCann, Richard. "To Embrace or Kill: 'Father and Sons.'" *Iowa Journal of Literary Studies*. vol. 3, no. 1-2, 1981, pp. 11-18.

McHaney, Thomas L. "Oversexing the Natural World: *Mosquitoes* and *If I Forget Thee, Jerusalem [The Wild Palms]*." *Faulkner and the Natural World: Faulkner and Yoknapatawpha, 1996*, edited by Donald M. Kartiganer and Ann J. Abadie, UP of Mississippi, 1999, pp. 19-44.

Mellow, James R. *Hemingway: A Life Without Consequences*. Da Capo. 1992.

Meyers, Jeffrey. *Hemingway: A Biography*. 1985. Da Capo, 1999.

Miles, Caroline. "Little Men in Faulkner's 'Barn Burning' and *The Reivers*." *Faulkner Journal*, vol. 15, no. 1-2, 1999-2000, pp. 151-68.

Moddelmog, Deborah A. "Sex, Sexuality, and Marriage." *Ernest Hemingway in Context*, edited by Moddelmog and Suzanne Del Gizzo, Cambridge UP, 2013, pp. 357-65.

Moreland, Richard C. "Looking Back at Social Change in *The Reivers*." *Fifty Years after Faulkner: Faulkner and Yoknapatawpha, 2012*, edited by Jay Watson and Ann J. Abadie, UP of Mississippi, 2016, pp. 243-53.

Nakjavani, Erik. "The Fantasies of Omnipotence and Powerlessness: Commemoration in Hemingway's 'Fathers and Sons.'" *Hemingway: Up in Michigan Perspectives*, edited by Frederic J. Svoboda and Joseph J. Waldmeir, Michigan State UP, 1995, pp. 91-101.

Pitavy, François. "'You Can't Know. You're the Wrong Color': Faulkner's Copernican Revolution in *The Reivers*." *Fifty Years after Faulkner: Faulkner and Yoknapatawpha, 2012*, edited by Jay Watson and Ann J. Abadie, UP of Mississippi, 2016, pp. 236-42.

Rieger, Christopher. *Clear-Cutting Eden: Ecology and the Pastoral in Southern Literature*. U of Alabama P, 2009.

Schedler, Christopher. "The 'Tribal' Legacy of Hemingway's Nick Adams." *Hemingway Review*, vol. 19, no. 1, 1999, pp. 64-78.

Strong, Amy. "Race and Ethnicity: American Indians." *Ernest Hemingway in Context*, edited by Moddelmog and Suzanne Del Gizzo, Cambridge UP, 2013, pp. 323-31.

Strong, Paul. "Gathering the Pieces and Filling in the Gaps: Hemingway's 'Fathers and Sons.'" *Studies in Short Fiction*, vol. 26, no. 1, 1989, pp. 49-58.

Taylor, Walter. "Faulkner's *Reivers*: How to Change the Joke without Slipping the Yoke." *Faulkner and Race: Faulkner and Yoknapatawpha, 1986*, edited by Doreen Fowler and Ann J. Abadie, UP of Mississippi, 1987, pp. 111-29.

Towner, Teresa. "'How can a black man ask?': Race and Self-Representation in Faulkner's Later Fiction." *Faulkner Journal*, vol. 10, no. 2, 1995, pp. 3-21.

Tyler, Lisa. "'Dangerous Families' and 'Intimate Harm' in

Hemingway's 'Indian Camp.'" *Texas Studies in Literature and Language*, vol. 48, no. 1, 2006, pp. 37-53.

Young, Philip. "'Big World Out There': The Nick Adams Stories." *The Short Stories of Ernest Hemingway: Critical Essays*, edited by Jackson J. Benson, Duke UP, 1975, pp. 29-45.

Vanderwerken, David L. "Faulkner's Anti-*Bildungsromane*." *Journal of the American Studies Association of Texas*, vol. 25, 1994, pp. 50-58.

Wainwright, J. Andrew. "The Far Shore: Gender Complexity in Hemingway's 'Indian Camp.'" *Dalhousie Review*, vol. 66, no. 1-2, 1986, pp. 181-87.

Eden Wales Freedman

"He could do so much more": Hemingway and Faulkner's Androcentric Treatment of Gynocentric Trauma

This essay analyzes representations of women and fetal and maternal death in the novels of Ernest Hemingway and William Faulkner to explore how two modern American male authors treat the gynocentric traumas that can accompany pregnancy, particularly for impoverished women lacking community support. The paper concludes that Hemingway, in *A Farewell to Arms* (1929), utilizes his female protagonist, Catherine Barkley, who dies in childbirth, to speak to the ideological fragmentation of male soldiers during World War I. As a result, the novel reveals more about the position of modern men and male trauma than about Catherine's individual struggles or the marginalization women faced in the modern era and beyond. Faulkner, conversely, depicts poor, pregnant Charlotte Rittenmeyer in "The Wild Palms" (1939) and Dewey Dell Bundren in *As I Lay Dying* (1930) as victims of a sexist and classist society, thereby acknowledging the difficulties impoverished, pregnant women can face. Whereas Hemingway uses Catherine's death to reflect the modern condition, appropriating her individual trauma to speak to a general and—for Hemingway—predominantly masculine sense of brokenness, Faulkner's fiction addresses the actual oppression poor women face in a patriarchal, capitalistic world—whether they die, as Charlotte does, or live like Dewey Dell. Faulkner's writing *can* have an androcentric focus, a tendency for which his novels have been criticized (Clark 143, Davis 441). In both "The Wild Palms" and *As I Lay Dying*, however, Faulkner breaks this pattern to represent women empathetically when he sometimes has not: Faulkner upholds women not as mere reflections of men (as Hemingway does in *A Farewell to Arms*) but as multifaceted persons in their own right.

Hemingway and Faulkner's fiction is characterized by the modern era's self-conscious break with traditional styles of writing to reflect the psychic shattering and disillusionment of the First World War. Throughout *A Farewell to Arms,* Hemingway underscores that his protagonist, Frederic Henry, suffers both physically and psychically from the trauma of war. Perhaps for this reason, Trevor Dodman suggests that the novel "stand[s] as a record" for modernity's "narrative collision with the violence of trauma" (249)—what Faulkner describes as a "sustained" and "universal fear" ("Upon Receiving" 119). Both authors display psychological insight into postwar trauma years before post-traumatic stress disorder was identified or diagnosed.[1] Hemingway's psychological acumen, however, applies predominantly to male characters' consciousness. Despite a nuanced understanding of modernity, trauma, and (male) psyche, Hemingway struggles to enter into and write out of female characters' perspectives. Perhaps accordingly, critics censure the modernist for his "unrealistic" and "one-dimensional characterization of women" (Brillhart 5). This problematic treatment of women is clearly evinced in *A Farewell to Arms'* Catherine Barkley. In contrast to Frederic, who narrates the novel, Catherine is not given a narrative voice, nor are readers welcomed into her perspective. Instead, Hemingway touches on Catherine's experiences only insofar as they pertain to Frederic's. For this reason, feminist scholar Judith Fetterley describes Catherine as a mere "reflection of male psychology," a character who is "understandable only when seen as a series of responses to the needs of the male world that surrounds her" (66). Catherine's experience and her strength are repeatedly co-opted to serve Frederic's needs.

Frederic is traumatized by World War I in particular and by the modern condition in general. As he travels across a battle-scarred landscape, he discovers that war destroys everything in its path. For Frederic, Faulkner's question to describe the modern condition—"When will I be blown up?" ("Upon Receiving" 120)—becomes both a philosophical and a physical concern. Though she has not seen the front, Catherine is also traumatized from having confronted broken bodies and psyches that, even as a nurse, she cannot heal. She also suffers when her fiancé dies in the Battle of the Somme (23). Instead of exploring Catherine's response to the trauma of war and the modern condition, *A Farewell to Arms* uses her character to speak to Frederic's shattered consciousness.

When Catherine tries to tell Frederic how her fiancé died, she speaks in a detached style, signifying psychic constriction, what psychiatrist Judith Herman describes as a "numbing response," symptomatic of post-traumatic stress disorder (42). "He was a very nice boy," she recounts rather robotically. "He was going to marry me and he was killed" (18). Frederic asks perfunctory questions in response: "Had you been engaged long?" and "Why didn't you marry?" (19), but the constricted Catherine is unable to answer. When she finally attempts to explain her previous relationship, Frederic quickly silences her: "I don't want to hear about it" (115). Frederic may resent that Catherine was previously engaged. He may not wish to hear about another man on a date. He may feel emasculated if he senses Catherine has had sex when he has not yet. He may not want to listen to a story about young men dying when he has witnessed so much death. Whatever his reasons, Frederic does not permit Catherine to share her experience, and neither does Hemingway. Catherine's grief at the death of her fiancé is elided to focus on Frederic's wounds (his fear of emasculation, his avoidance of death and pain). Moreover, Hemingway never returns to Catherine's point of view after Frederic silences her. The novel remains focused on Frederic's suffering, eclipsing Catherine's trauma to illuminate his.

Whenever Catherine does not say whatever—or act however—Frederic wants, he becomes resentful. On their last night together before Frederic returns to war, the couple rents a hotel room. Catherine's admission that the arrangement makes her feel "like a whore" irritates Frederic (141). "Oh hell," he thinks, "do we have to argue now?" (141). Catherine's distress, Fetterley explains, is something Frederic can respond to "only in terms of how it affects him" (59). Accordingly, Frederic does not dispel Catherine's concerns but focuses instead on his desire not to argue. Catherine, in turn, suppresses her pain to cater to Frederic's pleasure. She erases the "flatness" (or constriction) from her voice to perform the fantasy Frederic wants. "Come over," she purrs. "I'm a good girl again" (142).

Ironically, Catherine's behavior evokes that of a prostitute who flouts her desires to cater to those of her client. And Frederic, not unlike a john, approves of Catherine's performance: "You're my good girl" (142). Note Frederic's use of the possessive: Catherine is *his* "good girl"; she is not her own person. The adulation is also diminutive: Catherine is a good "*girl*," not an equal partner. Frederic Henry and Ernest Hemingway are not the same person, and Hemingway does not necessarily agree with everything his characters do.[2] In fact, *A Farewell to Arms* could suggest through such moments that Frederic is selfish and dismissive if the novel did not also celebrate Catherine's proclivity to submit to his fantasies. "I'm certainly yours" she capitulates (142). Earlier, she assures Frederic: "I'll say just what you wish and I'll do what you wish ... You see, I do anything you want" (100). If critics correctly read Catherine as one of Hemingway's "saintly" female characters (Brillhart 7), what makes her "good" is her ability to sublimate her needs to Frederic's.

On the few occasions when Catherine does not directly submit to Frederic, he overpowers her. When Frederic first meets Catherine, he puts his arm around her. She rebuffs him, but he is undaunted: "I kept my arm where it was" (29). Frederic then kisses Catherine against her will: "I kissed her hard and held her tight and tried to open her lips; they were closed tight" (30). This scene reads not as romantic but as assaultive, but, in the novel, no one (not even Catherine) seems terribly bothered by it. Although Catherine's first response is to cry and slap Frederick for kissing her against her will, she immediately apologizes for her behavior: "I'm dreadfully sorry ... I didn't mean to hurt you" (29). Frederic predictably does not apologize but reasserts dominance by kissing Catherine again (29). Rather than reevaluating his behavior, Frederic is annoyed by Catherine's initial resistance: "What the hell, I thought" (30). This combative start to the protagonists' relationship could demonstrate how the violence of war contaminates otherwise loving connections, but Frederic's abusive treatment still sends the message that what makes a woman "saintly" is her ladylike attempt to spurn a man's advances before ultimately yielding to them. What makes a man "masculine" is his ability to compel women to submit to him. For this reason, Dewey Ganzel characterizes Hemingway's "love story" as "badly flawed," depicting Catherine as "little more than an object of Frederic's appetite" as opposed to her own agent subject (576).

Catherine's pregnancy also becomes entirely about Frederic. When Catherine learns she is pregnant, she worries Frederic will feel trapped. The changes to her body, the responsibility of caring for an infant, the social shame she—not he—will face for having a child outside of marriage are all redirected toward Frederic. Catherine reassures her lover: "I'll try and not make trouble for you. I know I've made trouble now. But haven't I been a good girl until now?" (128). Catherine's declaration confirms that, as far as she and the novel are concerned, the only duty she has is not to "trouble" the man who got her pregnant. Catherine even blames herself for their failed contraceptive efforts, as if Frederic bears no responsibility for impregnating her. "I did everything," she professes. "I took everything but it didn't make any difference" (128). Whatever happens, Catherine is liable. Frederic is never to blame. Catherine, not Frederic, is at fault when Frederic assaults her: she should not have resisted him. Catherine, not Frederic, is at fault when she becomes pregnant: she should have used effective contraception. Catherine, not Frederic, is at fault when she dies: she should not have allowed Frederic to fall in love with her in the first place. Throughout, Catherine's traumas are appropriated to underscore Frederic's claim to her life experiences and his sense of loss at her demise.

Even Catherine's death is about Frederic. Catherine's passing, Pearl James explains, is "bloody, prolonged, frightening, and wasteful. She is young and has everything to live for. Her death [thus] epitomizes the shameful aspects of soldiers' deaths during World War I" (121). Catherine's "climactic death" (James 121) stands not for her own tragedy, but for the war in general and for the men like Frederic who are broken by it. In this way, Hemingway utilizes women's trauma (dying in childbirth) to comment on men's (dying in war). As Catherine dies, she repeatedly apologizes: "Oh, I wanted so to have this baby and not make trouble, and now I'm all done and all gone to pieces" (288). Catherine's phrase, "gone to pieces," reflects the shattering Frederic has experienced as a soldier. (In fact, Frederic uses this same phrase on the front [197]). Although Catherine has literally been cut to pieces by a cesarean section and now bleeds out, like a soldier on the field, Hemingway still makes her trauma about Frederic's.

Frederic's devastation at Catherine's death should not be dismissed. The problem is that Hemingway's novel focuses more on Frederic's *secondary* trauma than on Catherine's *primary* experience, and the text uses her death only to illuminate Frederic's pain. As Fetterley suggests, "if we weep at the end of the book," it is not for Catherine but for Frederic: "All our tears are ultimately for men, because, in the world of *A Farewell to Arms*, male life is what counts" (71). Catherine is expendable whereas Frederic is not: Frederic does not die in the war, but Catherine dies in childbirth because Hemingway needs her death to illuminate Frederic's pain. The last lines of the novel are Frederic's: "I ... left the hospital and walked back to the hotel in the rain" (332). Rain symbolizes Frederic's tears, the tears of a broken Western world, and the trauma of a modern landscape. Catherine's death becomes not about her own experience (or the dangers women face during childbirth), but about modern androcentric trauma.

Alongside Hemingway's, Faulkner's writing depicts modern rupture. His novels can also be androcentric, and women's traumas are repeatedly co-opted to speak to male concerns. What sets "The Wild Palms" and *As I Lay Dying* apart is that both texts celebrate women's agency and fortitude. "The Wild Palms" is one of two intersecting stories in the novel *If I Forget Thee, Jerusalem*, in which a woman becomes pregnant; her lover unsuccessfully attempts to terminate her pregnancy, and she dies of septicemia. Joseph Fruscione notes that the plot of "The Wild Palms" "borrows directly" from *A Farewell to Arms* (85). Harry is not a soldier like Frederic, but he shares with Hemingway's protagonist the modern, "tragic conviction" that nothing in life matters, a belief that causes him lasting and "profound despair" (Faulkner 95). Correlations abound between Catherine Barkley and Charlotte Rittenmeyer: Both women unintentionally become pregnant. Both die from blood loss. Both shout "don't touch me" as they die (Hemingway 330; Faulkner 240). Even Faulkner's depiction of Charlotte's dead body mirrors Hemingway's of Catherine's: Catherine's corpse is "flat under the sheet" (328); Charlotte's is "flattened beneath the sheet" (702). Both women suffer painful deaths, and both texts underscore men's agony when they lose the women they love.

"The Wild Palms" is not as androcentric as *A Farewell to Arms*, but Faulkner does at times use women's experiences to illuminate men's. Throughout the story, for example, Faulkner characterizes Charlotte's pregnancy as something that happens not to her or even to Harry and her together but to Harry alone. About Charlotte's pregnancy, Faulkner writes, "Then one day something happened to him [Harry]" (94). Later, Harry thinks about Charlotte's pregnancy: "*Something is about to happen to me*" (172). Philip Weinstein identifies "something" as a word Faulkner uses to connote trauma (e.g., Temple's "something is happening to me" as she is raped in *Sanctuary* [102]) (48). While Temple's rape actually happens to *her*, however, Faulkner appropriates Charlotte's "something" as Harry's. Moreover, Charlotte's death, like Catherine's, becomes less about her and more about the men who witness it. As Charlotte dies, her lover and landlord argue over who is responsible for killing her. The landlord shouts at Harry, "You have murdered her!" (23). Harry begs the proprietor to call an ambulance, but he calls the police instead (237). When the landlord tells his wife, "This woman is dying and this man must suffer for it" (243), he seems more concerned with blaming a man for a woman's death than with attempting to save the woman's life.[3]

In fact, "The Wild Palms" focuses so much on the men who behold Charlotte's pain (instead of on Charlotte's pain itself) that the story ends not with Charlotte's death but with Harry's trial and guilty verdict for *causing* her death (267). Moreover, when Harry confesses to having performed the abortion that killed Charlotte, Charlotte's husband, Rat, pleads in court on Harry's behalf. Rat also pays Harry's bail and gives him money to flee to Mexico to escape incarceration (269). When Harry refuses to leave, Rat offers him cyanide to kill himself so he will not have to exist without Charlotte (269). Throughout, Rat seems more concerned with saving the man, Harry, than with mourning the woman, Charlotte. When Harry rejects death-by-cyanide because he wants to live with the "forever and inescapable" grief at Charlotte's death (272), Charlotte's life is subsumed into Harry's, and her death—evoking Catherine's in *A*

Farewell to Arms—becomes not about the trauma she has suffered but about the heartache a man feels at her loss.

Despite these androcentric moments, Faulkner's treatment of women in "The Wild Palms" is more realized than Hemingway's in *A Farewell to Arms*. While Hemingway and Faulkner's plots are similar, their feminist content differs. Faulkner may even signify on Hemingway's novel, as Fruscione argues, to "differentiate his … concerns from Hemingway's" (86). Consider, for example, the deconstruction of gender norms in "The Wild Palms." Whereas Frederic is the stereotypical masculine, assertive (and assaultive) hero-protagonist, and Catherine is the feminine, "saintly" (and submissive) love interest, Charlotte is more "masculine" than Harry, and Harry is more "feminine" than Charlotte. When Harry meets Charlotte at a party, she takes immediate control of their relationship. "At ten oclock," Faulkner writes, Harry "said he must go. 'No,' she said, 'not yet.' So he remained" (37). Here, Charlotte recalls Frederic as she directs her lover's action. Harry's prompt submission to Charlotte parallels Catherine's submission to Frederic. Charlotte also makes more money than Harry does and maintains primary control over their finances (77). When Harry is fired from his job for "moral turpitude," i.e., for living with a woman who is married to someone else (81), his termination marks another reversal of gender roles. In the modern era, a woman would be more likely to be shunned socially for living with a married man while a man could be considered more masculine for conducting an affair. Here, however, Charlotte assumes the role of the dominant male, and Harry becomes the submissive female. Once Harry is fired, Charlotte continues to work while he stays home: "Each day she departed, … leaving him to move about the house empty" (94). Harry becomes domesticated, the stereotypical wife to Charlotte's stereotypical husband. Perhaps for this reason, Harry characterizes Charlotte as "a better man than I am" (113). Charlotte's very name reflects this gender-bending. Charlotte is the female form of Charles, the origin of which is "free man." Charlotte even introduces herself to Harry as "Charley" (37), presenting a masculine version of the feminine "Charlotte." Because, however, Charlotte is a masculine woman and not an actual man, she is still subject to patriarchal control—an inequity "The Wild

Palms" pointedly uncovers.

"The Wild Palms" also exposes the challenges non-normative women can face, especially when they lack economic privilege. Both Harry and Charlotte suffer financially during the Great Depression, but poverty does not affect them equally: Charlotte becomes pregnant and dies. Harry survives. If abortion had been legal and affordable in the 1930s, death-by-hemorrhage may not have been Charlotte's fate. Charlotte seeks an abortion primarily for financial reasons. When Harry does not want her to terminate the pregnancy, she reminds him: "Dont you see there is nothing else? ... We both know we cant have it [a child], cant afford to have it" (184). When Harry insists he wants a baby *despite* financial concerns, Charlotte counters: "I dont and you dont because we cant. I can starve and you can starve but not it" (173). B.W. Capo points out that Charlotte's argument echoes Margaret Sanger's regarding the "selfishness of bringing children into the world to starve" (38). With Sanger and other pro-choice advocates, Charlotte makes the provocative claim that aborting a fetus is more ethical than giving birth to a child who is likely to suffer.

Although "The Wild Palms" underscores the difficulties of being both poor and pregnant, the story does not suggest that poverty is the only justifiable reason to terminate a pregnancy. Instead, the text maintains that women can—and should—uphold their own wants and needs above those of an unborn child. Lanlan Du explains that Charlotte, in pursuing her own sexual desire, challenges traditional concepts of Western romantic love (63). Charlotte correlates her sexual relationship with Harry to her art, suggesting that sexual expression in women can itself be an art form. When she brings home her first paycheck, Charlotte tells Harry: "I like bitching, and making things with my hands. I dont think that's too much to be permitted to like, to want to have and keep" (75). Charlotte recognizes that society prohibits women from working and from enjoying sex; she wants to do both anyway. Charlotte's rejection of patriarchal norms insinuates that, in addition to financial concerns, a legitimate reason for a woman *not* to want a child is to join men in enjoying sex without having to link sex to reproduction.

"The Wild Palms" also challenges patriarchal norms by suggesting that women need neither seek nor remain in oppressive marriages. Faulkner depicts Charlotte's marriage to her husband, Rat, as a perpetuation of patriarchy: "*She had a father and then four brothers exactly like him and then she married a man exactly like the four brothers*" (70). Faulkner recognizes that women have limited options in modern society: they get married, have children, care for their husband and children, and die.[4] Frustrated with the restraints of patriarchal marriage, Charlotte leaves Rat and selects Harry as her lover. In contrast to her relationship with Rat, Charlotte and Harry's affair is based not on adhering to traditional gender roles but on subverting them. The fact that their relationship does not last (because they run out of money and Charlotte gets pregnant and dies) suggests that there is no escape from capitalist patriarchy. Rather than punishing Charlotte for the non-normative choices she makes, "The Wild Palms" underscores the oppression inherent in a system that does not allow women to make—or to enjoy freely—their own choices.

"The Wild Palms" also challenges patriarchal norms by suggesting that women cannot be equal, happy, or free until empowered to control their own reproduction. Charlotte, not Harry, insists on the abortion, viewing the procedure as a means to assert control over her fertility: she even "boil[s] the water" and "fetche[s] out the meagre instruments" herself (185). Harry, conversely, uses figurative language to refer to abortion. He tells Charlotte: "You just have to let the air in" (185), a phrase that recalls Hemingway's 1927 story "Hills Like White Elephants" (212) and demonstrates an urban legend regarding the procedure (Capo 138). By having a naïve and blundering man repeat Hemingway's original words, Faulkner signifies on Hemingway's fiction, suggesting that men (like Harry and Hemingway) do not understand abortion—even when they have trained at medical school, as Harry has. Women, conversely, understand their bodies, but society restricts their ability to control them. When Charlotte discovers that her friend, Bill, is pregnant and cannot afford to have a child, she convinces Harry to perform an abortion for her. Bill has the procedure without incident, and she and her lover, Buck, leave the area to pursue a better life together. Bill is not textually punished for terminating her pregnancy, and her abortion is not treated as a tragedy but as a medical necessity that allows her the freedom to pursue a happy life. Through such scenes, "The Wild Palms" presents women's reproductive freedom as a key component of their liberation.

When women cannot control their reproduction, "The Wild Palms" suggests, everything goes wrong. Charlotte practices post-coital douching, which Capo explains was "one of the most popular methods" of contraception in the 1940s since douche bags could be purchased at most drugstores (138). This method of birth control is successful until Charlotte's douche bag freezes in the cold, thaws, then bursts (172). Because they live in a remote, impoverished mining community, Charlotte cannot buy a replacement. Rather than penalizing Charlotte for having extramarital sex or becoming pregnant, Faulkner's story explores the ways in which lack of access to birth control affects women's health. Though the abortion is Charlotte's idea, a fact critics have used to argue her self-destructiveness as a character and punishment for being non-traditional (Craig 144), Faulkner's story emphasizes that it is not through Charlotte's choice but through society's restriction of her choices that her downfall occurs. Because of patriarchal social strictures, Charlotte must depend on Harry to solve the problem of her unplanned pregnancy. If Charlotte had had access to a more reliable contraceptive than a douche bag, if she had a safe alternative to obtain an abortion, her fate may have been quite different.

When Charlotte asks Harry to perform an abortion (as he recently and successfully has for Bill), he avoids her in an attempt to eschew both the problem (her unplanned pregnancy) and her proposed solution (an illegal abortion). Following Charlotte's request for an abortion, Harry makes every effort *"not to see her"* (174). His response is shortsighted and cowardly; Harry cannot solve Charlotte's predicament by ignoring it. In a final effort to shirk responsibility for Charlotte's pregnancy and his termination of it, Harry attempts to buy her an abortifacient pill. As a medical student, he knows that the pill will be less effective than an abortion. In fact, he knows the pill is unlikely to be effective at all.[5] The pill, however, temporarily relieves Harry of his fear of having to perform the abortion on Charlotte himself. Harry's reluctance to conduct the procedure results in Charlotte's death since the pill he buys is indeed ineffectual, he waits too long to terminate, and then has to perform the abortion anyway. Such moments expose the perils women face when denied reproductive care. If Charlotte had had access to reliable contraception, if she had not had to rely on a conflicted man to perform an illegal procedure, she would likely have survived to "bitch" again. When Charlotte bleeds to death, the story underscores not the shame women should feel when they accidentally become pregnant but the dangers women confront when choice is denied. In this way, "The Wild Palms" operates as a feminist text (and a response to Hemingway's *A Farewell to Arms*), testifying not only to androcentric modern anxiety (symbolized through Harry) but also to the compounded jeopardies women, such as Charlotte, encounter and the traumatic consequences that ensue when women are denied equity.

Faulkner takes up a similar theme in *As I Lay Dying*. The novel begins with seventeen-year-old Dewey Dell agonizing over an unplanned pregnancy. Unlike Charlotte, Dewey Dell does not seem to enjoy sex. She sleeps with her boyfriend, Lafe, not because she wants to but because she does not seem to know she can refuse him. When Lafe initiates sex, Dewey Dell offers minor resistance, asking, "What are you doing?" (27). When Lafe answers, "I am picking into your sack" (27), Dewey Dell silently endures his objectification (which treats her as a "thing" to be "picked into") and passively submits. "So it was," she recalls, "I could not help it" (27).[6] Here, Faulkner does not seem to blame Dewey Dell for having sex and becoming pregnant. Instead, he underlines the importance of affirmative consent, arguing—through Dewey Dell's example—that just because one does not clearly say "no" to sex does not mean one voluntarily agrees to it. Passive resistance and coerced acceptance do not constitute active consent, and, if Dewey Dell has not in fact agreed to sex, her intercourse with Lafe is not mutual but coercive. Some who oppose abortion argue that women who become pregnant should accept the consequences of sex and give birth. If a woman is ready to have sex, they maintain, she should be prepared to parent ("Ethics Guide").[7] *As I Lay Dying* challenges this claim: Dewey Dell is ready for neither sex nor motherhood, but is impelled into both by a coercive boyfriend and a patriarchal society that wrest control from her over her own body.[8]

Note that Dewey Dell is not violently attacked by Lafe but feels pressured into sex with him. She does not tell Lafe "no," but she does not say "yes" either. By her own admission, when they are about to have sex, "I didn't say anything" (27). Dewey Dell does not actively consent. She simply feels she has no other option. While pro-life advocates sometimes support terminating pregnancies that result from rape and incest (Varga 67), few uphold sexual coercion as a reason to abort. If Dewey Dell had been raped by her father instead of feeling manipulated by her boyfriend, some may more comfortably support her decision to abort. In framing Dewey Dell's impregnation as the result of coercion as opposed to more obvious forms of assault,[9] Faulkner challenges readers to reconsider what constitutes sexual assault and when a woman is entitled to full reproductive rights. A woman has been assaulted if she does not actively consent to sex, *As I Lay Dying* argues. She is entitled always to reproductive freedom.

Because abortion (or birth control for that matter[10]) is neither legal nor accessible, Dewey Dell faces additional risks when seeking to terminate her pregnancy, namely the persistent danger of sexual assault. In contrast to Hemingway's representation of assault as "romantic" in *A Farewell to Arms*, Faulkner depicts Dewey Dell's sexual encounters not as amorous but as assaultive. Indeed, the omnipresent risk of sexual assault pervades the narrative. When Dewey Dell enters a pharmacy, looking for an abortifacient, the clerk, MacGowan, takes advantage of her naiveté and desperation by pretending to be a doctor who can perform an abortion by having sex with her. Dewey Dell offers MacGowan ten dollars to perform the procedure, but the clerk tells her that her money is not enough. MacGowan then coerces Dewey Dell into sex as payment for abortion. The desperate girl agrees to MacGowan's terms, though it remains unclear whether or not she realizes precisely what Mac-Gowan expects from her. Again, Dewey Dell's sexual encounter is non-consensual. While she passively submits to what men demand, she does not actively consent to intercourse. Here, Faulkner seems to suggest that a poor, uneducated "country woman" (241) such as Dewey Dell has few options. They cannot control their reproductive systems via birth control or abortion, and men repeatedly exploit their vulnerability by coercing them into sex. Dewey Dell does not actively choose to have sex with Lafe or MacGowan or to become pregnant. She *does* choose to terminate her pregnancy (the only active choice she makes in the novel), but this choice is also denied to her.

As I Lay Dying also makes clear that the danger women face is not limited to one "bad" man but reflects systemic sexism in a patriarchal world. Impoverished women such as Dewey Dell cannot stop men from having sex with them, cannot keep themselves from getting pregnant, and cannot terminate their pregnancies. Faulkner underscores this reality when MacGowan and his co-worker, Jody, conspire to assault Dewey Dell. When he first meets Dewey Dell, MacGowan nearly sends her away until Jody tells him "she looks pretty good for a country girl" (242). MacGowan and Jody undercut Dewey Dell because she is poor. She is only "*pretty* hot" and only "for a *country* girl" (242; emphasis added). She *is* assaultable, however. Faulkner also suggests here that bystanders impact how women are treated: Jody could have let Dewey Dell go. Instead, he participates in a pattern of patriarchal control and sexual abuse by playing wingman to his friend. He then stands guard for MacGowan while MacGowan assaults Dewey Dell in the back of the pharmacy (242). The point is clear: sexual assault is convenient for men like MacGowan and Jody. Bodily autonomy is often impossible for women like Dewey Dell.

When MacGowan tells Jody he plans to assault the girl, Jody asks: "Aint you going to give me no seconds on it?" (243). That Jody asks his male friend, MacGowan, not Dewey Dell, to get in "on it" suggests the girl has no choice over what happens to her body. Men (MacGowan) not women (Dewey Dell) use and abuse women's bodies. Here, Jody's "it" refers both to the assault (the act of sex) and to Dewey Dell herself—who is again treated as an object, an "it," not a person ("her"). When MacGowan refuses: "What the hell do you think this is ... a stud-farm?" (243), he does not protect Dewey Dell from the violence of multiple assaults but takes control of the girl's body as his property: he does not want to share his sex object with another man. Note too that Jody refers to Dewey Dell as food. He asks for "seconds," and MacGowan treats her like an animal when he says he is not running a "stud-farm." Neither man recognizes the girl's humanity. Such scenes highlight the trauma women encounter when they seek bodily control only to face further violation. Mac-Gowan reflects: "Them country people. Half the time they don't know what they want" (243). MacGowan's dismissal of Dewey Dell (and all country people) suggests that she is too poor and stupid to know whether she wants an abortion or an assault. As a representative of the patriarchy, he decides for her and takes what he wants, independent of her desires. MacGowan's behavior toward his victim shows how little social power girls like Dewey Dell have to protect themselves against men who would harm them.

As I Lay Dying also exposes the slut-shaming women encounter when pursuing reproductive freedom. When the pharmacist, Moseley, realizes that Dewey Dell is pregnant, he asks her: "You are not married, are you?" (201). Moseley is one of the more benevolent men in the text. He does not assault Dewey Dell and thinks kindly, if paternally, about her. Instead, however, of trying to help her, he judges the teenager for becoming pregnant while unmarried. Mac-Gowan slut-shames Dewey Dell by assuming falsely that she has had multiple sexual partners simply because she is pregnant and unwed: "Which one" got you pregnant? he asks (244). When Dewey Dell tells him she has had sex with only one person, MacGowan does not believe her. Such sexist attitudes, which blame and shame women for getting pregnant without being married, make Dewey Dell want to have the abortion in the first place. She is already marginalized as a "country girl." Now she faces compounded stigmatization as a poor, pregnant "slut." Perhaps for this reason, Dewey Dell "don't say nothing" (247) in response to MacGowan's prodding. She does not know how to defend herself, so she remains silent, just as she is silent when first Lafe and then MacGowan have sex with her.

Repeatedly, Faulkner emphasizes how difficult it is to be a poor woman in a capitalistic patriarchy. After slut-shaming Dewey Dell, MacGowan tells her to come back at night so he can "perform the operation" (247) or have sex with her: "It wont hurt you," he assures her, "You've had the same operation before" (247). MacGowan assumes that, because Dewey Dell has previously had intercourse, sex with him "wont hurt." He presumes she must be promiscuous if she is pregnant and unwed. Dewey Dell is not promiscuous, but even if she were, her sexual history does not justify sexual assault. Through such scenes, Faulkner underscores that men control women's bodies, and women, denied choice, must rely on the men who blame, shame, and abuse them.

Even the ten dollars Dewey Dell offers MacGowan point to women's lack of control. Lafe, who gives Dewey Dell the money (presumably for an abortion), treats her like a prostitute, someone he can pay and leave for a minimal fee. When Dewey Dell's father, Anse, learns his daughter has ten dollars, he immediately takes it from her. Dewey Dell, coerced into sex by both Lafe and Mac-Gowan, refuses to give her father the money, shouting, "Dont you touch it" (255). Her body and psyche have been violated by Lafe and MacGowan. If she cannot control her mind or body, she wants at least to control her capital. When Anse takes the money anyway, his action represents another assault: Dewey Dell cannot control what should be hers. Men take what they want from her whether she submits silently (as she did with Lafe and MacGowan) or actively refuses them (as she does with her father). Leslie Fiedler argues that Faulkner "echoes in his fiction" Hemingway's "anti-feminism" in repeatedly suggesting that men are "helpless in the hands" of women and that women, possessing neither "morality" nor "honor," use their "sexuality with cold calculation to achieve their inscrutable ends" (26). *As I Lay Dying* seems to argue the opposite. In this novel, men take advantage of women, and women are not empowered to stop them.

Dewey Dell's second narrative section begins: "He could do so much for me if he just would. He could do everything for me" (58). "He" likely refers to Dr. Peabody, the Bundrens' family doctor and the first man in the novel to refuse to terminate Dewey Dell's pregnancy. "He," however, could also signify every other man Dewey Dell encounters in the text: Lafe, who could have chosen *not* to coerce her into sex (or to abandon her thereafter); her father and brothers, who largely ignore her (except for Darl, who taunts her about her pregnancy [26]); Moseley, who judges her, then turns her away; Jody and MacGowan who conspire to assault her; and the patriarchy in general—that overarching "he," which systemically controls all women. Perhaps, in a meta moment, "he" could refer to Faulkner himself, whose story exposes impoverished women's desperation without providing solutions to the challenges they face. At the end of the novel, Dewey Dell's story remains unresolved; her prospects are grim. She has not found anyone willing to perform an abortion. Her failed attempt to terminate her pregnancy results only in assault, and she is likely either to suffer harm from a botched procedure (as Charlotte does) or to struggle to raise her child alone in abject poverty.

To be a woman, Faulkner suggests, is often to be ostracized and alone. When MacGowan asks Dewey Dell, "what is your trouble?," she responds: "It's the female trouble" (243). Literally, she means her pregnancy, but her answer makes a larger point: her trouble is distinctly female, the "trouble" of being a woman who lacks agency over her own body. Both Charlotte and Dewey Dell want abortions because they are young, poor, and desperate. Charlotte wants an abortion because she is an artist, because she is sexual, because she wants to work and play and create art—not just babies. Dewey Dell seeks termination because she is poor, assaulted, unaided, and shamed. Whatever their reasons, Faulkner supports their quest. In this way, Faulkner's narratives, contra Hemingway's novel, operate as feminist texts, testifying to the "troubling" consequences that ensue when women are denied bodily autonomy.

Faulkner is not a perfect writer, and Charlotte Rittenmeyer and Dewey Dell withstanding, his novels' treatment of women is inconsistent at best. Nevertheless, as André Bleikasten argues, what is "admirable" about Faulkner's fiction is not its "embroilment" in patriarchal ideology but the fact that it "manages so often to give" sexism "the slip" (213). No writer, Bleikasten maintains, is "above" the limitations of his time (or, in Faulkner's case, his identity constructs as a white Southern male). It is "equally important to acknowledge," however, Faulkner's "keen sensitivity" to the violence done to the "downtrodden," such as Charlotte Rittenmeyer and Dewey Dell Bundren (Bleikasten 213). Could Faulkner do "so much more" for his impoverished female characters? Absolutely. Nevertheless, in "The Wild Palms" and *As I Lay Dying*, Faulkner still fares better than those, such as Hemingway, whose texts remain blind to gyno-centric trauma and (mis)appropriate female characters' experiences to speak to androcentric concerns. Moreover, what Faulkner *does* do for his heroines (especially in contrast to Hemingway's treatment of Catherine Barkley) is remarkable not only for the modern era but for all time.

Notes

1. Post-traumatic stress disorder (PTSD) was not officially recognized by the American Psychiatric Association until 1980. Writing in the early twentieth century, Faulkner and Hemingway would not have been able to classify their characters' symptoms of post-traumatic stress. Nevertheless, both authors' characters repeatedly (and realistically) demonstrate behaviors indicative of PTSD, perhaps because the phrase "shell shock"—an early attempt to define PTSD-like symptoms—was coined during World War I, and both Faulkner and Hemingway would have been familiar with that term and its symptoms.

2. The novel, however, is based on Hemingway's experiences serving in the Italian army during World War I, and the inspiration for Catherine Barkley is the real-life Agnes von Kurowsky, a nurse who cared for Hemingway in Milan while he was wounded (McIlvaine 445). Depending on how closely Hemingway modeled his novel on his own life, protagonist and author may be more similar than not.

3. The landlord seems more upset that Harry has performed an abortion than that Harry has killed Charlotte. This concern over Harry's behavior overrides any effort to save Charlotte's life. It is worth noting that Faulkner appears critical of this attitude (267).

4. The quotation continues: "*so she probably never even had a room of her own in all her life*" (70). The phrase "a room of her own" recalls Virginia Woolf's 1929 argument that women will not be as successful as men until they have their own space in which to work and create (3). Quoting Woolf, Faulkner suggests that women need both

physical and social space to "bitch" and "make things," to be free. Faulkner may even insinuate that because he, as a man, already has a "room of his own," he can profitably write and publish whereas Charlotte, a woman, cannot.

5. When Harry tells a pharmacist in another town that he "knocked up [his] girl" and needs "something for it," the pharmacist charges him five dollars for a pill they both know will not work: "Do you guarantee it?" Harry asks. "Nah," the clerk responds. "All right," Harry decides. "I'll take it" (180).

6. Dewey Dell also cedes agency to Lafe when she thinks, "if the sack is full, I cannot help it" (27) and "so it was full when we came to the end of the row and I could not help it" (27). Some might read this passage as her attempt to justify having premarital sex (i.e., since her "sack was full," she was destined to have sex at that point). It seems more likely, however, that Dewey Dell worries about Lafe's expectation that she will have sex with him ("the woods getting closer and closer ... I said will I or wont I ...?"), feels she does not have a choice in the matter ("I cannot help it. It will be that I had to do it all the time and I cannot help it"), and promptly disassociates from the imminent act ("when we get to the woods it wont be me") (27). Disassociation is another symptom of PTSD (Simeon and Abugel 17), suggesting that Dewey Dell feels anxious about (and even traumatized in anticipation of) having sex but has sex anyway because she feels she cannot refuse. While phrases such as "our eyes would drown together" (27) risk romanticizing the sexual encounter (and indicate that Faulkner does not consistently depict sexual coercion), the tone of Dewey Dell's monologue is more agitated than enthusiastic. Dewey Dell's "I could not help it" (27)—a line she repeats four times in just two sentences—does not read as a justification of sex-positive behavior, but as the anxious reasoning of a girl who knows she is about to have sex before she feels ready to do so. Dewey Dell's continued (and seemingly detached) lack-of-response to men who demand sex from her seems to confirm this reading. When men, such as Lafe or MacGowan, expect sex, Dewey Dell does not outwardly resist, but she does not actively consent either. She simply

feels she has no other choice. As she insists: "I could not help it" (27).

7. Such arguments focus their attention on a woman's duty to a fetus, not a man's. A pregnant woman must care for an unborn child; the man who impregnated her presumably need not. A position that holds women single-handedly responsible for the result of sex between a man and woman (pregnancy) encumbers women in holding them—and not their male partners—liable for pregnancy. In Dewey Dell's case, Lafe impregnates his girlfriend, then disappears. To those who take a "responsibility" stance against abortion, Faulkner's novel raises the question: why should Dewey Dell be forced to care for her unborn child when Lafe is not?

8. In "Tactics of Sexual Coercion," published in *The Journal of Sex Research*, Cindy Struckman-Johnson, David Struckman-Johnson, and Peter B. Anderson define sexual coercion as "the act of using pressure, alcohol or drugs, or force to have sexual contact with someone against his or her will" (76). Lafe presumably does not drug Dewey Dell, but he does appear to pressure her into having sex. (At the very least, Dewey Dell feels pressured to have sex with Lafe.) What constitutes "sexual pressure" can be difficult to define, but Struckman-Johnson et al. classify sexual pressure in relation to sexual coercion as "physical pressure, verbal pressure, or emotional pressure" (76). That we know of, Lafe does not physically pressure Dewey Dell. He may, however, verbally and emotionally pressure her by telling her that they are going to have sex—or that he is going to "pick into her sack" (27)—without bothering to discuss whether or not she wants to participate. Emotional pressure, Struckman-Johnson et al. explain, is the most "frequent" and "subtle" of all the coercion tactics. In such cases, the perpetrator convinces the victim that s/he must have sex with the perpetrator and makes the victim feel "obligated to participate in sexual acts," as if—as Dewey Dell insists—s/he does not actually have a choice (Struckman-Johnson et al. 76; Faulkner 27). In *As I Lay Dying*, it is unclear whether Lafe as an individual actively coerces Dewey Dell or whether, as a young, uneducated woman in a patriarchal and misogynistic society, she simply feels compelled to comply with any man who extorts sex. In

either case, Faulkner presents Dewey Dell's sexual experiences as coerced rather than consented to.

9. Struckman-Johnson et al. classify sexual coercion as falling on the continuum of sexual assault (76).

10. Birth control is not readily available to Dewey Dell, nor has she likely had comprehensive sexual education about various methods of fertility prevention. Heather Holcombe suggests that Dewey Dell's futile pursuit of an abortion recalls the "contraception controversy" in the United States in the 1930s when *As I Lay Dying* was published (204). Dewey Dell, Holcombe writes, is "burdened" by the Comstock Act, which "defined contraceptives as obscene and illicit, making it a federal offense to disseminate birth control through the mail or across state lines" (204). Accordingly, women could not often secure the contraceptives they needed to regulate their reproductive health.

Works Cited

Bleikasten, André. "Faulkner in the Singular Chapter." *Retrospect and Prospect*, edited by Donald M. Kartiganer and Ann J. Abadie, UP of Mississippi, 2000, pp. 204-18.

Brillhart, Kelly, "Women without Men: Hemingway's Female Characters" (1994). *Honors College Capstone Experience/Thesis Projects.* Paper 77. Western Kentucky University. https://digitalcommons.wku.edu/stu_hon_theses/77.

Capo, B.W. "Can This Woman Be Saved? Birth Control and Marriage in Modern American Literature." *Modern Language Studies*, vol. 34, no. 1/2, 2004, pp. 28-41.

Clark, Deborah. *Robbing the Mother: Women in Faulkner.* 1994. UP of Mississippi, 2006.

Davis, Bonnie. "Women." *William Faulkner Encyclopedia*, edited by Robert Hamblin and Charles Peek, Greenwood Press, 1999, pp. 439-42.

Dodman, Trevor. "'Going all to pieces': *A Farewell to Arms* as Trauma Narrative." *Twentieth Century Literature*, vol. 52, no. 3, 2006, pp. 249-75.

Du, Lanlan. "Abortion in Faulkner's *The Wild Palms* and Mo Yan's 蛙 (Frog)." *Mo Yan in Context*, edited by Angelica Duran and Yuhan Huang, Purdue UP, 2014, pp. 63-76.

"Ethics Guide: Responsibility of the Mother." *BBC*, 2014 www.bbc.co.uk/ethics/abortion/philosophical/responsibility.shtml. Accessed 1 Jan. 2017.

Faulkner, William. *As I Lay Dying*. 1930. Vintage, 1991.

—. *Sanctuary*. 1931. Vintage, 1993.

—. *The Wild Palms (If I Forget Thee, Jerusalem)*. 1939. Vintage, 1995.

—. "Upon Receiving the Nobel Prize for Literature, 1950." *Essays, Speeches, & Public Letters*, edited by James B. Meriwether, Modern Library, 2004, pp. 119-21.

Fetterley, Judith. *The Resistant Reader: A Feminist Approach to American Fiction*. U of Indiana P, 1981.

Fiedler, Leslie. *Love and Death in the American Novel*. Stein and Day, 1966.

Fruscione, Joseph. "Rivalry and Influence in the Afternoon: Faulkner, Hemingway, and 'If I Forget Thee, Jerusalem.'" *South Atlantic Review*, vol. 71, no. 4, 2006, pp. 78-98.

Ganzel, Dewey. "'A Farewell to Arms': The Danger of Imagination." *The Sewanee Review*, vol. 79, no. 4, 1971, pp. 576-97.

Hemingway, Ernest. *A Farewell to Arms*. 1929. Scribner, 2014.

—. "Hills Like White Elephants." *The Complete Short Stories of Ernest Hemingway*, Scribner, 1998, pp. 211-14.

Herman, Judith. *Trauma and Recovery*. Basic Press, 1997.

Holcombe, Heather. "Faulkner on Feminine Hygiene, or, How Margaret Sanger Sold Dewey Dell a Bad Abortion." *Modern Fiction Studies*, vol. 57, no. 2, 2009, pp. 203-29.

James, Pearl. "Regendering War Trauma and Relocating the Abject: Catherine Barkley's Death." *The New Death: American Modernism and World War I*, U of Virginia P, 2013, pp. 119-59.

McIlvaine, Robert M. "A Literary Source for the Caesarean Section in *A Farewell to Arms*." *American Literature*, vol. 43, no. 3, 1971, pp. 444-47.

Simeon, Daphne, and Jeffrey Abugel. *Feeling Unreal: Depersonalization Disorder and the Loss of the Self.* Oxford UP, 2008.

Struckman-Johnson, Cindy, David Struckman-Johnson, and Peter B. Anderson. "Tactics of Sexual Coercion: When Men and Women Won't Take No for an Answer." *The Journal of Sex Research*, vol. 40, no. 1, Feb. 2003, pp. 76-86.

Varga, Andrew. *The Main Issues in Bioethics.* Paulist Press, 1984.

Weinstein, Philip. "'A Sight-Drafted Yesterday.' Faulkner's Uninsured Immorality." *Faulkner at 100: Retrospect and Prospect*, edited by Donald M. Kartiganer and Ann J. Abadie, UP of Mississippi, 2000, pp. 45-52.

Woolf, Virginia. *A Room of One's Own.* 1929. Mariner Books, 1989.

Barry Hudek

"Mississippi on the Potomac": Sutpen's Hundred as Washington, D.C.

The founding of Washington, D.C. and the founding of Sutpen's Hundred in William Faulkner's *Absalom, Absalom!* (1936) share a variety of striking similarities: both have an original territory of one hundred square miles.[1] Both have been reclaimed from swampy bottom land.[2] Their namesakes are slave-holding planters from Virginia. Each was designed with help from a French architect and built with help from slave labor. Even after their founding, they existed in a raw, undeveloped state. Each lost territory as a result of the Civil War and each, at some point, had their central, white house burned down. As such, I argue that more than a passing connection exists between the founding of these two locales. In fact, John Padgett writes that "many of the events in Thomas Sutpen's story parallel or suggest similar key moments in American history," where these moments "both [summarize] the American story [...] even as [Sutpen's story] highlights [...] the 'mistakes' in that grand design that will eventually bring the design tumbling back to earth, its promise unfulfilled in the way originally intended by the designer" (272-73). Ultimately, Padgett writes, "[w]e can thus see many allegorical similarities or parallels between the depicted or constructed life of Thomas Sutpen and American history" (278). Additionally, Thadious Davis notes that since *Absalom* is primarily focused on interiority and mental constructions, "description of the objective natural realm [of Sutpen's Hundred] is noticeably absent." This, she writes, contrasts with many of Faulkner's other novels that "not only provide descriptions of the land, but also open directly in outdoor settings" (4). For Davis, Faulkner's depiction of Sutpen's Hundred is conspicuously nondescript, non-Southern. Just as Faulkner provides a description of Sutpen's Hundred that is not overtly Southern, Eric Sundquist argues further that "there is an analogy between Lincoln and Sutpen, each of whom labors heroically to build or preserve a magnificent 'house' symbolic of his national and personal dream" (105).

Thus, with *Absalom, Absalom!* being suggestive of "key moments in American history" and with the idea that the Hundred is a "conspicuously nondescript, non-Southern space," coupled with the idea of a house as a metaphor for nation, I argue that Sutpen's Hundred allegorically represents the founding of Washington, D.C. Through this allegory, Faulkner illustrates that D.C.'s and the nation's founding represents a "promise unfulfilled" where the reality of American history does not match the idealism surrounding the capital's formation and the idealistic promises inherent in the formation of the U.S. Instead, Faulkner shows a national past fraught with contradictions, with slavery being the most prevalent of those contradictions, and a national past that is dependent upon the South in the formation of the United States.

Moreover, I am interested in the ways Faulkner writes to a national audience. This exploration shows how Sutpen's Hundred as Washington, D.C. illustrates Faulkner reacting and "writing back" to his contemporary national culture that saw the U.S. South as retrograde and backward, a place where the underlying racism found a semi-acceptable home in the national culture. Furthermore, Faulkner's connection of D.C. to Sutpen's Hundred illustrates that a "concept of the South is essential to national identity in the United States of America" (Greeson 1). Indeed, Faulkner reminds his readers how integral the South was to the formation of the United States as a whole. I focus on aspects of similarity between Washington, D.C. and Sutpen's Hundred and then discuss what Faulkner might be saying in "writing back" from his position as a Southern writer to the national culture he occupied.

Beyond the direct comparisons of factual data between Sutpen's Hundred and Washington, D.C., several indirect corollaries exist as well. First, Washington, D.C. was appealing to Southerners comfortable with the capital's unfinished, rustic qualities. It had, according to Catherine Allgor, "[r]ough living conditions, physical, psychological, and political isolation, diverse populations, and an amorphous sense of impermanence" (43). Yet, out of this roughness, Southerners found D.C. appealing whereas their Northern and European counterparts were put off by the expansive wilderness and ramshackle development of the capital district. In fact, one early joke suggested that "Washington would be a beautiful city if it were built" (48). Additionally, stories abound about "Europeans, standing in forests or hip-deep in mud, asking directions to the city, only to be informed that they were in it," as sardonic jokes about the backwardness of the capital became "local sport" (48). To Southerners, though, Washington, D.C. looked and felt like home. Their own county seats or regional capitals—often consisting of dirt roads, open wilderness, and a few scattered buildings—clearly resembled the backwards aspects of early D.C. Allgor points out that:

> Washington City's unfinished state appalled northerners and Europeans more than it did southerners. This was owing partly to their preconceptions: people who came to Washington expecting to encounter a European or northeastern cityscape obviously expressed more surprise than local people. Southern cities and towns, such as Charleston, South Carolina, might be sophisticated, but many smaller state capitals and county seats were quite rustic. Southerners like the Madisons and Thomas Jefferson accepted more easily the abrupt juxtapositions of aspiring refinement and downright crudeness that struck others as an absurdity peculiar to Washington. (48-49)

In this way, Sutpen's Hundred and Faulkner's Jefferson clearly resemble this "aspiring refinement and downright crudeness" peculiar to the nation's capital in its early stages. They both had a "blank slate" quality to their crudeness that bespoke not only the transformation of wilderness to civilization but the opportunity to craft that blank slate to reflect the national or personal ideals of their creators.

This creation and transformation, too, is imbued with idealism and power. Faulkner describes the creation of Sutpen's Hundred in biblical terms:

> Out of quiet thunderclap he would abrupt (man-horse-demon) upon a scene peaceful and decorous as a schoolprize water color, faint sulphur reek still in hair clothes and beard, with grouped behind him his band of wild niggers like beasts half tamed to walk upright like men, in attitudes wild and reposed, and manacled among them the French architect with his air grim, haggard, and tatter-ran. Immobile, bearded and hand palm-lifted the horseman sat; behind him the wild blacks and the captive architect huddled quietly, carrying in bloodless paradox the shovels and picks and axes of peaceful conquest. Then in the long unamaze Quentin seemed to watch them overrun suddenly the hundred square miles of tranquil and astonished earth and drag house and formal gardens violently out of the soundless Nothing and clap them down like cards upon a table beneath the up palm immobile and pontific, creating the Sutpen's Hundred, the Be Sutpen's Hundred like the oldentime Be Light. (4)

Sutpen transforms his land almost in ex-nihilo fashion. For Sutpen, however, this is not a peaceful transformation nor a happy collaboration among the principle actors ("*tore violently a plantation*" [5], Rosa Coldfield says). Instead, the formation of Sutpen's Hundred is done against the will of its principal actors and, maybe, the "astonished" land itself. The location of Washington, D.C., too, was prized for its wilderness state. "From a political point of view," Allgor writes, "Washington City's very blankness constituted one of its greatest assets. Largely rural, removed from older, more 'corrupt' eastern seaboard cities, the new capital provided the Republican founders with a fresh slate" (45). On this slate, the founders wanted the capital to reflect the nation's character and idealism. Leland Roth argues that the "constitutional government was an experiment in

applied Enlightenment philosophy which rejected monarchial absolutism and attempted to recreate the natural society in which it
was believed men were meant to live." "Jefferson and Latrobe," he
continues, "suggested that architecture should be an instrument of
social reform, a tool to reshape men's minds and to enhance civil
intercourse" (53). In this way, the nation's founders sought to reflect
these ideals in the design and architecture of the capital. They sought
to create a more republican, more civilized culture of people through
the architecture and design of D.C.

Sutpen, too, wanted his transformation of land to reflect his
personal ideals and be a "blank slate" after his mistakes in Haiti. For
Sutpen, his home and land is an extension of his mission to combat
the planter class—a planter class that humiliated him when he was
a boy. Out of this mission then, Sutpen is fueled to recreate his
dynasty in Mississippi after repudiating his marriage to Eulalia and
disavowing Charles Bon as his son. His drive and determination
is so strong that he attracts the attention of the Jefferson community when he begins laying his plans and busily transforming the
wilderness so he can build his home and begin a cotton crop. His
methodologies (and how he can afford to do what he does) thus
draw much consideration from the Jefferson community. General
Compson imagines Sutpen imposing his will on the construction of
Sutpen's home this way:

> [It was] as though his [Sutpen's] presence alone
> compelled that house to accept and retain human
> life; as though houses actually possess a sentience,
> a personality and character acquired, not from the
> people who breathe or who have breathed in them
> so much as rather inherent in the wood and brick
> or begotten upon the wood and brick by the man or
> men who conceived and built them—in this one an
> incontrovertible affirmation for emptiness, deser-
> tion; an insurmountable resistance to occupancy
> save when sanctioned and protected by the ruthless
> and the strong. (67)

What is reflected here is Sutpen's indomitable will in achieving his aims. He (with the help of slave labor) transforms the wilderness and erects his plantation by brute force. The personality and character reflected in that creation illustrates Sutpen's ruthless and violent effort to enact his strange vengeance upon the planter class that humiliated him in the person of Pettibone's servant when he denied him entrance at the front door of the Pettibone mansion. The central house at Sutpen's Hundred, then, reflects Sutpen's malice, anger, and rapaciousness—his home and land takes on the aspects of his mission to combat the planter class. The once "blank slate" that Sutpen imprints upon now reflects his self-serving nature as his mission to combat the planter class goes awry in his own muddled understanding of his plan and how human relationships work. So, if Sutpen's Hundred reflects upon Washington, D.C., Faulkner seems to be suggesting that the national ideals upon which the capital is built are similarly fraught—that seedy motivations underlie the national project.

While the altered landscapes reflect the imprint of their owners/creators, the wilderness aspects of both Washington, D.C. and Sutpen's Hundred allowed for expansion—an expansion that would be rooted, in the case of D.C., in the United States' growing commercial and military might. In fact, Washington, D.C. was envisioned to be a dazzling display of grandeur and democratic idealism that spared no expense in achieving that aim. As L'Enfant himself notes, the plan for the capital "must leave to posterity a grand idea of the patriotic interest which promoted it" (quoted in Kite 19-20). Even though the initial space fell well short of this spectacle, L'Enfant was confident that George Washington should not be dismayed but should "conceive it essential to pursue with dignity the operation of an undertaking of a magnitude so worthy of the concern of a grand empire [...] over whose progress the eyes of every nation, envying the opportunity denied them, will stand judge" (quoted in Kite 19-20). For the principal designer and architect of the U.S. capital, the undertaking should reflect a future prominence, not a current state of emptiness. L'Enfant envisioned that despite humble beginnings, the United States and Washington, D.C. would rise to greatness and be the envy of the world. Similarly, Thomas Sutpen gradually transforms the wilderness of Yoknapatawpha County into grandeur by clearing land, building the big house, furnishing that house, and constructing more buildings as his wealth increases (his shady deal with Mr. Coldfield to furnish the house certainly aided him in this development). For Sutpen, the Hundred was commensurate with his stature in the community—a community he wanted to impress and, later, subvert through his plan to build a plantation and establish a dynasty.

Additionally, Sutpen's Hundred similarly reflects the design of its namesake. Just as Washington, D.C. was to be expanded as an edifice celebrating American nationalism, Sutpen's Hundred is a physical extension of Sutpen himself. Daniel Spoth writes that the "house represents both eminence and endurance to Sutpen; he erects it not only as a device for the creation of his reputation, but as an indelible mark on the landscape, something that will persist into perpetuity. These significances […] are endowed upon the house by Sutpen's all-consuming, brutal *wille zur macht*; he engineers its creation and maintenance with no more elegant tools than sheer stubbornness and violence" (121). Sutpen wants to establish this "indelible mark" to remind the Jefferson community of how important and powerful he is. Sutpen wants there to be no doubt of his preeminence in society—he must outdo the other planters and make sure they know how well he has done for himself. Spoth argues:

> The house has greater significance than its simple role as a backdrop for the events of *Absalom, Absalom!*, greater significance even than the concern with eminence, aristocracy and the influence of history that the Southern mansion traditionally indicates; it is an extension of Sutpen's will, not just a means to, but a participant in, his grand scheme. (121)

In fact, "the emphasis [is] on Sutpen's overriding will, but in this case that will acts both to literally *form*, that is, create, the house, and also to *formulate*, or construct, confabulate, it in his own image. This image, however, is one that, like Sutpen's will, works its own organic destruction" (121). Likewise, the nation's capital as a synecdoche is an extension of the will of government, of the nation. For both Washington, D.C. and Sutpen's Hundred then, expansion and development are crucial aspects of the underlying ethos of its creation—the development of D.C. reflects well on the nation, and the growth of Sutpen's Hundred personifies Sutpen's will to establish his dynasty in Mississippi.

So what might Faulkner be suggesting by linking Washington, D.C. and Sutpen's Hundred? Jennifer Greeson in *Our South* argues that the "master narrative of U.S. exceptionalism has depended, from the founding forward, on U.S. writers writing their South—a term that becomes legible in the first place as it is understood to deviate from the republican model of U.S. nationalism." Where the U.S. South exists as "an internal other from the start of U.S. existence, it lies simultaneously inside and outside the national imaginary constructed in United States literature" (3). In this way, the South, and writing about the South, becomes a place to deposit all things problematic within the U.S., as if these things exist only in the South. The South becomes a region of disavowal for the larger culture, a place to cordon off racism, white supremacy, and backwardness. Leigh Anne Duck describes the phenomenon this way:

> the logic of the gothic novel also provided U.S. intellectuals with a way to understand southern culture and to distance it, both spatially and temporally, from national culture [...] pathologies represented in Faulkner's characters were seen as endemic to southern subjectivity, the inevitable results of the interaction between an individual mind and a stagnating, aggressively backward culture—a condition said to paralyze the author himself. (147)

Even though Faulkner does not deny that such unsavory people populate his Southern worlds, he suggests that these traits are not particular to the South; the South, too, is the nation. Any attempts at disavowal from the national culture are faulty since the South played such a crucial role in the formation of the United States, and he seems to be remarking on the Southern touches prevalent in the symbol of the nation, Washington, D.C. Additionally, Virginia

ceded land for the creation of the district, and three early and influential presidents presided over the formation of the national capital.
Faulkner reminds readers of the importance Virginia and Virginians
played in creating the United States. I think it no accident that the
namesake for Sutpen's Hundred is a planter from Virginia.

In fact, Sutpen is from Appalachia, a region known in lore as
mythically connected to a pre-colonial, authentic ancestral America as its inhabitants purportedly exhibited a "pure" character in a
region within the nation untouched by changes. As such, looking
at the region is a way of looking at the nation's past.[3] Sutpen's origins in West Virginia thus cast him as a national figure linked to
the mythic origins of the United States, and Sutpen's rise from this
region invokes a similar mythology. In coming from this pre-revo-
lutionary area, Sutpen is connected to a time before the Civil War.
However, this Appalachian ancestry allows Quentin to try to distance Sutpen from the South, something Shreve does not allow him
to do. "Because he was born in West Virginia, in the mountains,"
Quentin says. But, not "in West Virginia," Shreve interjects. "And
there wasn't any West Virginia in 1808 because [...] West Virginia
wasn't admitted [...] into the United States until—" (179), Shreve
challenges. Quentin tries to position Sutpen as not quite Southern
since he came from a region that would not join the Confederacy.
In distancing Sutpen from the South, Quentin tries to suggest
that Sutpen is more national than Southern. This is, in part, true,
but Sutpen occupies both a national and Southern position in the
novel—a situation similar to what Greeson says of the South as "an
internal other from the start of U.S. existence, [lying] simultaneously inside and outside the national imaginary constructed in U.S.
literature" (3) much like how D.C. is both Southern and national.
Faulkner seems to remind readers that while the importance of Virginia has waned since the eighteenth and nineteenth centuries, it
played a crucial role in shaping the United States.

In connecting Virginia and the South to the importance of
national culture, Faulkner also shows the importance of slave labor
in formulating the land of the free. As Michelle Obama's speech
at the 2016 Democratic National Convention reminded the nation,
the White House and parts of D.C. were built by slaves. Allgor confirms this, writing that "[v]isitors [to D.C.] could not fail to notice

the active role of slaves in the city's construction, including the Capital and the White House, nor could they miss the coffles of human beings chained together or held in pens as they awaited transportation South" (49). These images clearly contradict the national ideals—images that may have left foreign visitors to D.C. wondering about the United States' stated mission in the world. Indeed, Abigail Adams makes the connection clear: "Two of our hardy N England men would do as much work in a day as the whole 12, but it is true Republicanism that drive the Slaves half fed, and destitute of cloathing [sic],…to labour [sic], whilst the owner waches [sic] about Idle, tho his one slave is all the property he can boast" (quoted in Graham). What is more, the nation at large has benefited from slavery regardless of region given that the White House itself was built largely on the backs of slaves. As David Graham argues, "to say slaves built [the White House] is to imply that they built the United States." Even though slavery was outlawed above the Mason-Dixon Line, the economic arrangement between North and South was still dependent on slave labor. Abraham Lincoln, of course, points this out in his second inaugural address: "He gives to both North and South this terrible war as the woe due to those by whom the offense came," so that "God wills that [the war] continue until all the wealth piled by the bondsman's two hundred and fifty years of unrequited toil shall be sunk, and until every drop of blood drawn with the lash shall be paid by another drawn with the sword" (quoted in Gardella 184). Here Lincoln argues that God's judgment is pouring out on both North and South because both benefited from slavery and the war is a necessary step in removing it from the country. Even though many writers and intellectuals from the antebellum period through Faulkner's own time wanted to disavow such unpleasantries by limiting them to the South, Faulkner does not allow us to forget the interconnected nature between North and South, showing the centrality of exploitation in the foundation of the nation instead. Put simply, as David Blight argues, "[s]laves were the single largest, by far, financial asset of property in the entire American economy" (quoted in Coates).

So, too, was slavery instrumental to the success of Sutpen's Hundred. Faulkner's connection between Sutpen's Hundred and

Washington, D.C. shows that what was disavowed by the nation at large was still part of the nation's cultural formations—it was not limited to the ring of states below the Mason Dixon Line and into Texas. John Padgett describes *Absalom* this way: "it can likewise be viewed against a historical backdrop in which American history, 'bright' with the potential of its founding ideals in 1776, saw much of that luster tarnished over the subsequent century as a result of sectional conflict, predominantly over the issue of slavery and race" (280-81). Faulkner indicates that just as Sutpen ignores those whom he exploits in order to achieve his dynastic aims, the United States disavows its connection to the peculiar institution as well. As such, Sutpen's failure to deal with his own inconsistencies results in the ruin of his dynasty. Faulkner might likewise be suggesting that the United States' own refusal to accept its complicity in racism and slavery undercuts its mission of peace and democracy on the world stage.

What is more, Faulkner reminds his readers that Sutpen, and the United States, would not have risen to prominence without slave labor and/or the subjugation of blacks. Sutpen's move to the West Indies in seeking his revenge on the planter class is what vaults him into success in Southern society; his entrée into their world could not have happened without the actions he undertakes in Haiti and elsewhere. As such, Sutpen's Hundred could not be purchased, nor could Sutpen's house be built, without slave labor—without the intentional suppression of others' liberty and humanity. Given that D.C. and the White House are extensions of national will, the land and the house of Sutpen's Hundred are living extensions of Sutpen's will and character; these foundational moments in Sutpen's life are rooted in oppression and subjugation, not freedom and equality. Sutpen's role in suppressing the revolt on Haiti is the springboard for his success, although the violence is chronologically incompatible with the Haitian Revolution. I agree with Richard Godden's account of Faulkner's anachronism regarding Sutpen's time in Haiti. Godden argues that Sutpen works in Haiti to subvert the "only successful black revolution" in order to "foreground the continuous potential for revolution within the institution of slavery," and Sutpen's violence highlights the "counterrevolutionary violence [...] necessary to the workings of the plantation system" (53).

In evoking the Haitian Revolution, Faulkner brings up a powerful fear in the U.S. South: the potential for slaves in the U.S. to enact a similar revolt. In Padgett's reading of the Sutpen story as an allegory for key moments in U.S. history, "Haiti allows the novel an allegorical portrait of the American Revolution and the creation of a new nation based on principles of liberty and equality while simultaneously pointing out the legally sanctioned contradictions of those ideals by the institution of slavery" (295). With this in mind, Sutpen's story of subverting a labor revolt in Haiti becomes an oblique commentary on U.S. Southern planters' desire to similarly suppress black agency in the U.S. In this way, the planters knew that the nature of their project ran counter to the ideals of the United States where plantation society works to camouflage its true nature, and Sutpen knows that his actions run counter to his desires to subvert the planter class. To disguise this fact from himself and others, he cannot allow himself to be known. In fact, Godden further suggests that Sutpen (and U.S. planters in general) sought to be "unreadable" in order to disguise the facts of plantation society's brutality. Likewise, *Absalom*, "as a record of an attempt by a planter and his class descendants to tell the story of planter accumulation it is the product of characters who, in order to live with themselves and their properties, have to make themselves more or less unreadable to themselves and to others" (77-8). Thus, all of Sutpen's talk of transforming planter society from within is merely a mask for his oppressive schemes.

In connecting Sutpen's Hundred to Washington, D.C., Faulkner points out slavery's hidden role in its creation. In fact, Michelle Obama's commentary on slavery in D.C. was a harsh wake up call for many. Washington, D.C. would not have been built without slave labor, and this fact is reflected, albeit obscurely, in the character and ethos of the nation's capital. Thus, Faulkner suggests that Washington, D.C. and the success of the United States are similarly rooted in an imperialism that intentionally suppresses others to achieve its aims—especially given that Faulkner composed *Absalom* during the U.S. occupation of Haiti (1915-1934). This occupation was promoted as a mission of uplift but was rooted in militaristic and economic imperialism with little humanitarian uplift offered to the Haitians, a way to disguise the "unreadable" imperial motivations of the U.S. Just as Sutpen represents the continual need to suppress black revolution in order for the planter class to succeed, the contemporary connection to the United States' role in Haiti reminds Faulkner's readers that this suppression and unfulfilled promise continue into the twentieth century.[4]

I see a lot of similarities between the founding of Washington, D.C. and the founding of Sutpen's Hundred that I think are no accident. In connecting Sutpen's Hundred with D.C., Faulkner "writes back" to a national culture that seems to think the South represents only the negative aspects of the country. Greeson challenges that rather "than looking to those writers who defend the 'South' side of the sectionalist binary, and in so doing simply reinforced the Slave South construct, we should look to writers who profoundly problematized the binary itself, asking to what ends it was being invoked" (208). Faulkner does this in *Absalom*. Through the figure of Thomas Sutpen, he problematizes the relationship between North and South, showing a nation dependent upon slavery and regions more alike than some are comfortable admitting.[5] Faulkner reminds his readers that those are part of the national culture at large, not merely regional quirks. My exploration opens up further research into Faulkner's engagement with national culture and ideology, the role of the South in the U.S. imaginary, and the way Faulkner may be "writing back" against stereotypes about the South in order to show how much a part of the national culture the South is. In fact, in exploring Faulkner writing to a national audience in *Absalom, Absalom!*, we might reimagine Quentin's haunting final lines about the South—"*I don't hate it. I don't hate it*" (303)—in the context that Faulkner is talking about the nation, not only the South. Quentin cannot single out the U.S. South in his assessment when the whole nation is implicit in the problems and issues inherent in the South that haunt Quentin and Shreve, leaving the reader to confront the idea that the South and the nation are inexorably linked.

Notes

1. Washington, D.C. is listed as having 99.9 square miles in its original territory. I am comfortable rounding up to one hundred.

2. The idea that D.C. was reclaimed from swamp land is, apparently, a legend. Swampy land did exist within its original territory, but it was in small portions and the main areas of D.C. did not have to be drained.

3. See Frost for more information on the subject. In fact, Ronald Lewis argues that all the myths about Appalachia—myths that would inspire further travel writing and shape national ideas regarding the region—come from Frost's essay.

4. A full exploration of the role of the United States' occupation of Haiti is beyond the scope of this article: however, see Schmidt as well as Renda as excellent histories on the motivations, results, and consequences of the U.S. involvement in Haiti. See Stanchich for Faulkner's use of Haiti in the novel.

5. Donald Trump's rise and subsequent victory seem to illustrate how much the supposed dark qualities that were relegated only to the South are part of the nation as a whole. In fact, a *Politico* article from August 2016 argues that Trump "brought into the mainstream the kind of race hatred that had flourished only in the shadows before he came along. But his presence also removed the scales from the eyes of sane Americans who had held onto the belief that the election of our first black president had ushered in a post-racial society. Trump's most enduring legacy, and it is an oddly beneficent one, is that he taught America how bigoted it still is, and that many among us who are not intentionally bigoted are willing to tolerate racism anyway, given the right circumstances and stakes" (Bailey). Part of Greeson's and Duck's argument is that the South allows the U.S. to disavow racism and bigotry, but the recent election cycle reveals, in part, how prevalent this thinking is throughout the United States.

Works Cited

Allgor, Catherine. *A Perfect Union: Dolley Madison and the Creation of the American Nation*. Holt and Company, 2006.

Bailey, Issac. "How Trump Exposed America's White Identity Crisis." *Politico Magazine*, 22 Aug. 2016. www.politico.com/magazine/story/2016/08/trump-race-whiteamerica-identity-crisis-214178. Accessed 15 Sep. 2016.

Coates, Ta-Nehisi. "The Case for Reparations." *The Atlantic.* 1 June 2014. www.theatlantic.com/magazine/archive/2014/06/the-case-for-reparations/361631/. Accessed 16 Sep. 2016.

Davis, Thadious. "'Be Sutpen's Hundred': Imaginative Projection of Landscape in *Absalom, Absalom!*" *Southern Literary Journal*, vol. 13, no. 2, Spring 1981, pp. 3-14.

Duck, Leigh Anne. *The Nation's Region: Southern Modernism, Segregation, and U.S. Nationalism.* U of Georgia P, 2006.

Faulkner, William. *Absalom, Absalom!* Vintage Classics, 1990.

Frost, William Goodell. "Our Contemporary Ancestors in the Southern Mountains." *Atlantic Monthly*, vol. 83, 1899, pp. 1-9.

Godden, Richard. *Fictions of Labor: William Faulkner and the South's Long Revolution.* Cambridge UP, 2007.

Graham, David A. "How Abigail Adams Proves Bill O'Reilly Wrong About Slavery." *The Atlantic.* 27 Jul. 2016. www.theatlantic.com/politics/archive/2016/07/bill-oreilly-andthe-long-tradition-of-slavery-apology/493223/. Accessed 16 September 2016.

Greeson, Jennifer Rae. *Our South: Geographic Fantasy and the Rise of National Literature.* Harvard UP, 2010.

Lewis, Ronald L. "Beyond Isolation and Homogeneity: Diversity and the History of Appalachia." *Confronting Appalachian Stereotypes: Back Talk from an American Region*, edited by Norman Billings, Dwight B. Gurney, and Katherine Ledford, UP of Kentucky, 1999, pp 21-46.

Lincoln, Abraham. "Second Inaugural Address." *American Civil Religion: What Americans Hold Sacred*, edited by Peter Gardella, Oxford UP, 2014, pp. 183-90.

Kite, Elizabeth. *L'Enfant and Washington, 1791-1792.* Johns Hopkins Press, 1929.

Padgett, John. "War and History in the Fiction of William Faulkner." Dissertation. University of Mississippi, 2004.

Renda, Mary. *Taking Haiti: Military Occupation & the Culture of U.S. Imperialism, 1915-1940.* U of North Carolina P, 2001.

Roth, Leland M. *A Concise History of American Architecture.* Harper and Row, 1979.

Schmidt, Hans. *The United States' Occupation of Haiti, 1915-1934.* Rutgers UP, 1995.

Spoth, Daniel. "The House that Time Built: Structuring History in Faulkner and Yeats. *European Journal of American Culture,* vol. 26, no. 2, 2007, pp. 109-126.

Stanchich, Maritza. "The Hidden Caribbean 'Other' in William Faulkner's *Absalom, Absalom!*: An Ideological Ancestry of U.S. Imperialism." *The Mississippi Quarterly*, vol. 49, Summer 1996, pp. 603-617.

Sundquist, Eric J. *Faulkner: The House Divided.* Johns Hopkins UP, 1983.

C. D. Albin

Courage and Verbena, Sartoris and Macomber

In April of 1947, the two most noted American novelists of their generation, William Faulkner and Ernest Hemingway, began a famous tiff over the term "courage"—or, more precisely, over competing nuances of the term. The issue arose when Faulkner, addressing a creative writing class at the University of Mississippi, remarked that Hemingway had "no courage." Faulkner intended the comment in the context of artistic creation, his argument being that Hemingway took fewer risks than contemporary authors whom Faulkner deemed more artistically adventurous. However, when the remark appeared in newspaper accounts and eventually reached Hemingway, the former Red Cross ambulance driver interpreted his rival's statement as an accusation of personal cowardice (Blotner 483). Hemingway even requested that Brigadier General C. T. Lanham, commander of the 22nd Infantry Regiment with which Hemingway had served as a war correspondent in 1944, write to Faulkner confirming Hemingway's bravery. Lanham complied, asserting that Hemingway was "without exception the most courageous man I have ever known, both in war and peace. He has physical courage, and he has that far rarer commodity, moral courage" (qtd. in Baker 461).

While this episode may seem oddly beneath the dignity of the authors concerned, it does suggest how resonant the issue of courage was for each man, perhaps calling to mind the various public poses they assumed. One thinks of the young Faulkner's false claim that he had been wounded in WWI, his frequent presence in hunting camps, or his persistent but poor efforts as an equestrian. Likewise, Hemingway's various personae of big game hunter, deep sea fisherman, and warrior seem calculated to align himself with familiar public concepts of male courage. Yet the 1947 episode, for which Faulkner was quick to apologize once he learned Hemingway had taken offense, suggests not only a high degree of sensitivity on the part of each man concerning the term "courage," but also a contest of sorts, a struggle over which version of courage—artistic, physical, or moral—should take precedent.

Nearly a decade prior to this disagreement, each author had published a short story—Hemingway's "The Short Happy Life of Francis Macomber" and Faulkner's "An Odor of Verbena"—in which struggles over contested notions of courage become the crux on which each story turns. Few scholars have compared the two narratives, perhaps because they are set in different centuries, even different continents, and they explore strikingly different social settings. Yet both authors use verbena in the context of a courage/cowardice dichotomy, and Thomas McHaney suggests Faulkner may have noted Hemingway's phrase "an odor like verbena" in 1936 when "The Short Happy Life of Francis Macomber" appeared in *Cosmopolitan* (20). The following year, in July of 1937, Faulkner began work on what would become "An Odor of Verbena." The story saw print soon after with the 1938 publication of *The Unvanquished*. Additionally, Maryanne Gobble has noted another basis of comparison, arguing that each story probes "different possibilities for courage within the context of a stressed man-woman relationship" (570). Joseph Fruscione holds a complementary view, arguing in particular that Hemingway's story "examines gendered courage on the hunt through [courage's] presence and absence" (230). Building on the work of these scholars, I contend that the relationship between "An Odor of Verbena" and "The Short Happy Life of Francis Macomber" deserves greater attention based upon the stories' common references to verbena and their distinct explorations of courage, particularly gender-contested notions of the term.

The solitary reference to verbena in Hemingway's story occurs the day after Francis Macomber has fled from the charging lion and Robert Wilson, Macomber's guide, has killed the lion for him and subsequently slept with Macomber's wife Margot. The narrative enters Wilson's mind as the hunting party sets out for another day of hunting, Wilson in the front of the vehicle with the driver, the

Macombers in back. Initially, Wilson is mindful of the marital tensions that his own actions have heightened: "Hope the silly beggar doesn't take a notion to blow the back of my head off .... Women *are* a nuisance on safari" (21). Then, as the jeep moves deeper into the wooded hills, Wilson's mood seems to alter:

> It was a good morning, Wilson thought. There
> was a heavy dew and as the wheels went through
> the grass and low bushes he could smell the odor
> of crushed fronds. It was an odor like verbena and
> he liked this early morning smell of the dew, the
> crushed bracken and the look of the tree trunks
> showing black through the early morning mist as
> the car made its way through the untracked, park-
> like country. He had put the two in the back seat
> out of his mind now and was thinking about buf-
> falo. (21)

Here the verbena reference attends the story's shift from the day of the lion (with its associations of fright, public cowardice, and cuckoldry) to the day of the buffalo, during which Francis Macomber will undergo his own shift from fear to courage.

To reach that brief and happy state, however, Macomber's male ego has had to endure the scalding of female scorn. Margot seems to consider his flight from the lion a personal affront, declaring at one point, "It's [my face] that's red today" (6), as if her husband's public exhibition of fear has diminished her standing as a woman. Her verbal jabs continue until he pleads, "Why not let up on the bitchery just a little, Margot" (10). In response, Margot chooses to sleep with Wilson, the man whose profession as a safari guide is associated with traditional notions of courage and who, unlike her husband, has stood before the charging lion and slain him. When Macomber declares, "You think that I'll take anything," she tells him, "I know you will, sweet" (19). Earlier in the story, Margot's caustic remarks to Macomber have caused Wilson to wonder, "How should a woman act when she discovers her husband is a bloody coward?" (10). Wilson's confusion does not keep him from welcoming Margot to his double-sized cot, nor, it seems, from empathizing with her disdain, but he also considers her "simply enameled in that American female cruelty" (9) when she fails to offer her husband emotional support.

Like Hemingway, Faulkner also explores female disdain for a male who does not exhibit courage of the culturally expected variety. At the outset of "An Odor of Verbena," University of Mississippi law student Bayard Sartoris learns of his father's death, the elder having been shot down on the streets of Jefferson by a former business partner. Bayard's Reconstruction-era culture expects him to honor the old code of a life for a life, and no one's expectations are more passionate than those of John Sartoris's widow Drusilla, a woman only eight years Bayard's senior and who only two months before had implored him, "Kiss me, Bayard" (228). Although as a boy during the war Bayard killed to avenge a loved one's death, nothing will dissuade Drusilla from her belief that he can now travel only one path and be a man. Bayard knows Drusilla so well that he can accurately imagine her in his mind's eye even before he arrives in Jefferson. He sees her "waiting for [him] beneath all the festive glitter of the chandeliers, in the yellow ball gown and the sprig of verbena in her hair, holding the two loaded pistols . . . the two arms bent at the elbows, the two hands shoulder high, the two identical dueling pistols lying upon, not clutched in, one to each: the Greek amphora priestess of a succinct and formal violence" (219).

Here verbena is associated with seductive femininity, set-piece elegance, pistols as phallic symbols, and a cult-like call to violence. It is a heady mix, and Bayard's arrival proves his vision right in the particulars, including the verbena, the ball gown, and the dueling pistols. They are all present as he and Ringo ride up the drive. When he dismounts and approaches Drusilla, "the scent of the verbena in her hair seemed to have increased a hundred times as she stood holding out to [him], one in either hand, the two dueling pistols" (237). Her voice is "fainting and passionate with promise" as she says to him, "Take them. . . . Do you feel them? The lone true barrels of justice, the triggers (you have fired them) quick as retribution, the two of them slender and invincible and fatal as the physical shape of love" (237). Yet Bayard is no longer the vengeance-seeking boy who killed during the war. He has grown in moral awareness and has become not only a student of American jurisprudence but also a student of an older law, one that declares he "who lives by the sword shall die by it" (214). Bayard's studies have shaped him so thoroughly that moments after learning of his father's death he concludes, "*At least this will be my chance to find out if I am what I think I am or if I just hope; if I am going to do what I have taught myself is right or if I am going to just wish I were*" (215).

Here Bayard's test of courage is not the traditional question "will I fight or will I run" but rather the differently nuanced "will I resist or will I kill." To answer the question as he hopes, Bayard must resist not only communal disdain but also the gale force of Drusilla's scorn. When she senses that Bayard does not intend to uphold her code of violence, a code she herself lived by as she rode and fought with his father during the war, her response proves more mocking and caustic than even Margot Macomber's:

> her eyes filled with an expression of bitter and passionate betrayal. "Why, he's not—" she said. "He's not—And I kissed his hand," she said in an aghast whisper; "I kissed his hand!" beginning to laugh, the laughter rising, becoming a scream yet still remaining laughter, screaming with laughter trying herself to deaden the sound by putting her hand over her mouth, the laughter spilling beneath her fingers like vomit. (239)

One can infer the social and personal pressure Drusilla's response places upon Bayard. He is derided in his own home, in the very room where rests his father's body, by an attractive woman who has herself demonstrated the physical courage their culture associates with masculinity. Outside the house, gathered on the lawn, are the men of his father's old troop who expect from him the same act of vengeance Drusilla demands. Only his Aunt Jenny is a dissenting voice: "You are not going to try to kill [Redmond]. All right" (240). Yet Bayard repeats her two-word declaration, "All right," as a question. When Jenny asserts, "I know you are not afraid" (240), Bayard answers with another question: "But what good will that do? . . . I must live with myself, you see" (240). At twenty-four, his heart has become the battleground for two conflicting cultural claims: "Avenge your father's death" and "Thou shalt not kill." Circumstances and societal demands have not allowed him even the time to grieve. George Wyatt, leader of his father's old troop, extracts from Bayard the promise of "Tomorrow" (234)—a word we may take to mean, *Yes, I know it can't wait. Whatever I do, I'll do it tomorrow*—even before he can enter the house and view his father's body in the parlor.

While Francis Macomber does not face the same dilemma as Bayard, he too feels the pressure of conflicting cultural codes. In the moments prior to his public disgrace, Macomber is waiting outside the bush where the wounded lion has retreated. He dreads going in after the animal and wishes himself free of the responsibility, as his conversation with Wilson suggests:

> "Why not just leave him?"
> "You mean pretend to ourselves he hasn't been hit?"
> "No. Just drop it."
> "It isn't done."
> "Why not?"
> "For one thing, he's certain to be suffering. For another, some one else might run onto him."
> "I see."
> "But you don't have to have anything to do with it."
> "I'd like to," Macomber said. "I'm just scared, you know." (15)

By publicly confessing to being afraid, Macomber is breaching a cultural taboo against a man acknowledging personal fear, but he may also be exhibiting a certain kind of courage rarely acknowledged by his society. When he answers "no" to Wilson's "You mean pretend to ourselves . . . ," Macomber appears to choose the psychological pain of cognitive dissonance over the emotional escape of personal deception and avoidance. In other words, he declines to suggest that the two men lie to themselves. As anxious as he may be regarding the danger ahead, he assesses himself honestly. He even recognizes the degree to which fear has paralyzed him: "He sat there, sweating under his arms, his mouth dry, his stomach hollow feeling, wanting to find *courage* [emphasis added] to tell Wilson to go and finish off the lion without him" (16). The fact that Macomber thinks of the term "courage" in this context—a context in which public admission of his own fear is conceived of as courageous—suggests the degree to which his notions of bravery may, on occasion, run counter to the accepted norms of the time.

Still, despite Macomber's candor, it is a near certainty that he would understand the layers of meaning in Bayard Sartoris's words to his Aunt Jenny when Bayard sets out to face Redmond the following morning: "You see, I want to be well thought of" (243). Macomber and Sartoris each recognize how vacuous many of the cultural claims are regarding courage, but each man is also a product of the culture and knows himself to be such. He cannot extinguish the wish to experience cultural approval. As Terrell Tebbetts argues regarding Sartoris, "the 'self' Bayard seeks to live with suggests a core personal identity, a skeleton on which he intends to build both the muscle of fuller personal identity and the skin of public identity as well" (83).

Bayard's decision as to how he will face Redmond—unarmed but unyielding, even as Redmond twice fires his own pistol—represents Bayard's bid to meet the dictates of his own conscience while fulfilling, in broad outline, his society's expectations regarding male courage. Robert Witt's view that "Bayard is becoming the priest of the New South as Drusilla has been the priestess of the Old South" (80) may be somewhat overstated. Nevertheless, Bayard has acquitted himself in such a way that, as he leaves town, a few men at the Holston House make a gesture indicating he has, by their lights, behaved in an acceptable manner: "A group of men stood before the door who raised their hats and I raised mine and Ringo and I rode on" (251). This mutual gesture, from Bayard to the men and they to him, offers confirmation that Bayard has forged a worthy union between his loyalty to the Christian ethic and his society's veneration of the masculine code of vengeance.

Prior to Francis Macomber's unfortunate death, he also performs acts that earn from Robert Wilson a modicum of public acknowledgement. The day after the lion fiasco, the hunting party pursues water buffalo, chasing the animals by car. In the midst of a frantic pursuit conveyed in a two hundred twenty-seven word sentence that may be aptly described as Faulknerian, Macomber's fear is transformed into hate for Wilson when the guide interdicts Macomber's attempt to fire from the vehicle. As the jeep skids toward a stop, "Wilson was out on one side and he on the other, stumbling as his feet hit the still speeding-by of the earth, and then he was shooting at the bull as he moved away, hearing the bullets whunk into him, emptying his rifle at him" (22). In these moments, Wilson appears to experience a reversal in his opinion of Macomber, telling him, "Now you're shooting" (22), and moments later, "You shot damn well" (23).

The assumption, of course, is that Macomber was successful in killing the first bull, but word comes back to the jeep that the wounded bull has risen. Tellingly, Margot is less quick than Wilson to praise her husband. Hearing that the bull will have to be tracked and killed, she says, "Then it's going to be just like the lion" (24). For his part, however, Macomber appears to have entered new emotional territory: "He expected the feeling he had had about the lion to come back but it did not. For the first time in his life he really felt wholly without fear. Instead of fear he had a feeling of definite elation" (24). As Macomber grows more confident, even excited about the prospect of pursuing the wounded bull, Margot grows more uncertain: "'You've gotten awfully brave awfully suddenly' [she] said contemptuously, but her contempt was not secure. She was very afraid of something" (26). For Virgil Hutton, Margot is "like her husband, a victim of Wilson's stereotyped notions of fear and bravery" (249). Ironically, while Wilson appears to have changed his views on Macomber, at least for the moment, Margot views her husband's former response to fear as determinitive. The prevailing cultural notion of courage has taught her to believe that once a man demonstrates cowardice, he will remain a coward at heart. Thus, as the bull charges toward her husband, Margot assumes the stock male role by taking action in a moment of crisis, even though in this instance her husband does not flee, but rather stands and fires. Whether Margot's aim from the jeep is accurate or off mark, whether the choice to fire is spurred by a desire to protect her husband or by fear that a more assertive mate will diminish her independence, she brings to quick conclusion Macomber's new self, his new life.

Despite the emphatic result of Margot's act, she finds herself in a relatively vulnerable position at the conclusion of the story. Suddenly widowed by her own hand, she is surely in shock, and Wilson's suggestion that she intentionally killed Macomber seems calculated to gain control over her by implying that she is at the mercy of whatever narrative he chooses to tell, shading his tale toward guilt or innocence depending upon his whim. His verbal manipulations prompt her to respond three separate times with the declarative "Stop it," then with a more desperate-sounding series, "Stop it. Stop it. Stop it." Only when she amends her words to "Please stop it" does Wilson utter the concluding line of the story, "Please is much better. Now I'll stop" (28). Despite the power that Margot has asserted throughout the narrative, she seems to relinquish control to Wilson in the end.

Whether Drusilla relinquishes control at the end of "An Odor of Verbena" is less certain. When Bayard returns home on the evening of his encounter with Redmond, he learns from his Aunt Jenny that she has chosen to leave the house. She is traveling to Montgomery to stay with her brother Dennison, thus outwardly adopting the traditional role of the young widow. Yet there is little that is conventional about Drusilla, and through her departure she denies Bayard the literal last word in their contest over courage. Moreover, a woman who has lived so free of traditional societal constraints is unlikely to accept those constraints as a natural or proper condition.

Figuratively, though, Faulkner does give primacy to Bayard's perspective on the issue of courage. As the man who is now "the Sartoris," Bayard passes through the parlor and notices that he can "still smell the [funereal] flowers above the verbena in [his] coat" (252). Previously, Drusilla has told him, "verbena was the only scent you could smell above the smell of horses and courage and so it was the only one that was worth the wearing" (220). Bayard's capacity to smell the other flowers over the verbena in his own pocket subtly contradicts Drusilla's assertion regarding verbena and, by implication, her own narrative regarding the cultural code to which she professes such loyalty.

Later, after he has ascended the stairs to his own room, Bayard discovers a single sprig of verbena on his pillow, its aroma "filling the room, the dusk, the evening with that odor which *she said* [emphasis added] you could smell alone above the smell of horses" (254). Scholars have noted the omission of the word "courage" in this final rendition of Drusilla's phrasing, and one can wonder whether its absence means Bayard is uncertain whether to interpret Drusilla's gesture as compliment or mockery. In either case, by charting a path free of violence yet absent of shame, Bayard has wrestled his own portion of cultural narrative away from Drusilla. He has struggled through the conflict between cultural expectation and personal conscience to make a choice he can live with. He has written his own story.

Although it is doubtful Faulkner had Bayard Sartoris or Francis Macomber specifically in mind the day he opined that Hemingway lacked artistic courage, the two characters do indicate the seriousness with which their respective creators contemplated courage, particularly male courage. Through Bayard Sartoris, Faulkner offers an outright challenge to the Southern code of vengeance, but it should not be overlooked that Hemingway, in allowing Francis Macomber the personal sturdiness to confess his own fear, also fashions a subtle critique of the masculine code. True, Macomber's subsequent exploits at the end of "The Short Happy Life of Francis Macomber" suggest Hemingway may not be as willing as Faulkner to mount a full-scale challenge to prevailing notions of male courage, but it is a mistake to read the story as a chest-thumping endorsement of those notions. Faulkner and Hemingway were different men who led strikingly different lives. They also took dramatically different approaches to the art of fiction. As a result, it is not surprising that each man would create different artistic renderings of male courage. The surprise lies in how much common ground they actually found.

Works Cited

Baker, Carlos. *Ernest Hemingway: A Life Story.* Scribner's, 1969.
Blotner, Joseph. *Faulkner: A Biography.* One-Volume Edition.
    Vintage, 1991.

Faulkner, William. *The Unvanquished*. Vintage International, 1991.

Fruscione, Joseph. *Faulkner and Hemingway: Biography of a Literary Rivalry*. Ohio State UP, 2012.

Gobble, Maryanne M. "The Significance of Verbena in William Faulkner's 'An Odor of Verbena.'" *Mississippi Quarterly*, vol. 53, no. 4, Fall 2000, pp. 569-82.

Hemingway, Ernest. "The Short Happy Life of Francis Macomber." *The Complete Short Stories of Ernest Hemingway*. Finca Vigia Edition, Scribner's, 1987, pp. 5-28.

Hutton, Virgil. "The Short Happy Life of Francis Macomber." *The Short Stories of Ernest Hemingway: Critical Essays,* edited by Jackson J. Benson, Duke UP, 1975, pp. 239-50.

McHaney, Thomas L. *William Faulkner's* The Wild Palms: *A Study.* UP of Mississippi, 1975.

Tebbetts, Terrell L. "'I'm the Man Here': *Go Down, Moses* and Masculine Identity." *Faulkner and Postmodernism*, edited by John N. Duvall and Ann J. Abadie, UP of Mississippi, 1999, pp. 81-94.

Witt, Robert W. "On Faulkner and Verbena." *Southern Literary Journal*, vol. 27, no. 1, Fall 1994, pp. 73-84.

Pennie Pflueger

Absurdity and Grace Under Pressure: Faulkner and Hemingway as Progenitors of Ellison's *Invisible Man* and Himes's *A Rage in Harlem*

"I would sit in my room and become hysterical thinking about the wild, incredible story I was writing. But it was only for the French, I thought, and they would believe anything about Americans, black or white, if it was bad enough. And I thought I was writing realism. It never occurred to me that I was writing absurdity. Realism and absurdity are so similar in the lives of American blacks one can not tell the difference."

Chester Himes, My Life of Absurdity

Chester Himes, and Ralph Ellison before him, found in Faulkner and Hemingway kindred spirits. Despite the fact that Himes never met either writer, and Ellison met Faulkner on only one occasion, they nevertheless drew from the older writers' art the sustenance that enabled them to produce their best work. The enormous influence cast by Faulkner and Hemingway, it could be argued, would be difficult for any writer who followed after them in the twentieth century to completely escape, including black writers who often saw their artistic vision diametrically opposed to that of both of the Nobel Prize winners. But for black writers to herald and even to be laudatory of Faulkner or Hemingway—as Himes and Ellison frequently were—is another matter. One need only to be reminded, for example, of the controversy in which Faulkner found himself in 1956 on the issue of civil rights, or Hemingway's heroic and *white* masculine ideal that runs throughout his fiction, to put Himes's and Ellison's reverence into perspective. Albert Murray and James Baldwin, to cite only two examples, found these "controversies" alienating and even indicative of a flawed artistic vision.[1] To be fair, Ellison himself had voiced misgivings about Hemingway—for example, his lack of fully depicted black characters, which for Ellison suggested that "the concern for the Negro and for the values which his presence connoted in American fiction were not just unspoken by Hemingway, they were *nonexistent*" (O'Meally 251). Ellison also found Hemingway's use of understatement and his prioritizing technical mastery over depth or complexity problematic. He states in 1946 in "Twentieth Century Fiction and the Black Mask of Humanity": "Artists such as Hemingway were seeking a technical perfection rather than moral insight" (*Shadow and Act* 38). Nevertheless, Ellison could not escape Hemingway, despite any misgivings he had. This influence appears in *Invisible Man* (1952), which Ellison began working on in 1945, and is explicitly acknowledged in "The World and the Jug," a later essay from 1963, in which Ellison expounds on why he considers Hemingway more important to him than Richard Wright: "I will remind you," he says, "that any writer takes what he needs to get his own work done from wherever he finds it," and he adds, "I needed instruction in other values and I found them in the works of other writers—Hemingway was one of them" (*Shadow and Act* 141).

Despite having a close personal relationship with Wright, Ellison increasingly distanced himself artistically from the writer whom many considered to be his primary literary influence. Ellison believed Wright's work to be constrained by ethnicity, a constraint he was not interested in preserving. In response to Irving Howe's essay, "Black Boys and Native Sons," an essay that praised Wright but faulted Ellison and Baldwin for being unable to surpass writing about black experience (despite their aspirations to do so), Ellison states, "No, Wright was no spiritual father of mine," and asserted that it was Baldwin "who found Wright a lion in his path." Ellison, however, because he was "older and familiar with quite different lions in quite different paths…simply stepped around him" (*Shadow and Act* 117). Ellison sought to surpass the limitations of what he saw as protest fiction to achieve an art that was universal and human rather than black and militant, which is why Ellison was willing to move beyond Wright and look to writers such as Hemingway and Faulkner. That Ellison and Himes do not feel compromised as black writers by any negative association that might be attached to

Faulkner or Hemingway is due at least in part to the interest they had in two specific strands of modernism in the white writers' work: the concept of Hemingway's grace under pressure, which is essentially an aesthetics of masculinity; and Faulkner's use of the absurd.

I. Hemingway and Grace Under Pressure

Grace under pressure, a concept most associated with Hemingway, reflects the changes and tensions that the early decades of the twentieth century brought and the anxieties that resulted, particularly for men. For Hemingway, grace under pressure encapsulated the masculine courage needed to confront and triumph over any perceived danger or complications imposed by modern and industrialized life. Ian Marshall has perceptively argued that Hemingway's primary concern in his fiction is that of (white) male self-actualization which requires exercise of will, a trait that Marshall identifies as "the central element of grace under pressure" (179). Notably, this exercise of will for Hemingway's characters cannot be achieved by blacks, women, or those of the working class, making Ellison's and Himes's appropriation of grace under pressure and the general Hemingway code hero particularly transgressive. The Hemingway male hero lives in the moment, is not afraid to take risks, frequently consumes alcohol, and pursues his desire with little regard for consequence. He keeps emotions in check and quietly endures. The code hero, when tested with danger and possibly death, does not flinch but confronts peril head on, testing masculine courage in what some readers have identified as a rite of passage. Recognizing that life itself is everything, Hemingway's masculine hero does not seek out death and thus does not enjoy darkness, instead preferring that lights remain on (giving Invisible's sabotage of power from the Monopolated Light & Power electric company for the 1,369 more expensive-to-operate filament bulbs in his hole particular Hemingway resonance). He also demonstrates restraint in speaking, another notable trait that gets re-worked particularly by Ellison in *Invisible Man* by having his protagonist intent on speaking and giving speeches. The minimalist style made famous by Hemingway reflects the restraint his code heroes exercise not only in their speech but in their emotions. The Hemingway masculine traits are seen by some scholars as evidence that Hemingway had deep insecurities about his own manhood (Strychacz 7). These traits also reflect Hemingway's attempt to recoup the anxieties experienced by white masculine culture after WWI, in particular, but also extending through mid-century and post-WWII. The loss of individual freedom, fear of the foreign (whether that be via xenophobia or any presence that might be rendered inscrutable), and the increase of women in the work place all contributed to white male anxiety and to the creation of several white male figure types in literature, one of which is Hemingway's masculine and romanticized hero. Megan Abbott identifies the white male figure who emerged in the 1930s-1950s in popular culture as well as literary works as "solitary" and "hard-bitten, street-savvy, but very much alone amid the chaotic din of the modern city" (2). Abbott's focus on the white male figure is situated within the hard-boiled tradition, but she argues that this figure "has forerunners in like-minded navigators of Western space or wilderness" and is also seen in "a relocation to the industrialized American city, combined with the influence of modernist themes of fragmentation and alienation, [which] created a unique new figure—a figure we can locate in Hemingway's Jake Barnes (*The Sun Also Rises*) and Harry Morgan (*To Have and Have Not*), Nathanael West's Miss Lonelyhearts, the marginal men of Nelson Algren and others, not to mention later incarnations in Henry Miller and Norman Mailer" (2).

But if white male anxiety could be assuaged—at least artistically—by the noir world or by Hemingway's ideal masculine hero, where did black men fit in? The toughness and hardboiled nature of the Hemingway hero appears oblivious to the plight of blacks and black males in particular, or perhaps worse sees black figures only in subordinate and undemocratic roles. Ian Marshall, for example, makes a compelling case that Hemingway needed and relied on the Other in order "to posit his idyllic white American identity" (178). Toni Morrison, in *Playing in the Dark* (1992), further elaborates on Hemingway's need for a subordinated literary black presence as it supports and enables the kind of masculine virility and supremacy the code hero (and white culture generally) must have in the desire for social and psychological dominance. Morrison states, for example, that Hemingway's fiction "is affected by an Africanist presence" (70) and that "Africanism becomes not only a means of displaying authority but, in fact, constitutes its source" (80). While grace under pressure could serve as a way to repudiate or offset any perceived threat that white masculinity was in peril or could potentially be "unmanned," there were compelling reasons for black artists such as Ellison and Himes to embrace that which was essentially exclusionary of their own ability to exercise male agency. Rather than dismiss or repudiate Hemingway, both Ellison and Himes appropriate Hemingway to expose the limitations in his masculine ideal in order to illuminate how black males, too, exercise grace under pressure in a racialized world.

II. Faulkner and the Absurd

Faulkner's use of the absurd also reflects concerns with modernism, the disjunction between ideals and reality. A sense of the absurd runs throughout Faulkner's work, perhaps most notably in *As I Lay Dying* (1930). But *Light in August* (1932) also implicitly conveys the absurdity of a racialized society in which a man destroys himself and allows himself to be destroyed because he believes himself to be black but is ultimately at an impasse in knowing who exactly he is. The absurd, with its concern with the paradox of seeking meaning in a meaningless environment, grew out of the nineteenth-century European philosophy espoused by Kierkegaard and later in the twentieth century by Albert Camus. Although Faulkner indicated that he was not familiar with Camus or his writings, his work demonstrates several absurdist traits: the irrationality of the human condition; the fallibility of discursive thought; the displacement and sense of loss felt by many of his characters; the lack of certainty to simply know; and a frequent tinge of the surreal, for example, in how a character is described or in how a character perceives his environmental surroundings.[2] While the absurd itself has received little attention in Faulkner, his use of humor and comedy have been recognized. For example, Faulkner, along with friends Phil Stone and Bess Storer, spent considerable time reading aloud Honoré de

Balzac's *The Human Comedy* (Brodsky and Hamblin 192).

Although Faulkner is not what readers would call a "humorist," his use of humor is unquestionably appreciated for its rich and complex contribution to his work. James Cox, for example, has stated that humor in Faulkner "is not a separate, subordinate aspect of Faulkner's world." Instead, Cox argues, humor is "at the very heart of his world. Thus we are not talking about scenes of comic relief that provide relaxation to some tragic intensity" (1). Along with the impact of Balzac, scholars have also identified the work of Henri Bergson as a source of influence for Faulkner's humor—in addition to Faulkner himself also acknowledging this debt. Patricia Schroeder, for example, in her analysis of the absurd or comic in *As I Lay Dying*, asserts that "for Bergson and Faulkner, life consists of movement, of flux, of inescapable change through time, and any effort to arrest this movement—with rituals, with unchanging truths, with imposed forms of any kind—produces comedy. Any sort of rigidity, postulates Bergson, elicits our laughter—which is, of course, the conventional response to the humorous. *As I Lay Dying* is full of this comedy of the rigid" (41).

But it is not just Faulkner's interest in what he once referred to as man's ability to be absurd that provides such fertile ground for later writers such as Ellison and Himes. Faulkner's interest in stylistically rendering the subconscious, that state between wakefulness and sleep, to use language representationally through signs and symbols rather than a linear or literal conveyance of thought—are, of course, modernist concerns with the novel that are evident in *Light in August* and are close to an absurdist or surrealistic quality. Eileen Bender has argued that surrealism serves as an intertext for *Light in August*, noting that Faulkner engages in word-amalgams that "blur linguistic distinctions and invite surrealistic readings" and that "the surrealists were fascinated by the mysteries of language, the inadvertent revelations of puns and slips, the dizzying whirl of associations set up by portmanteau words" (Bender 6). The wordplay, the dissonance, and what may appear as disparate images work to create what Bender identifies as Faulkner's "surrealistic canvas," aligning *Light in August* with that of a Salvador Dali painting.[3] Faulkner's use of the absurd in both style and theme, particularly as it relates to racialized American culture, are traits that Ellison and Himes found conducive to their own work.

III. *Invisible Man*: "An Ease of Movement within Explosive Situations"

"In our society it is not unusual for a Negro to experience a sensation that he does not exist in the real world at all. He seems, rather, to exist in the nightmarish fantasy of the white American mind as a phantom that the white mind seeks unceasingly, by means both crude and subtle, to lay to rest."

Ralph Ellison, "*An American Dilemma*: A Review"

Ellison's idea to write a story about a black man's search for identity began in 1945, and he would continue working on what would become *Invisible Man* over the next several years. While the novel is filled with a variety of influences ranging from Dostoevsky and T.S. Eliot, to folklore and jazz, to Booker T. Washington and Marcus Garvey (to list only a few), Ellison refers to Faulkner and Hemingway specifically in his 1948 essay "Harlem is Nowhere." Ellison invokes both writers to describe the plight of blacks who migrate to the North only to discover that they are in the land of nowhere, stripped of all support systems they may have had in the South (despite living in what Ellison alludes to as an "unhappy homeland") and who, nevertheless, inculcated techniques of survival—techniques which, according to Ellison, "Faulkner refers to as 'endurance,' and an ease of movement within explosive situations which makes Hemingway's definition of courage, 'grace under pressure,' appear mere swagger" (*Collected Essays* 323). That Ellison had Faulkner, Hemingway, and their techniques in mind in his conception of black alienation in post-war America is especially significant given that he was working on *Invisible Man* during the time this essay was published.

Ellison's allusions to Hemingway in *Invisible Man* have been identified by several scholars. Robert G. O'Meally, for instance, argues that the novel taken as a whole is a test of the narrator's ability to prevail in the face of life's battles. The narrator, like a Hemingway matador, must learn how to overcome the threats he faces, and he must also know how to discern what is at stake. When sitting in the El Toro Bar in Harlem with Brother Jack, he observes a bullfighting scene behind the bar and he thinks, "Pure grace." He then notices another bullfighting scene in which a matador is gored while Brother Jack instructs him on "mastering" the ability to balance ideology and inspiration in preparing his speeches for the people of Harlem (358-59). Tod Clifton's fight with Ras can also be linked with a Hemingway-esque bullfight. As O'Meally states: "bulls and bullfighting figure in *Invisible Man* in crucial ways. Metaphors that bring to mind the tragedy of the bull, as Hemingway glosses it, are, in fact, central to the novel's meanings" (260).

But unlike Hemingway's world, where men confront the dangers of life minus racial adversity or complication, Ellison's narrator must learn to exercise grace under pressure within the context of a racialized environment, which only adds to the absurdity of his plight. We first see Ellison draw attention to the absurdity of black life in *Invisible Man* with the famous "Battle Royal" scene in which the younger version of Invisible endures humiliation but is relentlessly intent on making a speech to a group of racist white men who have come together only for an evening of lewd and exploitative entertainment. Part of the pathos of this scene includes the naïve narrator who has not yet fully awakened to his plight and clings to his belief in educational progress in front of a white audience that conceives of him only as object. The chasm between this reality and the aspirations of the young black male establishes the alienation and disillusionment that will continue to haunt him through the novel. The Battle Royal scene is pivotal in that it shows Ellison laying the groundwork of his protagonist's racial identity and the subjugation of the black male in the context of white male entertainment.

Most readers see this scene as an early episode of emasculation and disempowerment of Invisible and the other black boys who are equally subjugated to the desires of the white men. The boys are punished whether they look at the naked white woman or not in what George Kent refers to as a "ritual…to stamp upon them the symbolic castration they are supposed to experience in the presence of a white woman" (99). The scene becomes particularly absurd in the way Ellison stresses the young protagonist's insistence on giving his speech despite the humiliation he has endured. By invoking Booker T. Washington as a role model for the young Invisible, Ellison underscores the important function that speech has played in the lives of blacks. And ironically, despite the laughter and humiliation he endures, at the end of the Battle Royal scene, Invisible receives a scholarship to the state college for Negroes on the basis of his speech. Whereas Hemingway's code hero is a man of few words and, in fact, refrains from using much speech at all, Ellison incorporates speech as essential in asserting identity. The code hero prioritizes action and courage over emotions as well as words and can afford to live without any reliance on others (indeed, doing so would only diminish his heroic qualities).

Ellison's narrator, however, must rely on others as well as speech to bring about awareness and organization in the absurd world in which he lives. He yells at a tall blond man in the opening Prologue to "Apologize! Apologize!" when the man calls him an insulting name and asks at the end of the novel, "Who knows but that, on the lower frequencies, I speak for you?" (581). The display of emotion, the outrage that Invisible experiences as a result of being insulted and defined by a white stranger, and the way in which he desires to take chaotic action in the moment all violate the Hemingway code. This violation is necessary, however, to illuminate the disparities between the hard-boiled fiction of Hemingway and the ambiguities Ellison stresses are part of the modern world that Invisible inhabits.

Speech allows Invisible to make sense of the world and of his place in it. In "Twentieth-Century Fiction and the Black Mask of Humanity," Ellison writes that "the essence of the word is its ambivalence, and in fiction is never so effective and revealing as when both potentials are operating simultaneously, as when it mirrors both good and bad, as when it blows both hot and cold in the same breath" (Shadow and Act 25). Ellison stresses the slippery nature of language not to control it but to draw off its complexity in shaping imagination and the possibilities that exceed a one-dimensional or reductive perspective. Invisible himself experiences a range of discourse possibilities: moments of uncontrolled rhetoric; stilted and rehearsed speech predicated on accommodation; and unplanned, extemporaneous speech. Invisible admits the possibility at the end of the novel that "perhaps, being a talker, I've used too many words" (579), but he also concludes that he must come out of hibernation ("a covert preparation for a more overt action" [13]) since "even an invisible man has a socially responsible role to play" (581). Violating the Hemingway code, however, is essential for Ellison's narrator since it is through speech-making and speaking that he is not only able to raise awareness of others and to make sense of his own experience but to convey that experience to the outer world. As O'Meally concludes, "Invisible Man is not a laconic Hemingway tough guy; he is a talker who says his piece in language more extroverted and southern than Hemingway's characters used" (268).

Although Invisible loses his Booker T. Washington ideology of accommodation as the novel progresses, the "Battle Royal" sets up the thematic concern with speech as a strategy Invisible uses to combat racial absurdity. This important scene also sets up the concern with the black phallus, castration, and the way in which white culture ascribes black men as voracious in their sexuality—or, at the very least, uncontained and uncontrollable, particularly in relation to white women. Themes of castration and racialized sex (and their implicit absurdity) parallel Faulkner's use of similar themes in *Light in August* and the tragedy of Joe Christmas, a man who is seen by the community as black and whose crime is not only the murder of a white woman, but possibly worse in the eyes of the town, one with whom he had been having a sexual relationship. Joe is eventually hunted down and killed by Percy Grimm but not before he castrates him and says, "Now you'll let white women alone, even in hell" (513).

Like Christmas, Invisible lacks a sense of identity or subjecthood that would allow him autonomy. Additionally, Invisible experiences others ascribing to him what they need, want, or interpret him to be. The encounter with Rinehart near the end of the novel (a character readers never actually know or experience) opens up the new possibility that identity is malleable and can be exploited. As he processes the potential power that conning identity has, Invisible thinks:

Can it actually be? And I knew that it was. I had heard of it before but I'd never come so close. Still, could he be all of them: Rine the runner and Rine the gambler and Rine the briber and Rine the lover and Rinehart the Reverend? Could he himself be both rind and heart? What is real anyway? . . . The world in which we lived was without boundaries. A vast seething, hot world of fluidity, and Rine the rascal was at home. Perhaps *only* Rine the rascal was at home in it. It was unbelievable, but perhaps only the unbelievable could be believed. Perhaps the truth was always a lie. (498)

With this new possibility opened to him, Invisible decides that he, too, will exploit identity, using a woman to gain inside information into the Brotherhood. Sybil, the wife of a fellow Brotherhood member, ascribes the identity "entertainer" and "big black bruiser" (522) to Invisible as part of her rape fantasy. Joanna Burden, likewise, attributes a black masculinity to Joe Christmas, one that allows her to engage in a socially prohibitive sexual relationship, and one that some readers have argued enables Joanna a subjectivity that infuriates and threatens Joe. Faulkner's exploration of the psycho-sexual episode in *Light in August* is revisited by Ellison via the Sybil section of *Invisible Man*, allowing his narrator to repudiate the mythology of hypersexual black masculinity. As Claudia Tate has argued, Sybil, along with the other female characters in the novel, help Invisible along the journey of peeling away illusions.[4] Sybil is his "last teacher" (Tate 170) who forces Invisible to confront her fantasy of sex with a black man as rape, a cultural taboo that seems to increase her desire for him. Notably, it is through the written word that Invisible refuses to enact the part of exploiting Sybil. Unlike Rinehart, Invisible refuses to fulfill or exploit others' fantasies about him. Instead, he chooses to use language in place of literal rape by writing in lipstick on Sybil's belly: "Sybil, You Were Raped / By / Santa Claus / Surprise" (522). Ellison's use of Santa Claus as a cultural symbol of white mythological gratification (combined with the phallic lipstick) indicates the extent to which he wants to signal Invisible's growing consciousness that both he and Sybil have been deluded.

Invisible's revelation that he will no longer participate in either being the object of others' desires or the exploiter of his own identity leads him to a final confrontation with Ras the Exhorter where he further solidifies his quest for identity by realizing that words alone will not be enough and that action is necessary. Once Invisible's illusions are stripped away, he engages in action (and not just speech) over the death of Tod Clifton. Invisible is aware that danger threatens him as the rioters loot businesses and burn an apartment building. The chaos that ensues and the terror Invisible feels is only further increased with the arrival of Ras the Exhorter, the black nationalist that Ellison's narrator refers to as Ras the *Destroyer*. Initially, the narrator attempts to persuade Ras and his men that they are all being used to destroy one another but quickly realizes it is not speech that will see him through. The ludicrous nature of the situation compels the narrator to contemplate:

> I looked at Ras on his horse and at their handful of guns and recognized the absurdity of the whole night and of the simple yet confoundingly complex arrangement of hope and desire, fear and hate, that had brought me here still running, and knowing now who I was and where I was and knowing too that I had no longer to run for or from the Jacks and the Emersons and the Bledsoes and Nortons, but only from their confusion, impatience, and refusal to recognize the beautiful absurdity of their American identity and mine. (559)

The pictures the narrator had previously observed while with Brother Jack in the El Toro Bar serve as a kind of foreshadowing of a matador in action. Confronted with the possibility that he will be lynched, the narrator uses a spear, which goes through Ras's face, causing both of his jaws to lock (560). The act of spearing Ras places the narrator in the role of a matador, one who must confront the risk of dying in order to know his reality completely and ultimately to gain the perspective necessary to tell his story. The narrator continues to contemplate death by reflecting on his identity:

> I, a little black man with an assumed name should die because a big black man in his hatred and confusion over the nature of a reality that seemed controlled solely by white men whom I knew to be as blind as he, was just too much, too outrageously absurd. And I knew it was better to live out one's own absurdity than to die for that of others, whether for Ras's or Jack's. (559)

Going underground and living in a warm hole full of lights where he hibernates, where he has mastered the art of the "joke," Invisible prepares his overt role. But this is after he comes full circle and completes a journey, one in which he achieves an autonomy that allows him to plan the next step. Ellison creates in his protagonist a complete person, African American, but also human, which is part of his attempt to redress what he saw as a deficiency in Hemingway. Ellison addresses the dearth of fully realized African American characters in American literature in "Twentieth-Century Fiction and the Black Mask of Humanity": "When the white American, holding up most twentieth-century fiction, says, 'This is American reality,' the Negro tends to answer (not at all concerned that Americans tend generally to fight against any but the most flattering imaginative depictions of their lives), 'Perhaps, but you've left out this, and this, and this. And most of all, what you'd have the world accept as *me* isn't even human'" (*Collected Essays* 82).

IV. *A Rage in Harlem*

What Ellison does in his attempt at expressing the chasm and absurdity between the shadows cast from American ideals and the realities of American culture, Chester Himes most fully addresses in his detective fiction that began with *A Rage in Harlem* (1957). Himes might have been considered unlikely to turn to a life of writing as he was sentenced to prison in Ohio for armed robbery and served seven and a half years there before being paroled in 1936. In prison, however, Himes began writing and publishing short fiction. After leaving prison, Himes continued to publish novels before moving to France. Detective fiction, however, was not a genre that Himes was initially comfortable with. It took Marcel Duhamel to suggest the idea that Himes try writing a detective novel for a French audience, but Himes quickly realized that he could make good money. Encouraged but still unsure how to actually become a writer of detective fiction for a French market, he turned to Faulkner and his novel *Sanctuary* (1931), as Himes has stated, "to give me courage."[5] Himes described his first foray into detective fiction with Faulkner leading the way by saying: "I have always considered the fiction of Faulkner the most absurd ever written and if I couldn't get any ideas from it I was stuck" (*My Life of Absurdity* 106). But with three hundred dollars in his pocket and Faulkner's novel in front of him, Himes finished *A Rage in Harlem*, which became the first detective fiction in a series using Harlem as his canvas and featuring the detectives Grave Digger Jones and Coffin Ed Johnson who would bring him wealth and fame.

Using *Sanctuary* as courage-inducing suggests the affinity Himes felt with a fellow, albeit white, American writer. Referencing Faulkner's *Sanctuary*, however, has other implications for Himes's use of the absurd. He would, for example, have been aware of the sensationalism attached to the book, as Edwin T. Arnold states in the Introduction to *Reading Faulkner: Sanctuary*: "*Sanctuary* defined Faulkner in the public mind as a writer of violent, sensational, semi-pornographic novels" (xiv). Himes may also have yearned for an American connection with a celebrity writer. The noir aspect of *A Rage in Harlem* also fits well with *Sanctuary*, which exhibits several noir elements, including that of aberrant behavior and violence.

A Rage in Harlem, like *Invisible Man*, focuses on the plight of blacks in the urban environment of Harlem. But whereas Harlem functions as a context that further alienates Invisible in his search for identity (but where it should be noted he also achieves identity), Harlem for Himes is a daily reminder of the consequences of being black in America. Himes's Harlem is grotesque, comical, and always infused with outrageous violence. Himes's characters expect violence and look for ways to exist despite being immersed in what Himes would characterize as the absurd reality of their day to day lives. Because the people in Harlem are surrounded by absurd events and situations, the concept of grace under pressure gets revised by Himes. It does not function as a code as Hemingway had envisioned it. A code of behavior assumes some sense of regularity, honor, and dignity, even in light of danger and the unexpected, and this is especially true for Hemingway's masculine hero who is able to function and perform regardless of circumstances. Himes's Harlem, however, has no sense of order. Therefore, the concept of grace under pressure takes on new meaning in the urban black environment. Jackson, Himes's protagonist, is described as "a member of the First Baptist Church of Harlem" and "a very religious young man" who crosses himself "whenever he was troubled" and "just to be on the safe side" (7). Yet, despite being religious, or perhaps *because* he is (which would make the situation even more absurd), Jackson endures intensely dangerous situations throughout *A Rage in Harlem*.

If Jackson is not at risk of encountering killer con men, he is being chased by cops. At one point in the story, Jackson is desperate to locate his girlfriend Imabelle and turns to his twin brother Goldy for help. Goldy is a drug addict and transvestite who disguises himself as a nun, sells tickets to Heaven, and has a wife but lives with two other men who all impersonate females. Despite being street savvy, Goldy is no match for the con men who kill him. After Goldy is killed by Hank and Jodie, the two con men who have come for the trunk that supposedly has gold in it, Jackson awakes to discover that the killers are right outside the apartment he is in and that they assume that he (or someone) is there who would have helped Goldy lift the heavy trunk onto the hearse that belongs to Jackson's boss (as Jackson works for an undertaker). The killers have already demonstrated that they are cold-blooded in their murder of Goldy (although Jackson is aware only that they are dangerous and not that his brother has been killed), and Jackson has nowhere to escape.

The risks Jackson confronts enable Himes to recuperate from Hemingway a searing understanding of racial injustices, injustices that Hemingway does not address in his conception of the masculine code. Whereas the Hemingway hero is able to conduct himself in predictable and honorable ways, the social, economic, and political structures in the Himes-ian world erase any possibility for such order. Nevertheless, Himes's characters confront life-threatening danger on a daily basis with the added complication that they must be prepared at all times to innovate. Himes opens the scene, for example, with immediate terror being felt by Jackson: "The short, sharp blast of a train whistle when it had crossed the river into Harlem awakened Jackson in a pool of terror" (106). Danger seeps into Jackson's dreams so that he immediately "jumped to his feet, overturning the chair. He sensed someone striking him from behind, ducked, and knocked the table aside. Wheeling about, he snatched the pipe from the table to knock Slim's brains out" (106). At this point, Jackson realizes that there is no one there. Although naïve and in many ways unprepared for the dangers and traps of con men, Jackson proves himself capable of pure nerve and determination as well as the ability to act quickly in chaotic situations, enabling Himes to counter Hemingway's inadequate depictions of black male characters.

When Jackson runs from the apartment to re-unite with Goldy, he becomes "petrified" to discover Hank and Jodie standing next to the hearse. Still unaware that Goldy has been murdered, Jackson "felt like damning Goldy to everlasting hell, but didn't want to commit blasphemy on top of all the other sins he'd committed" (109). Fearing that Hank and Jodie will enter the apartment building, Jackson hides in a closet underneath a set of stairs where he hears the killers ascend the flights of stairs back to the apartment, at which point Jackson runs for the hearse (which contains the body of his dead brother), starts the engine and says, "One more shave that close, Lord, and this brother ain't going to be here long" (111). In Harlem, though, almost every shave is that close. The environment itself poses considerable and consistent risk such that it becomes the fabric of living there. The collective community that makes up Harlem enables Himes to extend his detective series through seven additional novels, not so unlike the way in which Faulkner continued writing about Yoknapatawpha County. Angus Calder states that Himes's "presentation of Harlem is densely detailed, to the point of apparent redundancy, but this richness of 'background' is associated

. . . with a view of character in which character and environment are morally indistinguishable" (109).

Calder also notes that Himes is interested in creating works of fiction that "embody a splendidly intransigent refusal to come to terms with contemporary American values, to accept even one lie or subscribe to even one illusion" (109). This refusal to accommodate his work to the standards he found in American publishing, for example, ultimately led Himes to expatriate to Europe, where he hoped he might speak and create art more freely. Himes's intolerance for illusion, as Calder observes, carries over into his novels, so that a character unable to face reality is considered a "square," a gullible person who will be exploited.[6] Himes's "square" and Ellison's naïve narrator resemble Faulkner's naïvely absurd characters. In *Light in August*, for example, Joe Christmas's failure to discern that Bobbie Allen is a prostitute leads to his being taken advantage of. Likewise, in *As I Lay Dying*, MacGowan takes advantage of Dewey Dell when he tells her of the "hair of the dog" treatment that she hopes will abort her pregnancy. The naivety of the characters enables the absurdity of their situations to be even more pronounced and dramatic. The comic pathos also helps to underscore the inequities of the respective character's community as well as society at large.

In "So Much Nonsense Must Make Sense: The Black Vision of Chester Himes," David Cochran reminds his readers of an argument made by Jackson Lears about the recurrent theme of modernist artists who have "the belief that the commercial image of the sleek, successful twentieth-century American is neither as substantial nor as realistic as the pathetic, unfortunate and grotesque denizens of, for instance, Winesburg, Ohio, or Yoknapatawpha County, Mississippi." Cochran goes on to assert:

> Similarly, black modernists in the post-World War II period faced the slick, Sidney Poitier image of the successful black integrationist, one they knew did not convey the reality of their lives. But not in their darkest nightmares could Sherwood Anderson or William Faulkner conjure up the grotesqueries of Himes's Harlem, peopled as it is with a giant albino Negro idiot, a dwarf pusher, an elderly, withered

female faith healer/heroin pusher, a transvestite nun/con man/junkie who sells tickets to heaven, a ninety-year-old black Mormon with eleven wives and a brood of children who run around naked and eat from a trough. (27)

What Ellison's and Himes's work shows is that courage or grace emerges in the context of the absurd, that for African Americans one cannot exist without the other. Grace under pressure and absurdity are uniquely significant for black writers following in the footsteps of Faulkner and Hemingway because, as Ellison noted, post-World War II American culture provided no social or institutional acceptance and support for its black citizens, particularly those who had migrated north from the South, who had nothing from the past that would have prepared them for the alienating effects of urban living. Additionally, placing Ellison and Himes in the context of a Faulkner-Hemingway inheritance deepens our understanding of modernist concerns with individuals in their social environments and increases our awareness of the broader implications that modernism has for black writers.

Notes

1. In a letter to Ellison, Murray expressed outrage at reading Faulkner's interview in *Life*: "Son of a bitch prefers a handful of anachronistic crackers to everything that really gives him a reason not only for being but for writing. I'm watching his ass but close forevermore" (*Trading Twelves* 125).

2. One example of an almost "unreal" character is that of Popeye from *Sanctuary* who is described thus: "His skin had a dead, dark pallor. His nose was faintly aquiline, and he had no chin at all. His face just went away, like the face of a wax doll set too near a hot fire and forgotten..." (5); "Popeye's eyes looked like rubber knobs, like they'd give to the touch and then recover with the whorled smudge of the thumb on them" (6); and, "Ahead of him Popeye walked, his tight suit and stiff hat all angles, like a modernistic lampstand" (7).

3. Bender suggests that Faulkner may have been aware of "The Persistence of Memory," the famous Dali painting given to the Museum of Modern Art in New York in 1931. She states: "It is irresistible to speculate that Faulkner envisioned Dali's melting clocks, swarming insects, grotesque humanoid equines, and nightmarish, oddly-illumined landscape when he composed *Light in August*. He not only exploits similar images in his own narrative; the interpenetration of fantastic and substantial—hallmark of surrealism—gives even the most violent events of the novel a dreamlike quality. Perhaps most importantly, the persistent force of memory drives each of the major characters, functioning like fate in this multileveled drama" (Bender 5).

4. Tate's analysis is compelling, although it should be noted that in a novel that contextualizes women as intellectually inferior (in the Brotherhood as elsewhere), it is ironic that it is the female characters who, arguably, most assist the narrator in his journey of self-discovery.

5. Apparently, however, Himes was more naïve about the genre of detective fiction than even he acknowledges. He asked Duhamel after drafting eighty pages of *A Rage in Harlem*, "You think I should have some police? I asked, trying to sound intelligent" to which Duhamel replied, "You can't have a policier without police" (*My Life of Absurdity* 105).

6. Himes's original title for the novel was *The Five-Cornered Square*.

Works Cited

Abbott, Megan E. *The Street Was Mine: White Masculinity in Hardboiled Fiction and Film Noir*. Palgrave Macmillan, 2002.

Arnold, Edwin T. and Dawn Trouard. *Reading Faulkner: Sanctuary*. UP of Mississippi, 1996.

Bender, Eileen T. "Faulkner as Surrealist: The Persistence of Memory in *Light in August*." *The Southern Literary Journal*, vol.

18, no. 1, Fall 1985, pp. 3-12.

Brodsky, Louis D., and Robert Hamblin, editors. *Faulkner: A Comprehensive Guide to the Brodsky Collection, Vol. 2.* UP of Mississippi, 1984.

Calder, Angus. "Chester Himes and the Art of Fiction." *The Critical Response to Chester Himes*, edited by Charles L.P. Silet, Greenwood Press, 1999, pp. 101-116.

Cochran, David. "So Much Nonsense Must Make Sense: The Black Vision of Chester Himes." *The Midwest Quarterly*, vol. 38, no. 1, Autumn 1996, pp. 11-30.

Cox, James. "Humor as Vision in Faulkner." *Faulkner & Humor*, edited by Doreen Fowler and Ann J. Abadie, UP of Mississippi, 1986, pp. 1-20.

Ellison, Ralph. *Invisible Man.* Vintage Books, 1995.

—. *Shadow and Act.* Vintage Books, 1995.

—. *The Collected Essays of Ralph Ellison*, edited by John F. Callahan, Modern Library, 1995.

Fabre, Michel, and Robert E. Skinner, editors. *Conversations with Chester Himes.* UP of Mississippi, 1995.

Faulkner, William. *Light in August.* Vintage Books, 1987.

—. *Sanctuary.* Vintage International, 1993.

Hemingway, Ernest. *The Sun Also Rises.* Scribner's, 1954.

Himes, Chester. *A Rage in Harlem.* Vintage Crime / Black Lizard Edition, 1991.

—. *The Quality of Hurt.* Thunder's Mouth Press, 1971.

—. *My Life of Absurdity.* Paragon House, 1976.

Hochman, Brian. "Ellison's Hemingways." *African American Review*, vol. 42, no. 3-4, Fall/Winter 2008, pp. 513-32.

Kent, George. "Ralph Ellison and Afro-American Folk and Cultural Tradition. *Speaking for You: The Vision of Ralph Ellison*, edited by Kimberly W. Benston, Howard UP, 1987, pp. 95-104.

Marshall, Ian. "Rereading Hemingway: Rhetorics of Whiteness, Labor, and Identity." *Hemingway and the Black Renaissance*, edited by Gary Edward Holcomb and Charles Scruggs, Ohio

State UP, 2012, pp. 177-213.

Morrison, Toni. *Playing in the Dark: Whiteness and the Literary Imagination*. Vintage Books, 1993.

Murray, Albert, and John F. Callahan, editors. *Trading Twelves: The Selected Letters of Ralph Ellison and Albert Murray*. Modern Library, 2000.

O'Meally, Robert G. "The Rules of Magic: Hemingway as Ellison's 'Ancestor.'" *Speaking for You: The Vision of Ralph Ellison*, edited by Kimberly W. Benston, Howard UP, 1987, pp. 245-71.

Nieland, Justus. "'Enough to Make a Body Riot': Pansies and Protesters in Himes's Harlem." *Arizona Quarterly*, vol. 56, no. 1, Spring 2000, pp. 105-133.

Rosen, Steven J. "African American Anti-Semitism and Himes's *Lonely Crusade*." *Critical Response to Chester Himes*, edited by Charles L.P. Silet, Greenwood Press, 1999, pp. 221-39.

Schroeder, Patricia. "The Comic World of *As I Lay Dying*." *Faulkner & Humor*, edited by Doreen Fowler and Ann J. Abadie, UP of Mississippi, 1986, pp. 34-46.

Silet, Charles L.P., editor. *The Critical Response to Chester Himes*. Greenwood Press, 1999.

Steward, Douglas. "The Illusions of Phallic Agency: *Invisible Man*, *Totem and Taboo*, and the Santa Claus Surprise." *Callaloo: A Journal of African-American and African Arts and Letters*, vol. 26, no. 2, Spring 2003, pp. 522-35.

Strychacz, Thomas. *Hemingway's Theaters of Masculinity*. Louisiana State UP, 2003.

Tate, Claudia. "Notes on the Invisible Women in Ralph Ellison's *Invisible Man*." *Speaking For You: The Vision of Ralph Ellison*, edited by Kimberly W. Benston, Howard UP, 1987, pp. 163-72.

Weinstein, Sharon Rosenbaum. "Comedy and the Absurd in Ralph Ellison's *Invisible Man*." *Studies in Black Literature*, vol. 3, no. 3, 1972, pp. 12-16.

Matthew D. Sutton

"A Damned Big Book": Ken Kesey's *Sometimes a Great Notion* as Faulkner-Hemingway Synthesis

In 1971, Ken Kesey, acclaimed as the author of the massively popular *One Flew Over the Cuckoo's Nest* (1962), and notorious as the ringleader of the psychedelic-bus travelling troupe the Merry Pranksters, penned brief appreciations of his formative writing influences under the title "Tools from My Chest." In addition to the expected testimonials to current rock groups and contemporary counterculture writers like William S. Burroughs, Kesey extolled William Faulkner and Ernest Hemingway, declaring Faulkner "my admitted favorite" ("Tools" 183). Perhaps it is no surprise that Kesey, as part of the 1950s/1960s cohort that developed in modernism's shadow, looked to Faulkner and Hemingway as models when writing his second novel, the magnum opus *Sometimes a Great Notion* (1964). One contemporary review approvingly noted that *Notion* "out-Faulknered Faulkner" in its complexity (Christensen 97), while Kesey's publisher invoked the spirit of Hemingway in publicity materials. But *Notion* was conceived as more than a revisionist exercise in modernism. What makes the novel greater than the sum of its parts is its canny synthesis of Faulkner's and Hemingway's signature tropes. By adapting and recombining sources, character types, and stylistic techniques from Faulkner and Hemingway, Kesey committed himself—for the first and last time in his career—to writing what he called a "damned big book" in homage to his influences' most ambitious works (Tanner 54). More than fifty years after its controversial publication, *Sometimes a Great Notion* should be reconsidered and analyzed in light of its antecedents as both a conscious and unconscious synthesis of Faulkner and Hemingway, with the novel's experimental narrative shifts and multiple points of view in stark contrast to its more didactic (and dated) pronouncements on masculine authority and atavism.

It is more than a coincidence of chronology that Kesey's first publications gained attention soon after the passing of Hemingway in 1961 and Faulkner in 1962. As Nobel laureates, each possessed cultural capital that reached beyond the insularity of the writing trade. Hemingway's posthumous extraliterary fame as a man of action was burnished in mass-market biographies, features in men's magazines, and even a syndicated comic strip (Raeburn 167–79).[1] Even when his powers were diminishing in the 1940s and 1950s, he could still draw attention, for example boasting in a *New Yorker* profile that as the reigning heavyweight novelist of his age he could readily "defend the title again against all the good young new ones" (Ross 38). Though less taken in by authorial rivalry and the cult of celebrity, Faulkner's post-Nobel Prize public letters and speeches edged him toward the spotlight and informed early biographical works like Robert Coughlan's *The Private World of William Faulkner* (1953) and John B. Cullen and Floyd Watkins's *Old Times in the Faulkner Country* (1961). Among even casual readers, their respective trademark styles became familiar, with Hemingway's terse prose and clear plot development in contrast to Faulkner's prolixity and nonlinear narratives that were, in Robert Penn Warren's words, "the antithesis of simplification" (qtd. in Parini 153). Contemporaneously, Kesey came to prominence as part of an emerging group of American realist writers who sought to both challenge and carry on modernism's war against convention and gentility. As an undergraduate at the University of Oregon, Kesey attended a lecture by Faulkner and was duly inspired to create a Southern Gothic story titled "Cattail Bog," an imaginative stretch for a young author born and bred in the Pacific Northwest. Kesey sent other samples of his apprentice work directly to Hemingway, reportedly receiving a kind reply to keep writing (Dodgson 61).

Kesey pursued his ambitions further by enrolling in Stanford University's creative-writing graduate program in the early 1960s, joining an impressive pool of developing talents including Larry

McMurtry, Ernest J. Gaines, Tillie Olson, Robert Stone, and Wendell Berry. At Stanford, Kesey shared a personal connection with his most-admired literary forebears by taking a course in fiction with Malcolm Cowley. In a 1960 letter to editor Pascal Covici, tipping him off to new prospects, Cowley marveled in equal measure at his student's prodigious though still-rough literary output and his reputation as a championship wrestler and Hemingway-type "man's man" (Bak 549). Recalling Kesey in the 1980s, Cowley described him in larger-than-life terms as having "the build of a plunging halfback, with big shoulders and a neck like the stump of a Douglas fir" and compared his magnetism as a graduate student to Hemingway's charisma among his cohort in 1920s Paris (Cowley 325–26). Under the auspices of Cowley and writing-program director Wallace Stegner, Kesey began to construct an authorial persona equally made up of Hemingway-hero bravado and the provincial modernism of Faulkner.

Under the weight of readers' expectations and the success of his debut novel, *One Flew Over the Cuckoo's Nest*, Kesey bounded between elation and despair writing the much longer and complex *Sometimes a Great Notion* between 1962 and 1963. To a colleague, he lamented, "My book is trying maybe too goddamn much" (Tanner 53). The story's plot became so labyrinthine that he was forced to graph its structure on a wall at his home, just as Faulkner had in the writing of one of his most convoluted works, *A Fable* (1954) (Dodgson 178). As the manuscript neared completion, anxiety turned to near-hubris, as Kesey wrote his closest friend (and future Merry Prankster) Ken Babbs that *Notion* was "a big book. Possibly a damned big book. Certainly a remarkable book. Perhaps even a great book" (Tanner 54).

Kesey's grandiosity had precedence. Submitting the hefty manuscript of *Flags in the Dust* to Boni and Liveright in 1927, fledgling novelist William Faulkner congratulated himself for writing "the damdest [*sic*] best book you'll look at this year" (Hamblin 46). Faulkner's publisher, ultimately, did not reciprocate his enthusiasm. Over a decade later, in the process of assembling *The Fifth Column and the First Forty-Nine Stories* (1938), Hemingway urged Maxwell Perkins to bulk up the page count, admitting, "I'd like to have a pretty big one for a change" and claiming that the reviews savaging the just-published *To Have and Have Not* (1937) necessitated something, in his own words, "extra good and extra big" (Bruccoli 262, 264).

After the critical and commercial triumph of *Cuckoo's Nest*, the reading public initially seemed receptive to Kesey's second novel and first attempt at a "damned big book." Yet a backlash quickly ensued. The prepublication notices for *Sometimes a Great Notion* fixated on its outsized length—628 pages—and cost—$7.50 (Nichols BR8). The post-publication critical response was much more pointed, with the *New York Times'* initial review headlined, "A Tiresome Literary Disaster" (Prescott 29).[2] In decrying what he judged the "most insufferably pretentious [...] and totally tiresome novel I have had to read in many years," the *Times'* book critic Orville Prescott directed some curiously retrograde criticisms toward Kesey, criticisms the likes of which were once leveled at Faulkner and Hemingway as young iconoclasts by more decorous critics. Prescott singled out the book's reader-unfriendly narrative manipulation of time, shifting perspectives (the critic charged Kesey with changing point-of-view five times on one page, as if this was a violation of literary law) and, finally, dialogue he deemed "inordinately foul-mouthed" (29).

Kesey's publisher Viking Press, deeply invested in promoting its young charge as a major American author on the cusp of greatness, responded in the *Times* a week later with a half-page advertisement featuring some of the novel's more positive critical notices that celebrated *Notion* as "a big book in every way" and "a blockbuster of a book...628 pages of raw American power [...] with some of the old Hemingway spirit" (Viking 27). In interviews, Kesey admitted structuring the fraternal conflict at the heart of the book around Hank, the Hemingwayesque hero, and his more ambivalent, Faulkneresque half-brother, Lee. He based this on his own split sensibilities, telling *The Paris Review* years later, "The two Stamper brothers in the novel are each one of the ways I think I am" (Lish 24). Certainly Hank Stamper, the dominating presence in the novel and the analogue to the imperious Randle Patrick McMurphy in *One Flew Over the Cuckoo's Nest*, reflects Hemingway's influence, while Lee as well as Hank's wife Viv exert a more conflicted, fragmented sensibility in tune with Faulkner's characters.

Following the premise of many Faulkner novels, *Sometimes a Great Notion*'s plot revolves around the dynamics of a family in late-stage conflict. Set in the logging town of Wakonda, Oregon, in the winter of 1961 (with the exception of interspersed flashbacks), the novel focuses on the Stamper family, who make their living as "gyppo" loggers, or woodsmen unaffiliated with a lumber company or union. The family motto—"Never Give an Inch"—underscores the Stampers' obsessive nature and tenacity (31).[3] The Stamper men—patriarch Henry, his son Hank, and nephew Joe Ben—struggle with the physical challenges of clear-cutting the forest as well as meeting the terms of a contract they signed with a lumber company after the town's unionized loggers went on strike. Unable to recruit local workers to cross the picket line yet determined to honor the contract, Hank sends for help from his long-estranged half-brother Lee, a neurotic Yale literature student spiraling into madness and drug addiction after the recent suicide of his mother, Myra, who left Oregon with Lee twelve years earlier after having an affair with stepson Hank. With Hank fixated on defying the odds of clearing a forest with a small crew and Lee fixated on exacting revenge on Hank for his incestuous affair, the two engage in a long civil war, climaxing—perhaps inevitably—with a drawn-out *mano a mano* fistfight and the accidental deaths of Henry and Joe Ben before the half-brothers join together in leading a train of log booms downriver to a lumber mill.

In analyzing Kesey's endeavor toward a tour de force, the Stampers can be read as an amalgam of Yoknapatawpha families, particularly the Sutpens, Compsons, Bundrens, and Snopeses. Paralleling Thomas Sutpen's conquest of Jefferson, Mississippi, the Stampers' ancestors arrive suddenly in the Pacific Northwest and singlemindedly devote their energies to enriching themselves in the logging business. Reminiscent of Sutpen, Henry Stamper, Sr. transforms the land and "tears it out" in his own design to the mixed amazement and horror of the townsfolk (238). The family compound, a patchwork of additions and half-completed renovations, is lashed to the ground by steel cables and separated from Wakonda by a moat. Its partial collapse at the end of the novel recalls the apocalyptic fall of the house of Sutpen at the climax of *Absalom, Absalom!* (1936). By the novel's conclusion, Lee's inner turmoil, return to the family home, and attempted manipulation of his half-brother lead to the exposure of family secrets and the subsequent downfall of the patriarchal order in much the same manner that Charles Bon exacts revenge at Sutpen's Hundred.

The theme of family disintegration connects *Notion* to *The Sound and the Fury* (1929) as well. Just as the events of Easter Weekend 1928 exhibit the intergenerational decline of the Compson fortunes, Kesey compresses the Stamper family saga for maximum dramatic impact, beginning at Thanksgiving 1961. Though Lee indifferently attends a different Ivy League school than Quentin, Kesey imbues him with notable similarities to the eldest Compson son: he trades barbs with a cynical Northern college roommate and frequently considers suicide in his free-associative narration. Like Quentin, Lee harbors compulsive thoughts about female "purity" and his own failures as a protector of women, specifically his mother. His primal moment of witnessing Myra's assignation with Hank through a hole in a wall recalls Quentin's surveillance of Caddy (as well as the transgressive voyeurism of Popeye in *Sanctuary* (1931), the young Joe Christmas in *Light in August* (1932), and Otis in *The Reivers* (1962)), revealing a furtive, repressed sexuality. Through Lee, Kesey satirizes the excesses of high modernist discourse in internal monologues that exceed the second section of *The Sound and the Fury* in their verbosity, self-consciousness, and psychoanalytic obsessions: "Certainly there were all the run-of-the mill Freudian reasons beneath my animosity toward my dear brother, all the castration-complex reasons, all the mother-son-father reasons—and all especially deep-seated and strong within me because the usual abysmal longing of the sulky son wishing to do in the guy who had been diddling Mom were in me compounded by the malevolent memories of a psychotic sibling" (195). Like Quentin, Lee, on the verge of another suicide attempt, feels momentary elation when his watch temporarily stops, giving him the illusion that he has eluded the grip of time; fittingly then, Lee's sections of the main narrative suspend time and obsess over traumatic past events, intentionally delaying the forward momentum of the story.

As noted by both partisan and antagonistic critics, the

focalization in *Sometimes a Great Notion* manically shifts between the half-brothers' interior monologues, the dialogue between characters, and an omniscient narrator. Influenced by film-editing techniques like jump-cuts, Kesey juxtaposes narrators (twelve in all) in a much more rapid-fire fashion than in *The Sound and the Fury*, *Absalom! Absalom!*, and *As I Lay Dying* (1930), sometimes switching abruptly in mid-thought. Kesey freely borrows the composite narrative consciousness and other narrative devices from *As I Lay Dying*. In a bit of literary ventriloquism derived from Addie Bundren's sections, Henry's father Jonas (the first Stamper to migrate westward) makes lamentations from beyond the grave. In flashbacks, the narrator describes how Henry married Myra after a whirlwind trip to New York, replacing his recently deceased first wife as unexpectedly as Anse does at the conclusion of *As I Lay Dying*. Much like Jewel and his half-brother Darl, Hank and Lee experience a fundamental estrangement that complicates their bond and trust in one another. As insular, inscrutable and often as obnoxious to outsiders as the Bundren family, the Stampers boast a comparable fraternal conflict, an acquisitive father, and not one, but two troubled dead mothers as haunting presences.

But perhaps the Stampers can best be understood as a more ethical, self-conscious Snopes clan, if such a thing can be imagined. Henry Stamper is as uncompromising (and unlikely) a patriarch as Ab Snopes, establishing his family's antagonistic role in Oregon. Henry models the same crude adaptability that aided the Snopeses' rise, using automation to topple trees and clear the land to the consternation of more traditional logging men. Though similar to Ab and Flem in their obstinacy and dogged survival instincts, father and son Henry and Hank Stamper uphold many of the values corrupted by the Snopeses, such as an ethic of industriousness and plain-spokenness. The Stampers' forefather Jonas arrives in the logging country as unexpectedly as Flem and his kinfolk arrive in Jefferson, initially devoting himself and his family to "pursuits like business and community and church" (18). After Jonas abandons the family, Henry and his brood dedicate themselves to hard work and apply both the letter and the spirit of the law in their dealings. They quickly become the talk of the town as they seize control of the means of production in the area in defiance of the local co-op. Kesey introduces us to Jefferson's sister city Wakonda, Oregon, through the character of union president Jonathan Draeger, in appropriately Faulkneresque cadences:

> Man will oppose everything but a Hand Extended [...] he will stand up in the face of every hazard except Lonely Time; that for the sake of his poorest and shakiest and screwiest principles he will lay down his life, endure pain, ridicule, and even, sometimes, that most demeaning of American hardships, discomfort, but will relinquish his *firmest stand* for Love. (10)

Over the course of the novel, Draeger becomes an exasperated but bemused observer of rampant Stamperism, just as Flem's exploits are filtered through Ratliff's gentler sensibility in *The Hamlet* (1940). Still, Kesey indulges in imbuing some of the Stampers with less exalted Snopesian characteristics. Henry's brother Ben meets his end as a hermit in a shack full of pornography, a debasement even Faulkner might have thought twice about including in the Snopes trilogy (118). Ben's son Joe Ben is described as a human oddity like many of the auxiliary Snopeses, "issued a skin many sizes too small and chest and shoulders too large" (291). Such grotesquery ties the less adaptable Stampers to the more shadowy denizens of Yoknapatawpha while establishing the hardier Henry and Hank as the baseline for machismo and heroism on the new frontier.

The underlying conservative politics of *Notion* soon became retrograde due in part to Kesey's callow depiction of his female characters and the natural environment. Reviews of the novel and its 1970 Paul Newman-directed film adaptation regularly make superficial nods to the women or no mention at all, a startling omission, for one reason, given the centrality of the Hank-Viv-Lee love triangle to the plot (see Prescott 29; Knickerbocker 216). These selective readings can be partly attributed to Kesey himself; while no character in the novel exerts the same unrelentingly destructive force as the infamous Nurse Ratched in *Cuckoo's Nest*, the far more compassionate women in *Notion* lack development. Like the wives in *Absalom, Absalom!*, *As I Lay Dying*, and *The Hamlet*, the women whom the

Stamper men marry are acquired more than courted and are kept as far away as possible from the family's moneymaking schemes. While Hank's and Joe Ben's wives personify the same constancy and endurance found in what Mimi Reisel Gladstein calls the "indestructible woman" in Faulkner and Hemingway, they rarely take on a protagonist's role, instead echoing more passive earth-mother clichés (10). Viv, the most sympathetic woman depicted, ultimately serves as a device for the conflict between Hank and Lee, not fully understanding her circumscribed role in the Stamper household until she develops feelings for Lee. Her decisive departure from her husband and Wakonda at the end of *Notion* is arguably intended to invoke the tragedy of the likely end of the Stamper family line more than the triumph of her own personal liberation. In his strivings to portray an independent woman subordinate in a family of rapacious men, Kesey seems to have arrived at the same dead end Faulkner reached in *The Mansion* (1959) with Linda Snopes Kohl, essentially removing her from the scene once her relationships with the male characters have run their course.

Similarly, Kesey's writing recalls some of Hemingway's less nuanced characterizations of women. The broadly drawn prostitute character Indian Jenny stands as a particularly egregious example. A figure held in contempt by the Stampers and the union-affiliated loggers alike, Jenny's pidgin English, belief in black magic, and proclivities for alcohol and snuff mark her as the Other in a predominantly white community while simultaneously underscoring the pernicious stereotype of promiscuity and submissiveness Hemingway used as a key plot point in the short story "Ten Indians" (1927). Kesey's depiction of Joe Ben's wife Jan is less vicious, though also intended for comic effect. Her belief in faith healing and divine intervention run counter to the Stampers' self-reliance. She is seen mainly working in the extended family's household, chasing after her five children and thus serving as a foil to the more thoughtful, childless Viv. Viv, meanwhile, exemplifies a paradox also found in Hemingway's women: strong enough to support Hank in his endeavors, able to attract Lee intellectually as well as physically, and able to disappoint and/or betray both, yet not complex enough to truly influence the course of the story. Her sympathetic qualities connect her to Marie Morgan, the long-suffering helpmate of Harry in *To Have and Have Not*. Like Marie, though, her husband's failure to subvert a dominant system compounds her own alienation and ultimate lack of agency. Though ostensibly one of Hemingway's "indestructible" women, she is by nature of her sex excluded from the code that elevates men's heroic actions.

Kesey's treatment of nature also relies on the assumption that the Stamper men possess an inborn right to be indomitable. *Notion*'s syncretism of Faulkner and Hemingway is perhaps most pronounced in a scene where Henry leads his sons, Joe Ben, and Viv on an impromptu fox hunt. In contradistinction to the patriarchal Sam Fathers, Henry does not stand for conservation or old verities; when one of the family's hunting dogs confronts a bear, the elder Stamper neither venerates the bear as an untouchable foe (as the all-male hunting party does with Old Ben in "The Bear") nor initiates an obsessive pursuit, instead remarking on the dog's determination to "never give an inch." The woods serve a comparable role in the Stampers' self-aggrandizement. As Christopher Rieger shows, trees serve as a leitmotif in *Go Down, Moses* (1942), symbolizing concurrent changes in Yoknapatawpha's landscape, the human geography, and interpersonal relations (137). On the annual hunts, Ike McCaslin learns humility and respect in the "timeless woods" (Faulkner 192). But whereas Major de Spain's selling of the land to a lumber company signifies the end of the Big Woods, Henry and his family seem satisfied in having it both ways in relation to their own environment. Like logging, hunting provides Lee a belated initiation into the family's manly rituals and Hank with solace from past trauma. (As with Nick Adams in Hemingway's "Big Two-Hearted River: Part II" (1925), the narrative only alludes to Hank's past war experiences.) Yet none of the Stampers see a contradiction between escaping into nature for pleasure and clear-cutting the woods of old-growth trees for business. They consider no repercussions from the devastating boom-bust cycle inherent in the industry, illustrated elsewhere by the intrusion of the logging camp by Faulkner in "The Bear" and Hemingway in "The Last Good Country" (1972) at the high point of the cycle and the abandoned lumber mill that looms over Nick Adams in the story "The End of Something" (1925) after the forest is decimated. In contrast to Hemingway's message, as summarized by Wright Morris, that "Nature is good, man is a mess, but Nature will prevail," Kesey clings to a more anthropocentric (not to mention Faulkneresque) belief that man must prevail at all costs (Donaldson 74). In situations where the Hemingway hero typically faces atavistic nature alone, the Stampers collectively push the boundaries of the wilderness to gain advantage over their more civilized counterparts.

Hemingway foreshadowed Kesey's treatment of the machismo inherent in logging in the short story "The Doctor and the Doctor's Wife" (1925), as three Indian loggers intimidate Nick Adams's father to the point where the Doctor must retreat into the woods with a shotgun and hunt squirrels to recapture his manhood. Kesey picks up this thread in depicting the rugged individualists Henry and Hank Stamper as antagonists to disheartened, conformist loggers beholden to their bosses. Refusing to observe the strike by the union and keeping their contract with a lumber combine, the Stampers base their opposition less on ideological grounds than a stubborn self-reliance and a deep cynicism toward authority and groupthink.[4]

This fight for independence and self-determination also fuels the main conflicts for Hemingway's protagonists. Hank matches the criteria for a Hemingway hero by taking over the logging business and defending the family name with his fists on the one hand and seducing his father's second wife (Lee's mother) and lording a patriarchal authority over Lee on the other. In representing Hank's initial control of all that he surveys, Kesey adopts Hemingway's direct, unadorned style as the antithesis to his typical Faulkner-inflected prose, as in a description of Hank milking a cow: "He moved his ear to the animal's sleek bulk and could hear her guts working. He liked the sound. He liked the cow. He liked feeling her warmth and squeezing the rhythm of milk in the pail" (83). In contrast to Lee's recursive, stream-of-consciousness interior monologues, Kesey renders Hank's thoughts in lean, linear fashion, such as when he ponders the possibility of reuniting with his half-brother after their long separation: "You know? It's hard to talk to somebody you ain't seen in a long time and it's hard not to. And it's especially hard when you got a lot to say and no notion how to say it" (173). Throughout the novel, Kesey employs his sparest prose when representing

Hank's thoughts and actions.

Like Harry Morgan aboard his smuggler's boat in *To Have and Have Not*, Hank's command over his world is broken only by acts of outrageous fortune, including Lee's revenge-minded seduction of Viv and her subsequent departure. In a freakish chain of events, a tree that Hank is cutting on a job splits lengthwise, causing Hank to drop his buzz saw, which severs his father's arm. From there, the giant log rolls downhill, trapping Joe Ben beneath it, leading him to drown in the river's tide. The father's demise, especially, seals a connection with the downfall of the hero in many of Hemingway's late works: the wound and amputation of Henry Stamper's arm recalls the loss of Harry Morgan's own appendage. Old Henry lays dying at the end, like Robert Jordan after the destruction of the bridge in *For Whom the Bell Tolls* (1940), his achievement as lost to the world as Santiago's catch of the marlin in *The Old Man and the Sea* (1952). Like these characters' pursuit of masculine ideals, only literal mayhem can halt the Stampers' single-minded mission. Motivated in equal measure by family obsessions and an all-consuming passion/death drive, Hank's quest reaches a point where personal pride and integrity meet hubris, resulting in tragedy.

In the wake of these losses, Hank, who has up till now exemplified masculinity and absolutism, comes to a horrifying epiphany: "There ain't any true strength; there's just different degrees of weakness" (524). Unbeknownst to him, this realization comes at the same moment Lee and Viv betray him. Consumed with guilt for being the proximate and more general cause for his family's destruction and for not fulfilling the logging contract on his own, Hank's despair echoes Harry Morgan's final lamentation: "No matter how a man alone ain't got no bloody fucking chance" (Hemingway 225). For a moment, Hank's heroic mastery of his surroundings slips, as it does for Morgan, Jordan, and Santiago in their final hours. As compensation for this lack, in a crowning act of insolence, Hank hangs his late father's severed arm from a pole on the family's grounds, the hand closed in a fist save for a middle finger directed at the town that believes they have finally seen the end of the Stampers and their brand of rugged individualism.

Reduced to an uneasy two-man operation doing the labor of a full work crew, the book's conclusion shows Hank and Lee bound in mutual strife, ironically drawn toward cooperation by their seemingly inborn impetus to "never give an inch" in the face of likely failure. In this way, the pair cross over from obsessive self-interest to a more courageous (though likely doomed) mindset, akin to the Hemingway hero's exemplification of "grace under pressure." The stewardship of the family business and its underlying credo seem to be all that can reconcile the obstinate half-brothers' ideals. Ultimately, Kesey finds some resolution in his sprawling epic by taking the advice of the mentor he shared with his forerunners, Malcolm Cowley, and subjectively portraying his characters' defiant defense of their "little postage stamp of native soil" in the remote Pacific Northwest.

Though lacking a conventional ending, *Sometimes a Great Notion* closes as bleakly as *Absalom! Absalom!* or *To Have and Have Not,* with an individualist's Utopian grand design—his "Great Notion"—devolving into futility. The image of Henry Stamper's severed arm, with its middle finger extended to all who pass by it, underscores the irreverent, anti-authoritarian black humor Kesey and many of his peers employed in combination with the technical breakthroughs of the modernists. But this was a difficult balance to maintain. As literary historian Gordon Hutner summarizes, after World War II "no new Hemingway or Faulkner surfaced; in fact, not even the real Hemingway or Faulkner could serve as a luminous example for the next generation of novelists. By the late '50s, both were exhausted, and by the early '60s, both were dead" (271). Kesey too was exhausted. Having published only two novels, he retreated into other pursuits by the mid-1960s, such as nonfiction writing and filmmaking, and did not publish another novel under his own name until 1992.[5]

By that time, Kesey expressed disillusionment both with the detachment of writing and the draw of celebrity culture. Rapidly evolving mass media simply demanded more of post-World War II authors like Kesey than their Lost Generation counterparts. As Kesey biographer Mark Christensen surmises, "what America want[ed] was not a new writer but a protagonist," incorporating a crafted persona into his or her written art as an example to a young readership looking to current fiction for models for rebellion (103). Ambivalent about his fame, Kesey came to lament the divide between popular writer and private author, telling an interviewer, "If you really are interested in being a real straight old-fashion writer, it's better to live down in Mississippi like Faulkner and work out in the woodshed and not be seen but once every ten years. I think that being the observed always turns your eye back on yourself and you become kind of blinded by your own radiance" (Gross 111).

In light of this blinding radiance, *Sometimes a Great Notion* can be read today as an audacious errand into the wilderness to repopulate the ground cleared by American literary modernism's two titan novelists. To establish his reputation among a new generation, Kesey plotted his expansive family saga in the same spirit that Faulkner applied avant-garde techniques to "tell about the South" beginning in the 1920s and the same self-assurance that the young Hemingway displayed in "getting in the ring" with past masters of storytelling. In its synthesis of Faulkner and Hemingway, it is an anachronistic book written as the larger cultural generation gap was widening, and younger readers demanded their own representative voices, including those advocating for women's equality and environmental protection. As Lost Generation heroes became replaced by anti-heroes and postmodern irony and parody became the dominant discourse, Kesey attempted one last, grand retelling of past tales. Though his "big book" may ultimately have been "damned" by this ambition or the shifting tastes of critics and readers, it nonetheless reinforces the immense pull Faulkner and Hemingway still exerted among many of the best and brightest in the literary firmament of the 1960s.

Notes

1. For more on Hemingway's late-in-life fame as a pulp hero, see Earle.

2. Reflecting *Sometimes a Great Notion*'s mixed critical reception, a second, much more positive review appeared in the *New York Times* the following week (Knickerbocker 216). When issued in paperback in 1966, the novel was listed as a "best book" by the *Times* ("Some" BR 26).

3. Though "never give an inch" tersely encapsulates the pugnaciousness of any number of Hemingway's heroes, the exact phrase appears nowhere in the author's major works.

4. Years later, Kesey partly recanted his championing of strikebreaking in the novel on ecological grounds. See *Kesey's Garage Sale*, 218.

5. In the interim, Kesey published sections of a novel in progress in his occasional magazine *Spit in the Ocean*, two children's books, and *Caverns* (1989), a work written in collaboration with his University of Oregon creative-writing students under the pen name O.U. Levon ("Novel U.O." spelled backwards).

Works Cited

Bak, Hans, editor. *The Long Voyage: Selected Letters of Malcolm Cowley, 1915-1987*. Harvard UP, 2014.

Bruccoli, Matthew J., editor. *The Only Thing That Counts: The Ernest Hemingway-Maxwell Perkins Correspondence, 1925-1947*. Scribner's, 1996.

Christensen, Mark. *Acid Christ: Ken Kesey, LSD, and the Politics of Ecstasy*. Schaffner P, 2010.

Cowley, Malcolm. *The Flower and Leaf*. Viking, 1985.

Dodgson, Rick. *It's All a Kind of Magic: The Young Ken Kesey*. U of Wisconsin P, 2013.

Donaldson, Scott. *By Force of Will: The Life and Art of Ernest Hemingway*. Viking, 1977.

Earle, David M. *All Man!: Hemingway, 1950s Men's Magazines, and the Masculine Persona*. Kent State UP, 2009.

Faulkner, William. *Absalom, Absalom!* 1936. Vintage, 1987.

—. *As I Lay Dying*. 1930. Vintage, 1990.

—. *Go Down, Moses*. 1940. Vintage, 1990.

—. *The Hamlet*. 1940. Vintage, 1990.

—. *The Sound and the Fury*. 1929. Vintage, 1987.

Gladstein, Mimi Reisel. *The Indestructible Woman in Faulkner, Hemingway, and Steinbeck*. UMI Research P, 1986.

Gross, Terry. "The Fresh Air Interview." *Conversations with Ken Kesey*, edited by Scott F. Parker, UP of Mississippi, 2014, pp. 110-15.

Hamblin, Robert W. *Myself and the World: A Biography of William Faulkner*. UP of Mississippi, 2016.

Hemingway, Ernest. *The Complete Short Stories of Ernest Hemingway: The Finca Vigía Edition.* Scribner's, 1987.

—. *To Have and Have Not.* Scribner's, 1937.

Hutner, Gordon. *What America Read: Taste, Class, and the Novel, 1920-1960.* U of North Carolina P, 2009.

Kesey, Ken. *Sometimes a Great Notion.* Viking, 1964.

—. "Tools from My Chest." *Kesey's Garage Sale,* Viking, 1973, pp. 171-98.

Knickerbocker, Conrad. "Any Dream May Come True." *New York Times,* 2 Aug 1964, p. 216.

Lish, Gordon. "What the Hell You Looking in Here for, Daisy Mae?" *Conversations with Ken Kesey,* edited by Scott F. Parker, UP of Mississippi, 2014, pp. 15-28.

Nichols, Lewis. "In and Out of Books." *New York Times,* 24 May 1964, p. BR8.

Parini, Jay. *One Matchless Time: A Life of William Faulkner.* Harper Collins, 2004.

Parker, Scott F., editor. *Conversations with Ken Kesey.* UP of Mississippi, 2014.

Prescott, Orville. "Books of the Times." *New York Times,* 27 Jul 1964, p. 29.

Raeburn, John. *Fame Became of Him: Hemingway as Public Writer.* Indiana UP, 1984.

Rieger, Christopher. *Clear-Cutting Eden: Ecology and the Pastoral in Southern Literature.* U of Alabama P, 2009.

Ross, Lillian. "How Do You Like It Now, Gentlemen?" *Hemingway: A Collection of Critical Essays,* edited by Robert P. Weeks, Prentice Hall, 1962, pp. 17-39.

"Some of the Year's Best." *New York Times,* 27 Feb 1966, p. BR26.

Tanner, Stephen L. *Ken Kesey.* Twayne, 1983.

Viking Press. "Advertisement." *New York Times,* 4 Aug. 1964, p. 27.

Han Qiqun

Faulkner's Mink Snopes, Material Places, and "The Material Turn"

Harper's Magzine published William Faulkner's short story "The Hound" in August 1931, a story about Ernest Cotton, a poor white who, because of a lost pig, clashes with its owner, Jack Houston. Cotton later kills Houston as a result of not receiving compensation for keeping the pig for a whole winter. The story was later adapted into the novel *The Hamlet* (1940), with the character Ernest Cotton changed into Mink Snopes and the lost pig changed to a cow. The Snopes Trilogy, contrasted with the depiction of the conflict between Cotton and Houston in "The Hound," portrays how Mink and Houston were at odds with one another economically, leaving the image of Mink far more intricate than that of Ernest Cotton.

Mink, as simple as the intellectually disabled Eck on one side, and as stubborn as Ab Snopes on the other, aroused a deep concern among critics not long after the publication of *The Hamlet*. Cleanth Brooks made an initial analysis of Mink, claiming that Faulkner did not portray Mink as a positive character in the Snopes Trilogy. He argued that Mink "is indifferent and mean in response to any human demands or claims"; therefore, he is "selfish and self-centered," possessing only two things of value: "his identity and the savage pride with which he defends that identity" (230). Brooks's point of view is not echoed by most later critics. Crystal Greenawalt concludes that Mink "has shown honor within himself, maintained clan loyalty, and even more directly than Linda, has rid the world of an evil man" (72). This tolerant understanding of Mink's behavior is continued by T. Allan Hillman who, in his recent research, further points out that "no matter how mean or unjust his past actions, there is something comfortable—something morally comfortable-—about Mink. He has a genuine commitment to certain principles, and he acts according to them as a matter of honor" (273). In both *The Hamlet* and *The Mansion* (1959), published nineteen years later than the former, the economic disputes between Mink and Houston are repeatedly focused on the cow, but the latter novel details more fully how the conflict between Mink and Houston developed. During this process, Mink is affected psychologically when he sees the luxurious items of great variety during his visits to Houston's house. Barbara Booth Serruya and Nancy Eileen Gregory compare the representation of Mink in the Snopes Trilogy with that in previous short stories, but give less attention to the various changes in Mink's character in *The Hamlet* and *The Mansion*.[1] These are significant to the dynamic change of Mink's identity in the trilogy. Although some critics have noticed Mink's "curiosity and uneasiness upon entering into the new world" on his way home from the prison, there is no further research investigating how Mink's identity is shaped by modern industrial objects he sees on his return home (Gregory 132). In other words, Faulkner's various writings of things, especially those closely related with Mink, deserve further exploration since these ignored details can not only help to unveil the changes in Mink's identity before and after his incarceration for thirty-eight years, but can also describe the relationship of his imprisonment to those changes.

Over the past decade, Faulkner's writing of things has captured the imagination of Faulkner scholars, which corresponds with a cultural climate emerging from "the material turn" in contemporary intellectual thought.[2] "The material turn" in literary criticism, being nourished theoretically in material cultural studies, as well as thing theories, has been investigating "how the material world impinges upon literature, and how writers, in turn, use that world as a way of negotiating change" with an interdisciplinary approach (Green 1). One of the major concerns of "the material turn" in literary criticism, proposed by Bill Brown in his far-reaching essay "Thing Theory" is "how inanimate objects constitute human subjects, how they move them, how they threaten them, how they facilitate or threaten their relation to other subjects" (7). In addition to the influence of this new way of thinking about subject-object relations, "the material turn" also explores "the literary life of things,"[3] as often inspired by thing theorists, like Jane Bennett's "vital materiality" and Sherry Turkle's "evocative objects," who regard agency as simply the ever-present force of all things; there is not just a human subject creating agency but a distributive agency consisting of a "swarm of vitalities at play" (Bennett 32). The perception that "things have vibrant lives at different scales" leads to later thing theorists' insights on how "the social world of humans and the material world of things are entangled together by dependences and dependencies that create potentials, further investments and entrapments" (Hodder 89). As a new critical paradigm, "the material turn" in literary criticism not only encourages readers to pay special attention to those objects "mentioned repeatedly" and "often at crucial narrative moments" in a certain literary text (Freedgood 2), but encourages exploration of the materiality of the literary objects since "sometimes they [speak] through their form and shape, their decoration and the materials from which they were formed" (Richardson 4). Even trash and decayed objects are considered as the "heuristic site for thinking about the aesthetics of detritus," as Patricia Yaeger points out in her study of Faulkner's trash aesthetics (53). Over the past decade, "the material turn" has emerged as a new critical discourse, and it informs my understanding of the writing of things as related to Mink Snopes.

Faulkner, in the Snopes Trilogy, documents Mink's dynamic developments as a poor Southerner, a prisoner, an ex-convict, and finally a murderer, and uses things, especially things related with material places and home spaces, as an important means of characterization. While the poetics of space, mainly promoted by Gaston Bachelard and Walter Benjamin, have already provided insightful accounts of the emotional affiliations with the architectures of home, "the material turn" in literary criticism extends the study of material places and home spaces, especially the role of material places in the formation of social identity and gender subjectivity of literary characters. Attending to the different material places with which Mink is connected, this paper focuses on how Mink's identity is dynamically shaped by the places he inhabits during his life and how he deteriorates into a quasi-thing like status. While Faulkner's literary rival Ernest Hemingway proposed "the Iceberg Principle" which is extolled by many followers, and Willa Cather complained about the "overfurnished house" and the "decorating impulse" of some realistic writers in her famous "The Novel Démeublé," Faulkner creates his own style which is characterized by Balzac's abundant descriptions of things. Accordingly, reading the Snopes trilogy in terms of thing theory offers a new perspective on Faulkner's aesthetics.

I. House, Possession, and "Materialisation of Distinction"

Mink, a representative of poor whites in Faulkner's Yoknapatawpha novels, is usually associated with Ab Snopes in "Barn Burning" (1939) who tracks manure on Major de Spain's newly-bought rug and burns down his barn for the purpose of protecting his own dignity and rights. Mink, for the same reason, shoots Houston dead without touching a penny in Houston's wallet afterward. Mink's unwillingness to be controlled by money wins him sympathy from critic Debra MacComb who sees him as countering "the very real violence of capital" (357). She emphasizes several points of Mink's resistance to money in the Snopes Trilogy, regarding Mink as a force countering Flem who makes money his top priority in life.

Nevertheless, Mink's complex attitude toward material wealth is revealed through his observations of Houston's house. If the characterizations of Mink in *The Mansion* and *The Hamlet* are compared, the former does not provide more details about Mink's killing of Houston than the latter, nor does it say much about Mink's escape after the murder. Instead, it focuses on Mink's interactions with Houston, how Mink was driven by rage, and why he shot Houston dead. It is important to note that Mink's dignity was insulted by Houston's spacious house as well as his excessive, luxurious domestic items when he attempts to find the cow—"his only property"—on Houston's place. Mink's first impression is of Houston's big house "with two nigger servants, the man and the woman to cook, and the stallion and the big Bluetick hound that was as high-nosed and intolerant and surly as Houston himself" (*Mansion* 10-11). In juxtaposition to Houston's nice accommodation, Mink finds himself "with nothing but an empty and foodless house which did not actually belong to him" (*Hamlet* 247), and he had "paid rent but not taxes, paying almost as much in rent in one year as the house had cost to build" (*Hamlet* 243).

The contrast between Houston's comfortable home and Mink's depressing sharecropper's cabin is further strengthened by recurrent rotten images of Mink's place. Apart from "the rotting lattice which enclosed the well," "the rotted bench," and "the gaping and broken entrance," even Mink's "paintless two-room cabin" is rather dilapidated, "the roof of which already leaked and the weather-stripping had already begun to rot away from the wall planks" (*Hamlet* 243). When approaching Houston's spacious house, Mink spots Houston, in his warm and bright kitchen, holding "in his hand a toddy" or a glass of "good red chartered whiskey ordered out of Memphis," while Mink drinks "the stinking gagging homemade corn" (*Mansion* 22), and his kids can only play with makeshift toys and checkers salvaged "from a broken plate and a blue glass bottle" (*Hamlet* 272). Faulkner's accounts of each character's home illustrate that possessed objects are more like a sphere for establishing social difference and position than a practice of sustenance, as elucidated in the "materialisation of distinction," which is "the coding of cultural and status difference in objects themselves" (Woodward 113). Different social strata, indicated by the distinction of objects, heighten the conflict and change Mink's psychology.

In *The Mansion*, Faulkner employs a third person limited point of view to depict with subtlety and vividness how Mink encounters Houston's luxurious house, highlighting Mink's gaze on Houston's domestic possessions. When gazing upon Houston's roomy and bright house with two servants as well as the food and drink Houston enjoys everyday, Mink projects onto these objects his "own feelings, beliefs, or parts of self," a process which Nancy Chodorow concludes is "a dialectic of transference of energies at play in people–object relations" (quoted in Woodward 140). While possessions can "offer deeper psychological gratification around the psychic satisfaction of learning about self, and others," Mink feels his "extended self" is far more satisfying (Woodward 139). Mink feels that his simple place is not only far shabbier than Houston's spacious one, but even the house for the black workers is much better than his. This results in his hatred and jealousy toward Houston, which is then further exacerbated by the arrogance of the latter. Actually, even in the last moment when Mink murders Houston, objects as the "extended self" serve as an important reason for Houston's death since the dying Houston accuses Mink not of being a murderer, but of being poor: "God damn it, couldn't you even borrow two shells, you fumbling ragged—" (*Hamlet* 241).

II. Parchman Prison as a Site of "Discipline and Punish"

One prominent characteristic Mink manifests in the Snopes Trilogy is his concentration and commitment to realizing a single goal. One frequently mentioned detail is that he intends to murder Flem directly after being released from prison without the least intention of visiting his wife and daughter whom he has not seen for thirty-eight years. Faulkner's descriptions of Mink's firm belief in "Old Moster," as well as his fairness in *The Mansion*, provide critics textual proof that Mink, "a religious man" in some deep sense, was "one of Faulkner's many Calvinists who do not believe in a god of love or mercy, but do believe there is a final justice" (Brooks 232). These points can serve as strong evidence of Mink's demonstration of remarkable patience and singleness of purpose but cannot fully convince readers of Mink's quasi-thing-like existence in prison and trash-like existence after he is released. Parchman Prison, a long-neglected space in which Mink spends thirty-eight years, plays a vital role in shaping his identity, especially when viewed through the lens of thing theory.

Faulkner describes the prison's structure and the objects inside as well. Initially, Mink was imprisoned in the jail in Jefferson for eight months, then transferred to Parchman Prison in the Mississippi Delta region. Parchman, with "the tall wire stockade with its single gate guarded day and night by men with shotguns, and inside it the low grim brick buildings with their barred windows," leaves Mink under the gaze and control of guards at all times (*Mansion* 48). His actions are always monitored, and much of his information is kept in detailed records. Mink, "living in a detached wire-canvas-and-plank hut," is left alone and isolated from the outer world. He and other prisoners have to work and eat and sleep as "a gang, a unit"; furthermore, shackled to the same chain, "they went to the mess hall to eat, then to the field to work and, chained again, back to the hut to sleep again" (94). The controlled regimen and routine life inside the prison exert their discipline upon Mink's identity.

In addition to Parchman and Mink's hut, even the objects associated with the prison, such as the prison uniform, serve as important material tools in the establishment of cultural and political power rather than mere settings or environmental filler. Once in the jail, his "patched faded blue overalls and shirt" are exchanged for the "overalls and jumper of coarse white barred laterally with black," which marks the beginning of his new life of discipline and punishment (49). Since "dress makes the body," as proposed by thing theorists like Simon Gatrell (5), Mink's prison uniform, plus the white and black color, corresponds with the routine life and controlled power of the prison itself and gradually leads to Mink's machine-like automation.

Although Parchman may not be modeled on the "panopticon," the central motif in Michel Foucault's *Discipline and Punish* (1975), the power there clearly operates in accordance with hierarchy. Being under surveillance all the time and confined to an enclosed and segmented space, Mink is treated like an object, and he gradually becomes object-like too. In his first three years in jail, he is eager to get out, and "his only reason for wanting to get out was to go back home and farm" (48-49). But three years later, he has given up every effort to escape, living like a machine: "it was automatic now after three years; he had only to open his mouth and breathe" (50-51). Time does not work on him since he, object-like, does not even "count off the years" and simply exists in the present moment (49). Every night in the prison's wooden bunk, he "was now having to change overnight and forever for twenty or twenty-five years his whole nature and character and being" (49). The enclosed spaces of the prison and the hut/cell "changed the way a man looked at what he saw after he got in Parchman" (92). There, Mink's plan to seek revenge on Flem is consolidated, and Mink is reestablished and objectified. Parchman Prison, as a very important site of juridicial and political power, fails to compel Mink to repent for his wrongdoings despite the discipline and regulation, but instead drives him to be inanimate, which explains why he is highly persistent in realizing his single goal, as well as his inhumane behavior in not seeking his family after being released.

III. A Modern Space Without "Evocative Objects"

In the Snopes Trilogy, Faulkner, several times, makes the comparison between Mink and children, especially after Mink completes his revenge and hides in an old cellar. Debra MacComb notes Faulkner's association of Mink with the obvious characteristics of children, including his small body and simple mind, and argues that Mink is an opposing force against the money-corrupted society (355). This point stands to reason since innocent images of children are often employed by writers as vehicles either for idyllic principles or for contrasting the defects of modern civilization. Mink's child-like characteristics can also be further verified by what Mink sees and hears after his release on his way back to Jefferson, which serves as an indication of how Mink experienced another tremendous change of his identity after his release from prison.

Similar to Rip Van Winkle who slept for twenty years, Mink, when heading for Jefferson, finds that the outside world has undergone enormous change. The hickory was gone and "chopped into firewood or wagon spokes or single trees years ago" and "perhaps the very place where it had stood was eradicated now into plowed land" (*Mansion* 105-6). Apart from the geographical change, familiar objects from Mink's memory no longer exist. The familiar landscape and objects, viewed by thing theorists as "evocative objects," are very important for Mink to sustain his spatial identity since they "promote inner experience" and "are potential forms of transformation" (Bollas 4). Sherry Turkle further points out the importance of "evocative objects," which are not only "a testament to the ways in which particular artifacts can become imbued with specific meanings, associations and memories," but also to the ways in which objects can function as "companions in life experience" (5). Unfortunately, evocative objects for Mink have either disappeared or been replaced, resulting in a loss of Mink's spatial identification with his own past. The South in which he once lived is not "a place a man wants to go back to; the place dont even need to be there no more. What aches a man to go back to is what he remembers" (*Mansion* 105-6). Put differently, Mink has been uprooted from the familiar space of prison and has lost his identity in the face of a modern space that is unfamiliar.

Mink's crisis of spatial identification with his own past is further highlighted by his uncomfortable encounter with the modern space represented by a number of modern objects. Not only have the the prices of familiar foods increased exorbitantly, but some food, such as sardines and cola, are totally new to Mink, among which lunch meat is a typical example:

> "What is it?" he said.
> "Lunch meat," the proprietor said.
> "What is lunch meat?" he said.
> "Dont ask," the proprietor said. "Just eat it. What
> else can you buy with eleven cents?" (260)

The lunch meat episode, as well as Faulkner's description of the emergence of new products in the modern South, although regarded by some critics as Faulkner's portrayal of Mink's curiosity, also highlights Mink's fear of entering this new world and further proves Mink's loss of the spatial identity with "evocative objects," as the latter are essential to the materiality of the home space.

The biggest visual and psychological shocks Mink experiences are his confrontations with city landscapes, the most representative part of the modern space, especially when he passes by metropolitan Memphis at night:

> At night, the dark earth on either hand and ahead
> already random and spangled with the neon he had
> never seen before, and in the distance the low por-
> tentous glare of the city itself, he sitting on the edge
> of the seat as a child sits, almost as small as a child,
> peering ahead as the car rushed, merging into one
> mutual spangled race bearing toward, as though by
> the acceleration of gravity or suction, the distant
> city. (283)

Here, neon lights and lights of cars, though making the city daylike, lead him to feel distant from the city. Everything Mink once was familiar with is not what it used to be. Mink is now totally out of tune with this era and unfit for the modern space; he is overwhelmed by modern things and is himself cast as "waste" by the modern industrial society. Mink's loss of his spatial identity is not only revealed by a space without evocative objects for him, but implied by his corresponding homelessness in the modern city.

After revealing Mink's alienation and homelessness in the modern space, Faulkner continues describing how modern objects, animated and evocative, threaten Mink:

> he became aware of a convergence like the spokes of a gigantic dark wheel lying on its hub, along which sped dense and undeviable as ants, automobiles and what they told him were called buses as if all the earth was hurrying, plunging, being sucked, decked with diamond and ruby lights, into the low glare on the sky as into some monstrous, frightening, unimaginable joy or pleasure. (283)

In this passage, the personified modern objects are endowed with human power and capacity. On the contrary, Mink, passive and weak, is represented like an object. Even the city itself "engulfed him; it stooped soaring down, bearing down upon him like breathing the vast concrete mass and weight until he himself was breathless, having to pant for air" (285). If it is true that objects around him render his identity as waste in a modernized world after his release, then it is safe to say that the animation of the city similarly threatens Mink's value of existence and reduces him to an object of waste. Mink's homelessness and waste-like identity culminates in the episode in which he is harassed by police when looking for a place to sleep in Memphis. Left in a modern space without "evocative objects," Mink is reduced to a tramp with nowhere to call his own.

IV. Cellar as an "Intimate Space"

Mink does not flee Yoknapatawpha immediately after seeking revenge on Flem. Instead he finds an old cellar in which to rest. First narrated from a third person point of view limited to Gavin and Ratliff and then by a third person omniscient point of view, Faulkner describes how the two visitors see Mink and his dying fantasies. Since the end of Mink's life is set in the cellar, a typical domestic interior exemplified by Gaston Bachelard in *The Poetics of Space*, the correlations between Mink's inner space and his environment, especially how the structure and shape of the cellar become "mirrors of the inner life and secret recesses of self," are primary concerns in this section (Tischleder 36).

Before the direct presentation of Mink and his cellar, Faulkner first focuses on a few trash-related objects, establishing an atmosphere full of decay and decline. When Gavin and Ratliff arrive at the road where Mink's cellar is located, they find "a canted roof line where one end of the gable had collapsed completely," a "worn gnarled cedar" above it, a "fallen yard fence," and a "crumbling slant" marking the entrance to the cellar (*Mansion* 432). The literary life of trash in this scene establishes the correspondences between the ruined landscape and Mink's waste-like situation, especially when he approaches the end of his life.

When Gavin and Ratliff, the last witnesses of Mink's life, find the entrance of the cellar, "a black and crumbled aperture yawned at their feet as if the ruined house itself had gaped at them" (432). "Crumbled" further emphasizes the decay of the place where Mink hides; the sentence structure with the inanimate word as the agent, followed by the personified verb, endows Mink's environment with an oppressive and obsessional sense. With Gavin and Ratliff descending to the cellar, Mink's striking hideout is presented at the end of an extremely long and sprawling sentence:

> into the old cellar—the cave, the den where on a crude platform he had heaped together, the man they sought half-squatted half-knelt blinking up at them like a child interrupted at its bedside prayers: not surprised in prayer: interrupted, kneeling in the new overalls which were stained and foul now, his hands lying half-curled on the front of his lap, blinking at the tiny light which Stevens held. (432)

In this nearly breathless description, the cellar is equated with "the cave" and "the den," both of which, deeper and more hidden, refer to the innermost life of Mink. In addition, both "the cave" and "the den" remind readers of the places in which animals usually live or hide. In this instance, Mink is degraded as an animal, and his human part is minimized or erased; his dwelling in the cellar can be associated with his animal-like response to being hunted for murder. Furthermore, Mink "half-squatted half-knelt" on a crude platform he "had heaped together," his dependence on which exemplifies Ian Hodder's illustration of "entanglement between humans and things" (10). Accordingly, Faulkner's description of Mink's statue-like presence and his blurred boundary with the crude platform seems once again to suggest Mink's trash-like identity.

However, though portrayed as modern waste derived from his maladjustment in a modernized world, Faulkner here seems to endow Mink with a newly refreshed identity by his repeated depiction of Mink's eyes. When descending to the cellar, Gavin and Ratliff find the man they sought "blinking up at them like a child interrupted at its bedside prayers" (*Mansion* 432). The image of Mink's blinking eyes is repeated in the sentence, while Faulkner makes a slight change the second time as the blinking is directed to "the tiny light which Stevens held" (432). In addition, Mink, again, is compared with a child in his last stage of life, tinted with the sense of holiness. In this sense, both "blinking at the tiny light" and the child image, contrasted to the dark cave, drive Mink to become "a vital remainder," which can also be understood as "a sign of everything that's wrong with the outposts of modernity" (Yaeger 51). Therefore, Mink's meaningful experiences in the cellar, especially his entanglement with this "intimate space," indicate his psychological identity and thus provide an indispensable area for exploring to what extent Mink represents Faulkner's disillusionment with modernity. Mink's adoption of the cellar as his temporary home again demonstrates his child-like response to an industrialized world with which he is not familar; that the thing-like Mink is animated in the last part may suggest Faulkner's gentle and implied dissatisfaction toward the modern world.

V. Conclusion

In the Snopes Trilogy, Faulkner embeds Mink in a manifold of systematically related material places and vividly displays the dynamic change of Mink to thing-like and waste-like status. When situating the study of Mink within the context of the transforming South, Faulkner represents and responds to the confrontation between traditional and modern civilizations, displaying an interactive relationship between the social changes and the Southern citizens' identities during the transitional period into the modern South. Mink, an epitome of the effects of modernization, serves as a symbol of primitive civilization as antagonistic to modern civilization and implies Faulkner's attitudes toward the change, especially the urbanization of the modern South. The dynamic portrayal of Mink, especially his objectified identity, formulates the pain coming from maladjustment to the modern industrial world.

Moreover, Faulkner's manipulation of detailed things, typically represented by home spaces and their contents in the Snopes Trilogy, contributes to the uniqueness of his narrative style, especially when situating him in a context in which simplicity is highlighted as the major trait of modern writers. His detailed and complex writing of things not only marks his unique style as different from his contemporaries but also won him the praise of the Nobel Prize Committee as "a painter of landscapes" and a writer with a "hunter's intimate knowledge of his own hunting-ground" (Hellström 442).

Notes

1. See respectively, Nancy Eileen Gregory's "A Study of the Early Versions of Faulkner's *The Town* and *The Mansion*," and Barbara Booth Serruya's "The Evolution of an Artist: a Genetic Study of William Faulkner's *The Hamlet*."

2. In *Material Powers: Cultural Studies, History and the Material Turn*, Tony Bennett and Patrick Joyce point out that the crucial intellectual move in "the material turn" is one that "turns away from notions of a coherent social totality, and towards the erasure of familiar conceptual distinctions between the natural and the social, the human and the non-human, the material and the cultural, divisions that are all in the first place predicated on the immaterial/material divide" (4).

3. "The literary life of things" comes from the title of Babette Bärbel Tischleder's book, *The Literary Life of Things—Case Studies in American Fiction*, in which Tischleder claims that "the questions of how things are imagined to assume different forms of life in a literary context (and beyond) informs the methodology of this book" (19).

Works Cited

Bennett, Jane. *Vibrant Matter: a Political Ecology of Things*. Duke UP, 2010.

Bennett, Tony and Patrick Joyce, editors. *Material Powers: Cultural Studies, History and the Material Turn*. Routledge, 2010.

Bollas, Christopher. *Being A Character: Psychoanalysis and Self Experience*. Routledge, 2003.

Brooks, Cleanth. *The Yoknapatawpha County*. Yale UP, 1963.

Brown, Bill. *A Sense of Things: The Object Matter of American Literature*. U of Chicago P, 2003.

Faulkner, William. *The Hamlet*. Vintage International, 1991.

—. *The Mansion*. Vintage Books, 1965.

Freedgood, Elaine. *The Ideas in Things: Fugitive Meaning in the Victorian Novel*. U of Chicago P, 2006.

Gatrell, Simon. *Thomas Hardy Writing Dress*. Peter Lang, 2011.

Green, Anne. *Changing France: Literature and Material Culture in the Second Empire*. Anthem Press, 2011.

Greenawalt, Crystal. "The Human Spirit in Faulkner's Fiction." Dissertation. Florida State University, 2006.

Gregory, Nancy Eileen. "A Study of the Early Versions of Faulkner's *The Town* and *The Mansion*." Dissertation. University of South Carolina, 1975.

Hellström, Gustaf. "Presentation Speech." *Nobel Lectures, Literature 1901-1967*, edited by Horst Frenz, Elsevier, 1969, pp. 440-443.

Hillman, T. Allan. "Faulkner the Stoic: Honor, Evil, and the Snopeses in the Snopes Trilogy." *Philosophy and Literature*, vol. 39, no. 1A, Sep. 2015, pp. A260-A279.

Hodder, Ian. *Entangled: An Archaeology of the Relationships Between Humans and Things*. John Wiley & Sons, 2012.

Horton, Merrill. *Annotations to William Faulkner's* The Town. Garland, 1996.

MacComb, Debra. "Mink Snopes Deals in Post Holes: Countering the Violence of Capital in Faulkner's Snopes Trilogy." *The Mississippi Quarterly*, vol. 61, no. 3, June 2008, pp. 343-57.

Richardson, Catherine. *Shakespeare and Material Culture*. Oxford UP, 2012.

Tischleder, Babette Bärbel. *The Literary Life of Things—Case Studies in American Fiction*. Campus Verlag, 2014.

Turkle, Sherry. *Evocative Objects*. MIT Press, 2007.

Woodward, Ian. *Understanding Material Culture*. Sage, 2007.

Yaeger, Patricia. "Dematerializing Culture: Faulkner's Trash Aesthetic." *Faulkner and Material Culture*, edited by Joseph R. Urgo and Ann J. Abadie, UP of Mississippi, 2007, pp. 48-67.

Rachel Betts

"Like Nurse Shark": The Racial Economy in Hemingway's *To Have and Have Not*

Critics have never denied Ernest Hemingway's interest in race, but they have chosen to ignore it. In *Race and Identity in Hemingway's Fiction*, Amy L. Strong writes that "scholars have noted the presence of Native Americans, Africans, and African Americans in [Hemingway's] work, though few have viewed these characters as anything more than scenery; primarily as a backdrop to the more central issues of manhood, courage, and stoicism" (4). Carlos Baker, one of the most influential Hemingway biographers, echoes this sentiment in his work, stating that Hemingway was "constantly aware of [the Indians'] presence, like atavistic shadows moving along the edges of consciousness, coming and going without a sound" (13). Philip Young, considered by many to be the first serious Hemingway scholar, dismissed Hemingway's portrayal of Native Americans in "Indian Camp": "Here as elsewhere Nick is not recognized as protagonist unless one perceives that the last page of the five-page piece would be irrelevant if the story were about Indians" (4). His insistence that Native Americans were not the central focus of "Indian Camp" took hold: most early Hemingway scholars did not mention or allude to his depictions of race at all.

When they did, it was through the lens of primitivism. Joseph DeFalco identified these racial binaries in his book, *The Hero in Hemingway's Short Stories*, where he describes Native Americans as "primitive," "dark," "intrusive," and "irrational." Nick's father and the other white characters are conversely characterized by DeFalco as "civilized," "scientific," "secure," and "rational" (28-30). Although this work of criticism recognized the presence of Native American characters in Hemingway's writing and granted them significance within the stories as a whole, the Native American characters are still left in the shadows. Their significance is the light their darkness sheds on understanding the still more significant white characters.

By the 1970s, the critic Paul Smith declared that "there was nothing more to be said about Hemingway's fiction." His explanation of this grandiose claim was that "the patterns were clear; motifs, categorized" (1). At this point, Hemingway's nonwhite characters were rarely addressed in literary criticism, and, if they were, it was as savage, uncivilized, and primitive beings, fully grown humans with the mentality of children who existed complacently under the paternal care of the courageous and masculine white man. It was, in a way, Hemingway himself who jolted critics to attention. In the 1980s, the release of his private letters and unpublished manuscripts obliterated any claims that there was nothing left to be said about Ernest Hemingway's writing. In these manuscripts, women became men, black became white—the patterns previously identified in Hemingway's texts were not only deconstructed, but destroyed.

Accordingly, current Hemingway scholars have shifted their focus. Rather than ignoring issues of race in Hemingway's writing, scholars emphasize them. Marc Dudley refers to Hemingway's treatment of race as a "lifelong psychic possession" (1) and views his entire body of work as "a career-long experiment exploring a variety of identity issues, of which race is an integral part" (3). Amy L. Strong claims that "Hemingway paints the picture with a very broad brush, fusing together the history of Africans, Native Americans, and European Jews. He expresses a sense of shame about how whites have treated nonwhites throughout history, and seems angered by their continued power" (137). Hideo Yanagisawa calls critics out in his article, "Harry Morgan's Identity Crisis: Orientalism and Slumming during the Great Depression in Hemingway's *To Have and Have Not*," arguing that "little attention has been given to the representations of Asians in Hemingway's literary texts…even when other ethnic and racial elements are examined" (47). There is a push to bring Hemingway's nonwhite characters out of the shadows, a push to recognize them not as representations of scenery but as representations of people integral to his collective body of work and to American identity itself.

In the critical work *Playing in the Dark*, Toni Morrison questions what it means to be American, and she searches for answers through an extensive reconsideration of American literature. She claims that the images of blackness long thought to function as complementary to the images of whiteness can (and do) stand alone: "images of blackness can be evil *and* protective, rebellious *and* forgiving, fearful *and* desirable—all of the self-contradictory features of the self" (59). It is the white characters who are stagnant, unchanging, and frozen, immobile in the presence of their dynamic "Others." This analysis implicitly suggests that the reason early Hemingway scholars were so quick to identify binaries between black and white characters is because Hemingway's white characters are not depicted as fully formed individuals. The nonwhite characters—long regarded as nothing but scenery—provide another dimension to the white characters and also remind readers that white cannot exist without black.

Even though issues of identity, particularly race and gender, are now at the forefront of Hemingway studies, debate still exists regarding the treatment of these issues in literary criticism. Which of Hemingway's texts should critics analyze? Should his "lesser" texts be ignored? What passages within these texts are significant to developing an understanding of the text and of representations of race in Hemingway's fiction as a whole? How should they be interpreted? Because of the increasingly interdisciplinary nature of literary studies and the current racial climate, answering these questions and performing these types of analysis concurrently seem more relevant and sensitive than ever.

Furthermore, the newfound critical interest in issues of race, gender, and sexuality has figuratively resurrected one of Hemingway's "lesser" novels, *To Have and Have Not* (1937). This novel follows the adventures of Harry Morgan, a charter boat captain, struggling to survive during the Depression. Although acknowledged as one of Hemingway's "abject failures" (Curnutt xvii), the novel was developed into three films, piquing the interest of movie fanatics and Hemingway readers alike. Additionally, *To Have and Have Not* is the only Hemingway novel set on American soil, which is intriguing for critics invested in answering questions concerning Hemingway and American identity. The hardboiled nature of the novel is off-putting to some, however, and Harry Morgan's singular obsession with proving his masculinity becomes repetitive and one-dimensional. Couple that with the fragmented form Kirk Curnutt identifies as a "blatant hodgepodge of two previously published short-stories with a longer third section tacked to its end" (xviii), and it is no wonder Toni D. Knott writes in her book, *One Man Alone: Hemingway and* To Have and Have Not, that the novel is "the most neglected of the Hemingway texts" (Knott 228).

Despite being the most critically neglected of Hemingway's writings, recent critical interpretations of *To Have and Have Not* have begun to play a role in teasing out the convoluted issues of race, gender, and identity in Hemingway's oeuvre. In *Playing in the Dark*, Morrison offers the most notable and controversial interpretation of the novel when she dissects a curious piece of dialogue, using it as a springboard to ground her idea that black women function as "caretakers" and "predators" in American literature. The conversation in *To Have and Have Not* occurs as Harry is in the midst of a sexual tryst with his wife, Marie. Marie asks Harry:

> "Listen, did you ever do it with a nigger wench?"
> "Sure."
> "What's it like?"
> "Like nurse shark"
> "You're funny. Harry, I wish you didn't have to go." (113)

Morrison's work on this passage functions to demonstrate the self-contradiction she argues is inherent to the images of blackness found in American fiction. For Morrison, black figures in literature are like nurses: figures of kindness, healers, and helpers, and also, like sharks: devouring predators who pose immediate danger to those around them. In the space of a single image, the black female clearly becomes a contradictory self—"they are predators, sharks, unnatural women who combine the signs of a nurse with those of a shark" (84). The conjunction of nurse and shark in the dialogue provides Morrison with a clever and seemingly surefire way to close the argument she makes in *Playing in the Dark*.

However, Morrison's analysis of this passage has been

challenged by both Knott and Curnutt. Knott, though sympathetic to many of Morrison's claims, feels that the dialogue, to which Morrison attributes so much significance, cannot be used to support her argument. Morrison's analysis depends on splitting the term "nurse shark" into two signifiers rather than one: the nurse and the shark. Instead of dividing "nurse shark" into two distinct descriptors, Knott recognizes that "nurse shark" is a particular species of shark and uses her understanding of nurse shark behavior to complicate Morrison's argument. Because nurse sharks are "passionate love makers," Knott argues that Harry's comparison may in fact be complimentary. If meant in a complimentary fashion, the signifier, "nurse shark," would not function in a contradictory manner, but in a manner of affirmation. Knott continues her argument, pointing out that Harry refers to himself as a "loggerhead" and that Conchs (slang for the Florida locals descended from Bahamians) are described as "mollusks" in the text. According to Knott, the association of other nonhuman images to nonblack characters in the novel "dilutes" Morrison's overall argument (87).

Curnutt, who views the passage as "another lamentable lapse into racism," provides two possible interpretations. He begins by offering information regarding nurse shark (*Ginglymostoma cirratum*) biology: "nurse sharks are distinguished by their small mouths and deep throat cavities, which cause them to consume their prey like suckling infants" (104). From this, he interprets the passage to either mean that "black women are sexually omnivorous" or that "Hemingway intends a specific fellatio connotation." Whatever the intent, Curnutt deviates from both Morrison and Knott in his ultimate analysis that the meaning is "unclear and, in the end, irrelevant" (104).

Morrison, Knott, and Curnutt center their interpretations of this passage upon the idea of the "nurse shark" as a type of biological organism—for Morrison, the stereotypical shark, and for Knott and Curnutt, a more specific shark—the species *Ginglymostoma cirratum*, which occupies an ecological space separate from that of a human organism. These interpretations, like most interpretations of animal metaphors, emphasize the biological characteristics of nurse sharks. The problem is that when viewed under a biological framework, it seems that the nurse shark passage becomes, as Curnutt indicates, convoluted, unclear, and irrelevant.

But can the nurse shark dialogue be interpreted in any other way? Extant Hemingway scholarship has focused on teasing apart animal metaphors, the blurring lines between racial identities, and the emergence of a "racial hierarchy" stemming from a tourist economy, but no studies have specifically focused on the development of a "racial economy" or the racial commodification of people in Hemingway's writing. What happens when nurse sharks are regarded not as organisms, but as commodities? When nurse sharks are regarded as commodities, the misunderstandings and contradictions in the nurse shark dialogue disappear, and the meaning behind the dialogue becomes singular, illuminating the role the economy plays in Hemingway's racial characterizations as a whole.

Before examining the racial economy in *To Have and Have Not*, it is necessary to deviate slightly into the explanations behind the biological metaphors in the nurse shark comparison. The following descriptions of nurse shark copulation practices cannot be extended to stand as an analysis of the passages in *To Have and Have Not*. Rather, the descriptions are used to elucidate the misunderstandings both Morrison and Knott make and to suggest that an accurate understanding of the concepts they assign importance to would fail to support either of their arguments, rather complicating them or even insinuating an opposite claim.

Morrison bases much of her argument upon the idea of sharks as dangerous predators: the figure of the nurse shark "evokes a predatory, devouring eroticism and signals the antithesis to femininity, to nurturing, to nursing, to replenishment" (85). Central to Morrison's claim is the assumption that nurse sharks are dangerous and pose a potential threat to humans; however, nurse sharks prey upon small fish, shrimp, sea snails, crabs, lobster, sea urchins, and corals (Castro 15). Furthermore, none of these prey items are very difficult to catch, especially when compared to the larger prey items many species of shark are known to hunt. In fact, other shark species, including the tiger shark, hammerhead shark, lemon shark, and the bull shark, are predators of the nurse shark. Nurse sharks are slow moving and are not aggressive (Castro 16).

Harry's specification of the species of shark in his conversation with Marie certainly seems significant, but the significance is not because the nurse shark is an exemplary representative of the *Elasmobranchii*, a dangerous and ruthless predator, but rather because, in comparison, the nurse shark is much less threatening. Morrison's argument depends upon the referent of the nurse shark evoking an image of danger; however, this image is in contrast to actual nurse shark behavior relative to the behavior of other shark species. Using a reference that is curiously not cited, Knott introduces the idea that a comparison to a nurse shark could be complimentary because "the female nurse shark is a slow-moving, graceful fish and a choosy lover, often leaving its mate collapsed on the bottom of the sea after a spectacular ritualistic lovemaking session" (87). Carrier et al., in the most recent study regarding nurse shark copulation, write, "It is notable that no discernable, *ritualized* [italics added for emphasis] recognition or acceptance behavior was displayed by females observed in the present study" (651). Fertilization in sharks is internal and involves complex and necessary behaviors to bring a male and female into the correct alignment. The female shark is also relatively unable to choose mates—multiple males have been observed copulating with a single female. The males have been documented to work together to pin the female to the ocean floor, allowing for easier access to her cloaca (Carrier et al. 651). Courtship involves the male persistently following and biting the female until she swims upside down (Carrier et al. 649). To avoid unwanted copulation events, the female's only discernable defense is escape to shallow waters. Copulation among sharks is violent and not demonstrative of a graceful lovemaking session. Males compete for access to the female cloaca and will sink their teeth into the pectoral fin of the female to anchor her down (Dempster and Herold 1-7). The duration of a copulation event for males is limited by oxygen, which may explain why Knott describes the males as "collapsed on the bottom of the sea after" (87). However, the reason oxygen is limited for the male shark is because of the necessity of biting the pectoral fin so hard that the pharynx is effectively blocked (Carrier et al. 655).

Knott proceeds, stating that "the categories of fish parody all of humankind, including variations in color and temperament" (87).

This may be true in certain cases, but the temperament of humans, which can be extrapolated from the comparison to nurse sharks, is that of the basest interactions as far as copulation is concerned. Color variation is prevalent in nurse sharks as well; however, it does not support either Morrison's or Knott's claims: courting males are considerably darker than receptive females, which are a light brown (Carrier et al. 655). Applied to the passage in Hemingway's novel or to Morrison's model of the contradictory Africanist self in American literature, it would appear that lighter women are more attractive to males and that males function as dark savages, working together to pursue a common goal: the taking of light-skinned women through whatever means necessary. Using these tidbits of biology, Knott's initial suggestion is unsubstantiated: the comparison of a "nigger wench" to a nurse shark cannot work as a means of complimenting black women.

Because these biological considerations do not result in a satis-factory literary analysis, it is simple to claim that this passage is an example of crude and insignificant racism. But neither Hemingway nor Harry Morgan were scientists, so why should we expect them to write and think like biologists? Furthermore, is it worthwhile to attempt to reimagine the dialogue as if we were Hemingway or Harry Morgan?

Knott does agree with Morrison's statement regarding Heming-way as an author: "It would be irresponsible and unjustified to invest Hemingway with the thoughts of his characters. It is Harry who thinks a black woman is like a nurse shark, not Hemingway" (85-6). Maybe to attempt to understand Hemingway's writing, we must move away from a consideration of Hemingway, the author, and into a consideration of the character who is speaking. Who is Harry Morgan? What does Harry Morgan mean when he makes this comment? And how can we reconcile Hemingway's influences with Harry's character to develop an understanding of this dialogue, the novel, and Hemingway's larger body of work as a whole?

The fact that Harry Morgan is speaking, and that Hemingway and Harry are regarded as separate entities, limits the possibility for interpretation of these lines. What does Harry know? What could he know? Where is his frame of reference in relation to this comment? Returning once again to the biological descriptions of nurse sharks, it becomes clear that Harry did not have access to this knowledge. As of 1980, brief incomplete observations of copulation behavior in sharks had been reported for only nine of the 376 species (Carrier et al. 1994). At the time of *To Have and To Have Not*'s publication in 1937, only one brief study regarding nurse shark copulation had been published (Gudger 148-50). Obviously, Harry Morgan did not have access to this publication. What Harry knew about sharks, especially the nurse shark, would have been from first-hand experience.

Harry Morgan surely encountered nurse sharks enough times to know that nurse sharks are a distinct species of shark, at least. It must, for the sake of any of these arguments, be assumed that he knows enough about nurse sharks to have meaningfully selected their species for the comparison he makes in this dialogue. But Harry's knowledge is not abstract, like the analysis Morrison and Knott make. Nor is his knowledge biological, like that of a scientist. If nurse sharks are, for Harry, neither symbolic figures of abstract meaning nor biological entities with a specific set of adaptive characteristics and a natural history, what are they?

To answer this question, it is essential to examine Harry's profession. Harry works mainly as a fishing boat captain—chartering his boat out to tourists. He is described as doing "a little bit of everything" and also as a "fisherman" (137). From this description, it follows that Harry is a man for hire. Because he does "a little bit of everything," it seems that he (and his boat) can be hired to do many things, even illegal things, for the right price. As a fisherman, Harry must be knowledgeable about fish from a basic physical and behavioral standpoint—he must know how to identify and catch them—and also from an economic one—he must know how much each fish is worth. Early in the novel, Harry is teaching Mr. Johnson, a tourist who has chartered his boat for sport fishing, how to fish. A fish bites, and Harry identifies it immediately as "the biggest black marlin I ever saw in my life" (19). As Johnson continues fishing, Harry remains in awe of the marlin's size: "He was huge. I bet he'd go a thousand pounds" (20). Instead of saying, "weigh," Harry says, "go." He is thinking about how much the fish would be worth.

Harry's profession requires him to not only calculate the value of fish, but of every item he owns. After Johnson loses the fish and Harry's bait and tackle, Harry catalogues the price of all the gear that was lost: "the reel cost two hundred and fifty dollars. It costs more now. The rod cost me forty-five. There was a little under six hundred yards of thirty-six thread" (21). After all his calculations, Harry concludes that Johnson "owe[s] [him] two hundred and ninety-five dollars" (24). From this statement, it becomes clear that Harry instructed Mr. Johnson not to teach him a new skill, but, rather, to protect the goods that he determined had value. Therefore, Harry's profession is not simply as a man for hire or as a fisherman. His profession is to construct value judgments and, subsequently, put a price on everything. Marc Dudley writes, "Hemingway's narrative reduces people to an occupation" (32), but from this analysis, it is evident that Harry Morgan is not only reduced to an occupation, but also that his occupation has become reduced to a determinant of monetary value. As a man for hire, his occupation is to put a price on himself.

If Harry essentially views himself and the objects around him as items to be priced and given value, Harry would have understood nurse sharks not as metaphorical abstractions or biological organisms, but as economic entities. The numerous comparisons of humans to fish and other animals throughout *To Have and Have Not* reinforce the idea that the novel is structured upon Harry's categorization and assignment of economic value. Toni Knott observes the many comparisons of humans to other animals in the novel; however, she does not make this conclusion. In her assessment, Knott argues that the presence of many of these metaphors reduces the significance Morrison attributes to the nurse shark comparison. Knott cites, in particular, Harry's reference to himself as a "loggerhead" (87). But what Knott fails to notice, and what gives this metaphor significance, especially when placed alongside the nurse shark comparison, is that Harry does not compare himself to a loggerhead turtle; rather, he compares his arm stump to a loggerhead turtle's flipper:

> "Listen, do you mind the arm? Don't it make you
>   feel funny?"

"You're silly. I like it. Any that's you I like. Put it
across there. Put it along there. Go on. I like it, true."
"It's like a flipper on a loggerhead."
"You ain't no loggerhead. Do they really do it three
days? Coot for three days?" (113)

In this awkward, yet somewhat touching, banter, Harry uses his
knowledge of loggerhead turtles to make a judgment about his own
value. A flipper, though useful in marine environments, is anatomi-
cally worthless on land. Similarly, without an arm, Harry regards
himself as physically and emotionally maimed. He is not whole.
Harry's dialogue reveals that the arm stump feels foreign and useless
to him. He says, "do you mind the arm" instead of "do you mind my
arm," for example. He refuses to associate the arm stump with himself, believing that in doing so he will subsequently reduce his value.

Harry Morgan associates humans with animals in an attempt to
justify and bring meaning to his declarations of value. Ryan Hediger
writes in his essay, "Becoming with Animals: Sympoiesis and the
Ecology of Meaning in London and Hemingway," that Hemingway
and London "[rely] on animal otherness to think through dimensions
of human life that tend to remain unacknowledged and marginalized" (5). Harry's arm stump is certainly an unacknowledged and
marginalized form. Though physically visible and impossible to
ignore, Harry refuses to acknowledge that it represents an absence.
The absence of an arm disables Harry, turning him into an unwilling, but marginalized character. It follows that Harry uses animal
metaphors or referents to turn attention away from his marginalized
self and to highlight the marginalization and devaluation of other
characters.

Harry's treatment of Bee-Lips, his lawyer, echoes this sentiment.
After Harry's boat is repossessed by the Customs Officer, Harry
confronts Bee-Lips saying, "You're poison ... everything you touch
is poison." Bee-Lips responds evenly, "Is it my fault a truck could
see it? You picked the place. You hid your own boat." In response,
Harry tells Bee-Lips to "Shut up" (121). Harry is unable to take
responsibility for the repossession of his boat because if he does, he
will have to accept the fallibility of his carefully constructed identity.

Bee-Lips continues to attempt to reason with Harry, wanting him to recognize that he must hold himself responsible for the loss:

> "'I let you know as soon as it happened.'"
> "'You're like a buzzard.'"
> "'Cut it out,' Bee-Lips said." (121)

This short section of dialogue evokes a slew of well-known associations, none of them positive. By calling Bee-Lips a buzzard, Harry is stating that Bee-Lips is a villain, a thief, and a selfish scavenger, stealing objects of value for his own gain. In addition, his nickname, Bee-Lips, is also a comparison, indicating that Bee-Lips has lips large enough to look as though they have been stung by a bee. The implication behind this comparison is that Bee-Lips is biracial. Imagery of the bee, a black and yellow bi-colored organism, furthers the implication of miscegenation. Even the colors of the bee, black and yellow, are descriptors of race or skin tone. Bee-Lips's racially charged nickname undermines his professional and economic status as a lawyer, and Harry, who identifies him solely by this nickname, takes advantage of Bee-Lips's racial identity in order to elevate his own status. The descriptor "Bee-Lips" is not an animal comparison in the straightforward way that the loggerhead turtle, buzzard, and nurse shark comparison are, but it is used similarly to devalue and create marginalization. In this case, the comparison functions to devalue occupation and suggests that identity is not decided through occupation alone. Race can outweigh occupation in Harry's determination of value.

Although Harry makes each of these animal comparisons, and each comparison is a value statement grounded upon the association of an animal to a human, Harry's language in the comparison of "nurse shark" to black woman deviates from that of any of the other comparisons in the novel. This deviation demonstrates the integral importance of this dialogue in the novel. The difference between the other comparisons in the novel and the nurse shark comparison is the article, *a*. Harry's arm stump is like a loggerhead flipper. Bee-Lips is like a buzzard. He is called Bee-Lips because his lips look like a bee stung them. However, intercourse with a black woman is not like intercourse with a nurse shark. It is "like nurse shark." The article is omitted.

The other comparisons refer directly to the perceived anatomical and behavioral characteristics of the organisms described. Harry makes a direct comparison of his arm stump to a loggerhead flipper, and Marie, with her questioning of turtle reproduction, "Do they really do it for three days? Coot for three days?" (113), follows Harry's anatomical comparison with a behavioral one. When Harry compares Bee-Lips to a buzzard, he makes a direct comparison of Bee-Lips's personality to a common behavioral allegorization: the buzzard as a villain or thief. Bee-Lips's name combines a behavior of bees (stinging) with a symptom (swollen lips) to perpetuate a stereotype attributed to people of African American descent and to reduce them simultaneously to the colors black and yellow. The animals in these comparisons function grammatically as count nouns in the sentence. They are organisms with distinct behavioral and anatomical characteristics that can be compared directly to human behavior and anatomy. They provide, as Hediger argues, a way to think about marginalized beings. However, upon closer analysis, the nurse shark comparison does not seem to be a relation between human and animal.

The lack of an article removes the possibility of the nurse shark functioning in the dialogue as an individual organism with distinct behavioral traits and anatomical characteristics. If so, the noun "nurse shark" would have operated grammatically as a count noun, and Harry would have responded, "it's like a nurse shark" or even, "it's like having sex with a nurse shark." The use of the article would indicate that this comparison could be read like the others: a specific nurse shark behavioral or anatomical characteristic is being associated with and compared to intercourse with a black woman. However, his response, "like nurse shark," appears to refer to a collective body of nurse sharks, a body of nurse sharks without a personality, as the buzzard comparison implies, without any distinctive physical characteristics, as the loggerhead comparison demonstrates, and even without a distinct sex, as Morrison, Knott, and Curnutt assume when they associate black women to female sharks. When Morrison writes, "It is Harry who thinks a black woman is like a nurse shark, not Hemingway" (85), she neglects to recognize that, grammatically, the dialogue does not indicate that Harry thinks a black woman is "like a nurse shark." He thinks that "doing it" with black women is "like nurse shark" (113).

Morrison is partially accurate when she states that, according to Harry, intercourse with a black woman is so removed that the black female is not human, "not even mammal, but fish" (85); however, the argument must be taken a step further. A black woman is so removed from humanity that she is not even female. She is so removed from living that she is not even fish. The noun "nurse shark" in "like nurse shark" functions grammatically as a mass noun. Because of this, the black woman is being compared to a fish, a nurse shark, but not in its living animal form. She is being compared to "nurse shark," the fish, as an undifferentiated commodity. The characteristics that intercourse with a black woman share with the nurse shark are the commodified characteristics, the characteristics existing only when the shark has been stripped of life and is subjected to the value system found in a consumer market.

The consumer market does not consider nurse sharks valuable. They are not hard to catch and are often found inadvertently hooked on fishing lines. Because of this, fishermen consider them to be a nuisance (Castro 18). They are slow moving, sluggish, and can easily be caught with a variety of bait. Because they are not very valuable, they generally are not worth even the minimal effort required to catch them. When fishermen do intentionally catch and sell them, it is because they cannot catch anything else, and they need money. Their tough skin can be used to make leather; their liver can be used to produce oil (Castro 16-17). They can be consumed. However, in each of these cases, they are supplements. There are better sources for leather and oil. There are better fish to eat. They are good enough only when there is nothing else.

This is how Harry Morgan would have understood and experienced nurse sharks. These descriptions of nurse sharks contain the essential information that Morrison, Knott, and Curnutt do not address: nurse sharks are trash fish to Harry Morgan; they are not good for much. In the context of the dialogue, "like nurse shark" means that sex with a black woman is a cheap catch, serviceable, just enough to satisfy a demand, but not great, not even good.

When considering this, it becomes evident in *To Have and Have Not* that Harry Morgan's description of a "nigger wench" lover as nurse shark is based primarily upon his experience of the nurse shark as an inferior commodity and something of a nuisance. It follows that Harry Morgan regards black people as commodities to be utilized for a specific purpose that benefits him. Black humans are commodities in the same way that nurse sharks are commodities. Concurrently, intercourse with a "nigger wench" is a supplement to the intercourse Harry has with white women like Marie. Because of this, he chooses to engage in physical intimacy with black women for the same reason that people sometimes choose to catch and sell nurse sharks: because they cannot get anything else. The comparison of human beings to fish, more so than implying black women are "the furthest thing from human, so far away as to be not even mammal but fish" (Morrison 85), implies that Harry categorizes people, both black and white, the way material goods are categorized: around scales of economic value. Identity for Harry Morgan is not based on personality, behavior, or even occupation. The price Harry puts on everyone is based primarily on racial identity; it is based on the active marginalization and categorization of people around an economy of race.

To Have and Have Not may be the only Hemingway novel to take place in America, but both the cultural and economic system of Key West are very different from that of the continental United States. Key West is an island located only ninety miles from Cuba, and it is the southernmost point one can travel to while still remaining within the fifty states. Adam Pridemore notes that because Key West is "so close to the Caribbean and its colonial/postcolonial culture, many times the borders between the two regions blurred. Key West therefore contains the multiplicity of cultures normally found within a colonial/postcolonial situation" (96). Therefore, Harry Morgan is not a white man in a sea of white men. He is a white man living amongst Cubans, African Americans, Asians, and, perhaps most significantly, tourists.

One of the reasons tourists flocked to Key West during the Great Depression was to see this heterogeneous mix of cultures and skin tones. Yanagisawa describes this phenomenon using the example of Chinatowns: "Once [the Chinese immigrants] walked into these communities, it felt like being in China…. However, an expatriate community was not the only thing Chinese immigrants expected Chinatowns to provide in the 1930s. Despite the Great Depression, Chinatowns created jobs by developing the tourist business" (52). Americans viewed Chinatowns as "quaint" and "mysterious" sections of cities; they were foreign colonies on U.S. soil (Takaki 246). Yanagisawa notes that "local government agencies were even known to support tourist businesses such as Chinatowns with the hope of increasing tax revenue" (53). This form of tourism, labeled "slumming," attracted large numbers of educated white people. In Key West, immigrants and Key West natives became like animals in a zoo, attractions for well-to-do white people seeking foreign entertainment on U.S. soil.

Harry, physically disabled and also a "native Conch," quickly becomes subjected to the value system of the racialized tourist economy. At the start of Chapter 15, three wealthy white American tourists chat mindlessly at Freddy's bar. When Harry walks in, one of the tourists referred to as "the tall tourist's wife," remarks, "Isn't he wonderful? That's what I want. Buy me that, Papa" (130). Here, Harry is valued in the same economic manner he often uses to judge others. His value is based entirely upon his physical appearance, and his physical appearance renders him a souvenir, a cheap toy, a plaything. He is not taken seriously, but rather mocked to his face. For the tourists, Harry is an amusing, cheap catch.

Harry initially does not respond to the tourist, instead turning his attention to Freddy and asking him, "Can I speak to you?" (130). Freddy does not respond; the tourist answers for him, "Certainly. Go right ahead and say anything you like" (130). Harry, suddenly unable to suppress his anger, retorts back, "Shut up, you whore" (130). Ironically, the tourist is not the "whore" in this conversation; rather, Harry is the character objectified with a price tag.

Freddy, a Conch just like Harry, does not defend Harry; rather, he chastises Harry for his behavior: "'Listen,' Freddy said. 'Cut it out. You can't get away with that. You can't call my trade names like that. You can't call a lady a whore in a decent place like this'"

(130). Harry cannot call her a whore, but she can call him whatever she wants. Freddy refers to her as "my trade," but really Freddy represents the tourists' trade: they are buying what he sells. They own him; he is a commodity.

Freddy's inability to see his own commodification is, for Harry, an act of betrayal. Pridemore identifies the first stage of decolonization as "the sense of direct community" (95). However, judging from Freddy's response to Harry and to the tourists, the Key West Hemingway portrays in *To Have and Have Not* is not in the process of decolonization and independence, but in the midst of total consumption by the tourism industry. When Bee-Lips tells Harry that Freddy is the "only son-of-a-bitch in this town I *would* trust," Harry replies that he "wouldn't trust anybody" (133). The tourist economy has led to Harry's feelings of betrayal, and this is seen when Harry tries to explain the results of tourism to Al:

> What they're trying to do is starve you Conchs out of here so they can burn down the shacks and put up apartments and make this a tourist town....I hear they're buying up lots, and then after the poor people are starved out and gone somewhere else to starve some more they're going to come in and make it into a beauty spot for tourists. (96)

Additionally, Harry appears to have distanced himself from his people. He says, "you Conchs," despite the fact that he is a native of Key West as well. By distancing himself, Harry indicates that he wants nothing to do with the tourist economy and that he is willing to forge his own independent and decolonized path by whatever means necessary.

It follows that Harry's treatment of Mr. Johnson in the beginning of the novel represents much more than an attempt to illustrate Harry's tedious preoccupation with monetary value. Harry's brash treatment of Mr. Johnson is juxtaposed to Freddy's treatment of the tourists in his bar. When Mr. Johnson asks how he managed to lose the black marlin, Harry tells him, "You figure it out" before cataloguing the price of all the goods he has lost (21). Eddy, the boat hand, attempts to console Mr. Johnson, telling him he was just "unlucky" and that what happened was "the rarest occurrence I ever saw in my life" (21). By this point, Harry is "plenty sore" (21). Harry also describes himself as sore when Al claims his viewpoints of the tourist economy make him "talk like a radical" (96). These snippets of dialogue illustrate that Harry's preoccupation with monetary value are driven by his desire to separate himself from the colonized Conchs and establish himself as equal to the colonizing tourists. Pressure from wealthy tourists, a changing economy, and an influx of more educated and qualified workers force Harry and his peers not only to assign prices to everything, but also to create an illusion of their own power and masculinity.

Power and masculinity in Hemingway's writings are often linked to sexual prowess. Harry finds solace because he can still please Marie sexually despite his "flipper" of an arm stump. In fact, Marie even encourages Harry to use his arm stump to bring her to orgasm—an act that directly gives his arm stump value. The arm stump functions as a sexual object, becoming, in Harry's mind, not a disability, but something that can be ignored. It neither increases his value nor decreases it. He is no less of a man because he is missing an arm. He emphasizes this to Al as they both lament their inability to find work. When Al comments, "Losing your arm don't make you feel better" (97), Harry immediately responds, "The hell with my arm. You lose an arm you lose an arm. There's worse things than lose an arm. You've got two arms and you've got two of something else. And a man's still a man with one arm or with one of those" (97). A rationale emerges for Harry's ruthless and singular insistence of his own *cojones*: Harry's standing as a white man equal in value to the white tourists is built off the illusion that his arm stump does not make him marginalized. If Harry accepts his disability, all his hopes of eventual financial freedom will be crushed.

It is not only Harry who uses sexuality to create an illusory identity. In Chapter 22 of *To Have and Have Not*, Richard Gordon is drinking with a group of veterans at Freddy's when a veteran described as "the red-headed one" comments that he has "the finest little wife in the world" (211). The veteran continues his description of her saying, "And that girl is nuts about me. She's like a slave.

'Give me another cup of coffee,' I say to her. 'O.K., Pop,' she says. And I get it. Anything else the same way. She's carried away with me. If I got a whim, it's her law'" (211). The word "slave" associates his wife with monetary value. She is a person to be bought and sold. She works not with him, as one does in a partnership, but for him. The last line of the dialogue, "If I got a whim, it's her law," enforces the idea that he owns her. He makes the demands, she follows them. To be "the finest little woman in the world," she must not only obey his every whim as if it were law, but she must also adhere to the physical standards of the entertainment industry. The veteran likes to think "that maybe she is Ginger Rogers and that she has gone into the moving pictures" (212). This woman exists only in the veteran's imagination. She is a wartime fantasy who keeps "the home fires burning" (212). By creating this illusion (not only of his fake wife's servitude and beauty, but also of his own masculinity and ability to exert power over her), the veteran is able to conceal his anxieties that stem from fighting in the First World War.

Through the veteran's story, national identity is explicitly recognized as a construct—the veteran, an American hero, is left drinking at Freddy's run-down bar ranting about the wartime fantasies he created in order to survive. When the veteran first tells his tale, it seems as though this woman actually exists and is waiting for him back at home; however, as the story goes on, the veteran's reality is revealed to be nothing more than fantasy. The constructs throughout *To Have and Have Not* function similarly to those in Hemingway's Indian stories. Marc Dudley writes that "each of Hemingway's Indian stories works as a complement to the others in exposing these fallibilities and in showing national and cultural identities for what they are: constructs" (10). It is no accident that the wartime veteran—a symbol of American nationality and independence—relies so heavily on constructs. By breaking down a figure largely thought of as a hero, Hemingway subtly suggests that American identity, founded on masculinity and whiteness, is not based on the reality of the consumer market.

It is the image of the servile wife at home that furnishes the veteran with some sense of value in his life. Harry constructs a similar image of himself that keeps him fighting for his own freedom from the financial constraints of the tourist economy in Key West. After he is shot, he wonders, "I wonder what she'll do. I wonder what Marie will do? ... I wish I could do something about Marie. ... I wonder what she'll do?" (174). Here, Harry is marginalizing Marie, making her entirely dependent on him. It is only after Harry is fatally wounded that he confronts the reality he attempts to hide: his physical disability has rendered him a marginalized being in a world where marginalization is commodified. It is only right before his death that Harry accepts his status not as a white male, but as "nurse shark," a cheap catch in a racialized tourist economy.

The white male characters in *To Have and Have Not* seem driven by the subconscious fear of becoming "like nurse shark." Freddy twists the reality of his occupation by describing the female tourist as "his trade"; the veteran creates a slave-wife to get him through the war, where his status as a soldier renders him expendable, and Harry, perhaps the most enlightened character in terms of the realities of the tourist economy, is bent on proving his arm stump is not a disability and that the whiteness of his skin is enough to result in equality and freedom from the tourist industry. The black and female characters in the story do not seem to have the same fear, however. For example, when Mr. Johnson is finished fishing, Harry takes responsibility for the black boat hand's payment:

> "You want to pay off the nigger?"
> "How much do I owe him?"
> "A dollar. You can give him a tip if you want." (23)

Harry appears to be in control of both Mr. Johnson and the black boat hand; however, his need for monetary control can be read as evidence for his deepening anxiety over his employment, his masculinity, and the power he has over his own town's economy. The black man's silence reveals not dimwittedness or stupidity, but a lack of concern for these very things—a lack of concern that is essential to highlight Harry's insecurities. When Harry gives him the money, which amounts to a dollar and forty Cuban cents, the black man appears confused: "'What's this for?' the nigger asks me showing the coins" (23). Harry, who is now provided with the chance to patiently explain, in Spanish, that the coins are a tip, can once again be falsely assured that he has command over the people around him.

Similarly, Harry is concerned with his value while sleeping with Marie, and she cannot grasp the meaning behind his questions and responses. When Harry compares his arm stump to a flipper on a loggerhead, Marie quickly dismisses his worry and asks a question regarding loggerhead turtle behavior. As quickly as Marie dismisses Harry's anxiety regarding his sexual performance with an arm stump, Harry dismisses Marie's curiosity in loggerhead turtles. He responds, "Sure. Listen, be quiet. We'll wake the girls" (113). Only a few lines later, Harry dismisses Marie's concern about his sexual experiences with black women in the same manner. When she asks, "Listen, did you ever do it with a nigger wench?" he responds, "Sure" (113). Although they are physically connected, they are worlds apart. Marie concerns herself with relationships—the bond between the turtles, as well as her bond with Harry. Did he ever have someone better? Someone more exotic? When they are intimate, does he think only of her? Harry worries about his masculinity, his physical abilities, and how he is perceived physically. Neither picks up on this dissonance, but the parallel structure of their language suggests that Hemingway crafted these lines purposefully with the hope that readers might. This interpretation of *To Have and Have Not* exposes Harry's anxiety and permits his behavior to be understood not as mean-spirited or racist, but as desperate and pitiful, a call for an identity in a place he once thought of as home. Their insecurities are so different: Marie is concerned with building physical intimacy, and Harry is concerned not with his relationship with Marie, but with the racial hierarchy he has so carefully constructed.

Harry's construction of a racialized hierarchical economy may protect him from facing the reality of the economic situation around him, but it causes others to reduce him in the very way he most fears. When Wesley, a black boat hand, and Harry are both shot during a bootleg run, Harry, despite his injury, keeps steering the boat while Wesley rests in the cockpit. Harry jokes with him saying, "You'll feel worse when the old doctor probes for [the bullet]" (86). Here, Harry is attempting to establish physical masculinity and assert his value through his ability to deal with physical pain. Wesley responds to Harry, "You ain't human. …You ain't got human feelings" (86). This response underscores Harry's behavior. If Harry is not human, what is he? An animal? Or is he so far removed from human, so far away as to be not even mammal, not even fish, but commodity? Wesley does not say, but the implication is that Harry's very quest for masculinity, equality, and financial freedom has led him away from humanity and resulted in the creation of a farcical and expendable commodified tourist attraction. Marie and Wesley, marginalized characters whose concerns seem to be grounded not in the economy but in relationships, retain their humanity.

In many ways, Harry's treatment of others is similar to the way early critics viewed race in Hemingway's fiction: as scenery. From Harry's dismissal of Marie's questions to his dismissal of Wesley's injury, Harry makes sure that he takes center stage. Harry's world-view takes on the lens of primitivism when he begins categorizing people as Conchs or Other, black or white, strong or weak, disabled or able. What Harry fails to recognize is that humanity does not divide so easily into binaries or racial hierarchies: he can be strong *and* weak, disabled *and* still able; he can be a white Conch without buying into the tourist economy, and he can create an identity for himself without creating a racial hierarchy of value.

Reading the nurse shark not as a biological animal but as a com-modified object allows for the exploration and analysis of another identity issue Hemingway confronted in his fiction: what happens when being white is no longer enough to guarantee financial stability, equality, or masculinity? Perhaps it is unavoidable to construct nar-ratives explaining one's identity as an individual and as an American, but when those constructions become based on the dehumanization and marginalization of others, people fall into Harry Morgan's trap. Instead of raising themselves up, they are only dehumanized and marginalized by others. More often than not, it appears to be the pressure from their precarious state within a capitalist economy that encourages this active discrimination and dehumanization. They become invested in turning others into "nurse shark" because they know that before too long they will be "like nurse shark" themselves.

Works Cited

Baker, Carlos. *Ernest Hemingway: A Life Story.* Scribner, 1969.

Carrier, Jeffrey, et al. "Group Reproductive Behaviors in Free-Living Nurse Sharks, *Ginglymostoma cirratum.*" *Copeia*, vol. 1994, no. 3, 1994, pp. 646-56.

Castro, Jose. "The Biology of the Nurse Shark, *Ginglymostoma cirratum,* off the Florida East Coast and the Bahama Islands." *Environmental Biology of Fishes,* vol. 58, no.1, 2000, pp. 1-22.

Curnutt, Kirk. *Reading Hemingway's* To Have and Have Not." The Kent State UP, 2017.

DeFalco, Joseph. *The Hero in Hemingway's Short Stories.* UP of Pittsburgh, 1963.

Dempster, R.P. and E.S. Herald. "Notes on the Hornshark, *Heterodontus francisci*, with Observations on Mating Activity." *Occ. Pap. California Academy of Science,* vol. 33, 1961, pp. 1-7.

Dudley, Marc. *Hemingway, Race, and Art: Bloodlines and the Color Line.* Kent State UP, 2012.

Gudger, E.W. "Summary of Work Done on the Fishes of Tortugas." *Carnegie Inst. Washington Yearbook,* vol. 11, 1912, pp. 148-50.

Hediger, Ryan. "Becoming with Animals: Sympoiesis and the Ecology of Meaning in London and Hemingway." *Studies in American Naturalism,* vol. 11, no. 1, 2016, pp. 5-22.

Hemingway, Ernest. *To Have and Have Not.* Scribner, 1937.

Knott, Toni D. *One Man Alone: Hemingway and* To Have and Have Not. UP of America, 1999.

—. "Playing in the Light: Examining Categorization in *To Have and Have Not* as a Reflection of Identity of Racism." *North Dakota Quarterly*, vol. 63, no. 3, 1997, pp. 82-88.

Morrison, Toni. *Playing in the Dark: Whiteness and the Literary Imagination.* Random House, 1992.

Pridemore, Adam. "Decolonizing the Native Conch in Ernest Hemingway's *To Have and Have Not:* Harry Morgan as a Cautionary Tale Against Tourism." *Florida Studies Proceedings of the 2006 Annual Meeting of the Florida College Annual English Association,* edited by Claudia Slate and Steve Glassman, Cambridge Scholars, 2006, pp. 92-99.

Smith, Paul. *New Essays on Hemingway's Short Fiction.* Cambridge UP, 1998.

Strong, Amy L. *Race and Identity in Hemingway's Fiction.* Palgrave Macmillan, 2008.

Takaki, Ronald. *Strangers from a Different Shore.* Penguin, 1989.

Yanagisawa, Hideo. "Harry Morgan's Identity Crisis: Orientalism and Slumming during the Great Depression in Hemingway's *To Have and Have Not.*" *The Hemingway Review,* vol. 34, no. 1, 2014, pp. 47-60.

Young, Philip. *Ernest Hemingway.* G. Bell & Sons, Ltd., 1952.

Renee Mattos

Cultivating Curses: Plants and African American Folklore in *The Sound and the Fury*

Descriptions of nature abound in virtually all of William Faulkner's novels and short stories. The Faulkner and Yoknapatawpha Conference chose "Faulkner and the Natural World" as their theme for the 1996 conference and published a book on the subject in 1999. Since then, ecocriticism of Faulkner's work has only continued to grow. His use of nature imagery and associated symbolism is well established in scholarship ranging from Lawrence Buell to André Bleikasten. The symbolism of the natural world in relation to regional folklore in Faulkner's novels has also received critical attention in the scholarship of Charles Peavy (1966), David Middleton (1977), and Daniel Hoffman (1989). However, much of the criticism that examines the connection between flora and folklore in *The Sound and the Fury* (1929) overlooks or minimizes the extensive inclusion of African American folk practices in the novel. Because the influence of African American folklore has remained largely obscured in the scholarship on nature in Faulkner's work, a deeper analysis of its role in *The Sound and the Fury* is needed.

While the most memorable plant imagery in the novel is undoubtedly that of Caddy wearing muddy drawers while climbing a pear tree—the symbolic moment of her loss of innocence—several passages connecting Benjy, Jason, and Quentin with nature are equally important for what they reveal about the presence of African American folklore in the text. African American folk beliefs identify the plants associated with the brothers as poisonous, destructive, or valuable in conjure rituals. In this way, African American conjure motifs and folk practices function as symbols of the damage and grief that define the brothers' lives in Caddy's absence. Thus, African American folk culture emerges from the peripheries of *The Sound and the Fury* to illuminate the emotional lives of the white Compson brothers.

Faulkner's familiarity with the folk practices of Southern blacks likely had roots in his personal life. His childhood caretaker Caroline Barr, born into slavery but freed at age sixteen, acted as a "second mother" to Faulkner and was known amongst the family as an avid storyteller (Blotner 13). In addition to telling stories, Barr also taught Faulkner and his brothers about the natural world by taking the children "out into the woods, where she would teach them how to recognize the different birds" (Blotner 15). Considering her knowledge of nature and love of storytelling, it is reasonable to conclude that Barr contributed to Faulkner's knowledge of African American folktales and practices—a knowledge that likely continued to grow through his frequent contact with the rest of his family's servants and the other black residents of Oxford.

Faulkner's awareness of African American folklore is evident early in *The Sound and the Fury*. Following the discovery that her youngest child is mentally handicapped, Mrs. Compson changes his name from Maury to Benjy. Versh tells him, "*Your name Benjamin now. You know how come your name Benjamin now. They making a bluegum out of you*" (84). In her study of African American hoodoo, Katrina Hazzard-Donald notes that "Faulkner's work references components from the old Hoodoo belief system. Statements about 'blue-gummed' Negroes, for example, though viewed as pejorative, reflect old tradition Hoodoo belief in markings, particularly the belief in birthmarks" (88). Applying the term "blue-gum" to Benjy is significant because it emphasizes his identity as "marked" by a cognitive disability. His existence effectively becomes evidence of the "bad luck" that surrounds the Compson family: "'They aint no luck on this place.' Roskus said. 'I seen it at first but when they changed his name I knowed it'" (35). Benjy's name change is his symbolic birthmark. It sets him apart as the manifestation of all the misery that afflicts the Compsons and makes him a seeming harbinger of the family's grim destiny. Frony also views Benjy as a sign of bad luck, and she fears that Benjy will conjure Luster by sharing a bed with him: "'You take Luster outen that bed, mammy.' Frony said. 'That boy conjure him'" (38). The supernatural qualities that Frony attributes to Benjy suggest a connection between Benjy's mental handicap and the African American folk belief that witch-doctors or hoodoo doctors were thought to possess an "unusual mentality and often show physical peculiarities as well" (Puckett 201). With various members of the black Gibson family convinced that Benjy's mental disability is evidence of bad luck and conjure, the novel begins to establish African American folklore as a marker of damage, destruction, and loss.

Benjy's feelings of loss regarding Caddy are first manifested in African American folk practices connected with the jimson weed. The symbolism of the jimson weed and its connection to Benjy has been discussed in much of the Faulkner scholarship that examines folklore and nature in his work.[1] Peavy notes the weed's association with male genitalia and argues that Faulkner "was doubtlessly aware of the phallic implications of the closed jimson flower clutched in the fist of the castrated Benjy" (438). While castration symbolism is one way to read Benjy's connection with the jimson weed, his link to the plant should also be examined in conjunction with the weed's use in African American folk medicine. Certain African American folk beliefs identify the jimson weed as an abortive agent (Bleikasten 68). In the opening scene of the novel, Benjy carries a worn stalk of jimson weed as he wanders the Compson property with Luster, who tells him, "You dropped your jimson weed. …You needs a new one. You bout wore that one out" (65). Although Benjy cannot under-stand Caddy's reasons for leaving him or the abortive possibilities of the worn stalk in his hand, the medicinal capabilities attributed to the plant symbolize his longing for Caddy. Caddy leaves home because of an unplanned pregnancy and her resulting marriage to Sydney Herbert Head. This makes Benjy's choice to carry the jim-son highly ironic because it is a plant with the potential power to end pregnancy. Its use in folk medicine further underscores Caddy's expulsion from her family and the termination of her relationship with Benjy. She is, in some sense, both in need of and a victim of the folk practices that utilize the plant. Understood in the context of African American folklore, the jimson weed thus highlights Caddy's absence from Benjy's life as well as the reason for that absence in the form of an unwanted pregnancy.

In his analysis of the jimson weed's symbolism, Peavy notes that it is often associated with the loss of Caddy because of its strong smell.[2] However, the plant's use as a component in various African American conjuration practices better illustrates Benjy's grief following the loss of Caddy. In his anthology of Southern folk beliefs, B. A. Botkin remarks that "charms make use of all things connected with the body ... and garments worn next to the person. ... These are mixed with a wide variety of symbolic substances including plants (snakeroot, devil's shoestring, Jimson weed, asafoetida, clover, tobacco)" ("Southern Folk Beliefs" 632). The creation of a charm is significant when considered in relation to Benjy's obsession with Caddy's abandoned slipper.[3] In combination with the worn stalk of jimson he carries, the slipper can be read as one component of a charm that Benjy uses to attempt to control the chaotic world around him that Caddy's absence has created. Benjy's attachment to the slipper is described as he sits in the dark holding his only physical remnant of Caddy: *I squatted there, holding the slipper. I couldn't see it, but my hands saw it ... my hands saw the slipper but I couldn't see myself, but my hands could see the slipper* (88-9). The repetition of the phrase "my hands saw" emphasizes the importance Benjy places on physically holding on to reminders of Caddy. In this way, the passage harkens back to the opening scenes of the novel when Benjy walks around the pasture gripping the worn stalk of jimson weed. When Benjy alternately clings to the jimson and the slipper as symbols of mourning and sources of comfort, the two objects are metaphorically brought together to create a charm meant to bring Caddy back into Benjy's life. Yet, as Benjy grasps the slipper and the jimson weed, the only thing that is brought into his life is a permanent sense of absence and loss. Rather than forming a magical charm, the worn slipper and poisonous weed only underscore Benjy's fate to be cast aside by his family.

African American folklore also shapes Benjy's longing for Caddy in that he experiences her absence as a kind of death in a manner that resonates with the many other associations between sex and death in the novel. Throughout the novel, Benjy visits his "graveyard": "Ben squat[ted] before a small mound of earth. At either end of it an empty bottle of blue glass that once contained poison was fixed in the ground. In one was a withered stalk of jimson weed" (393). The placement of the jimson weed in an old bottle of poison underscores the poisonous nature of the plant (Peavy 437), yet the bottle is more significant than its relationship to the jimson. Decorating graves with colored bottles and other household items was a common practice amongst blacks in the South (Puckett 105), and in some accounts, conjure doctors used blue glass to ward off evil spirits (240). Marking an empty grave, the bottle of blue glass stands as a statement of Benjy's anguish. It signifies both Caddy's metaphorical death and the evil that must be guarded against in her absence, for without Caddy to protect him, Benjy is under threat from a world that does not want to try to understand him. Forever being hushed by Luster, Mrs. Compson, and Jason, Benjy no longer has the possibility of comfort in the question, "What is it ... What are you trying to tell Caddy" (5). As he continues to visit his makeshift graveyard, all that really awaits Benjy is the internment of hope.

As with the folk beliefs associated with jimson weed, African American folk medicine's use of sassafras also underscores Benjy's experience of loss. Benjy watches Caddy's wedding ceremony through the parlor window while he and T.P. drink sarsaparilla.[4] The beverage was originally "made with *sassafras*, birch bark, and other flavors, but no actual sarsaparilla" (Stewart 191, italics mine), meaning Benjy consumes sassafras as he drinks. African American medicinal practices assert that drinking a tea made from the root of the sassafras tree can cure blindness (Puckett 383). This belief in the curative property of sassafras takes on tragic significance when put in context with Benjy. As he watches Caddy get married, Benjy becomes increasingly upset: "Caddy. I clawed my hands against the wall Caddy" (47). While Benjy's agitation is likely heightened by the alcohol in the sarsaparilla, his reaction to Caddy's wedding is nonetheless genuine as a response to the change taking place before his eyes. With its supposed ability to cure blindness, the sassafras contained in the sarsaparilla represents Benjy's ability to metaphorically see the fundamental change that Caddy's marriage represents. Even if he does not yet realize that Caddy is leaving or that her absence will be permanent, Benjy's desperate clawing at the wall suggests that he knows he is losing Caddy in some way. The sassafras figuratively restores Benjy's sight by opening his eyes to a world where everything he sees, from Caddy's wedding day forward, is a reminder that she is gone.

It is also noteworthy that Benjy observes the placement of the moon several times during Caddy's wedding, as it reflects off the branch and the steps of the cellar (42, 47). Taken together, moonlight and the consumption of sassafras are significant because both play an important role in African American conjure folklore. In his research on black Southerners, Puckett notes that "Conjures ... in the case of the Southern Negro, are set oftentimes with the dark or light of the moon to cause things to waste away or to grow" (349). Puckett also writes that "druggists throughout the black South report a large sale of such things as snakeroot, *sassafras*, lodestone, brimstone ... to the colored people for the purpose of hoodooing" (237, italics mine). Benjy is metaphorically cast under a spell wherein he is powerless to stop the damage resulting from Caddy's wedding. As he drinks sarsaparilla and looks longingly at Caddy through the window, the moonlight illuminates Caddy's growing distance from him: "Caddy put her arms around me, and her shining veil, and I couldn't smell trees anymore and I began to cry" (48). Their relationship wastes away as the invisible conjure cast in the moonlight and aided by the sarsaparilla—serving as a sassafras-filled charm—traps Benjy in a life without Caddy.

While Benjy's narrative reveals his deep sense of grief, conjure elements in Jason's narrative section underscore his inability to respond to Caddy's loss of innocence with anything other than anger and desperation. Throughout the novel, Jason suffers from near-debilitating headaches, which Mrs. Compson attributes to the smell of gasoline: "'You know gasoline always made you sick,' she says. 'Ever since you were a child'" (296). Although they typically occur while he is driving, Jason's headaches are more than the symptom of a sensitivity to gasoline. His headaches are persistent and hard to treat: "It's not something to cure it I need it's just an even break not to have to have them" (298). He has no control over the physical pain that afflicts him; the headaches are like a curse he must bear and reflect his sense of victimhood. Jason's inability to prevent or relieve his headaches parallels the suffering of a conjure victim. One African American conjure tale tells of a woman who suffered a constant headache until she discovered and removed a charm from her pillow (Puckett 227). Jason's headaches are often associated with Caddy and her daughter, suggesting that Jason is somehow under their spell. This is evident in the fact that Caddy's behavior is viewed as the catalyst for all the major events that shape Jason's adult life—Miss Quentin's birth, his brother's and father's deaths, and the lost bank job. Both women seemingly thwart Jason at every turn, appearing akin to conjure women whose actions have the power to fundamentally alter Jason's life.

Jason believes himself to be the rightful recipient of the money Caddy sends to her daughter (383). Thus, the fact that Miss Quentin steals the money makes Jason's anger more meaningful because he finds himself, through the actions of his niece, once again powerless against the machinations of Caddy. When Jason discovers that Miss Quentin has fled with his money, his headache only grows in intensity: "He was trying to breathe shallowly, so that the blood would not beat so in his skull" (384). His headaches are essentially the physical manifestation of the powerful hold Caddy and her daughter have over him. Not only are his desires for money, respect, and power continually crushed by Caddy and Miss Quentin, his body succumbs to their influence as well. The sound of beating blood in Jason's skull is simply a reminder of his sister's control over his circumstances. Like an invisible charm, his Compson blood keeps Jason constrained by the past and in pain.

While Jason frantically drives around in search of his runaway niece, he inhales the scent of camphor to try to counteract the odor of gasoline: "When it was necessary for him to drive for any length of time he fortified himself with a handkerchief soaked in camphor" (383). Considering the argument that Jason's headaches are a symptom of conjuration, it is notable that African American folk beliefs often call for the use of camphor as a curative for spirit-possession. Several accounts of conjuration or hoodoo recommend soaking counter-charms, often a piece of red flannel, in camphor to cure the conjured (Botkin, "Southern Folk Beliefs" 633). Jason is metaphorically trying to free himself from the "spell" under which Caddy and Miss Quentin have placed him. His sense of victimization and injustice is evident in his confidence that the search for Miss Quentin will be lengthy and that a pounding headache will be inevitable. Jason views his niece and Caddy as the embodiment of all the injustice he thinks he has suffered: "together they merely symbolized the job in the bank of which he had been deprived before he ever got it" (382). He cannot prevent Caddy or her daughter from leaving him feeling defeated and outraged. Inhaling the fumes from a camphor-soaked cloth is Jason's attempt to combat the defeat and outrage that manifest themselves through his headaches. Read in this way, his use of camphor oil serves as a counter-charm, albeit an ineffective one, against both the raging headaches and the "bitches" in his life.

Despite the camphor's ineffectiveness—"in either case, his head would be splitting" (283)— Jason continues to put his faith in the tree's oil, stubbornly clinging to the hope that it will free him from pain. Similarly, Jason clings to his obsessions with money ("it just belongs to the man that can get it and keep it" [241]), revenge against Caddy, and control of Miss Quentin. These obsessions underscore his inability to move beyond the familial obsession with the past and, in turn, the sense of loss and failure that haunt the Compson brothers in the wake of Caddy's fall from grace. With his brother and father for grim examples, Jason scorns their deaths by suicide and alcoholism. He, instead, relies on camphor oil as his inadequate means of counteracting the conjure-like effects of Caddy's actions and the pain that threatens to consume him.

Like the various items and practices that characterize African American conjure beliefs, the folklore associated with tree planting also illuminates Jason's feelings of anger and loss. According to Mississippi folk belief, African Americans "never plant a cedar tree except in a cemetery" (Botkin, "Bayou Pierre Plant Lore" 424). Shortly after Mr. Compson's funeral, Jason lingers in the cemetery and recalls watching workers fill in his father's grave saying, "I began to feel sort of funny and so I decided to walk around a while. ... I went back toward the nigger graveyard. I got under some cedars, where the rain didn't come much" (250-51). It is no surprise that Jason seeks shelter under cedars. As graveyard trees, cedars are directly linked to ideas of death, loss, and mourning. In sheltering beneath their branches to avoid the rain and his "funny" feelings, Jason tries to escape the loss and ruin that characterize his and his family's lives—the loss and ruin that can only be outrun by the grave. In the context of African American planting lore, however, the protection Jason seeks in the graveyard essentially highlights his inability to escape the decay and destruction he fears. Confined to cemeteries, cedars really only provide shelter to the dead, which leaves Jason vulnerable to his unwanted feelings and the ghosts of family and heritage.

Given the tree's association with graveyards and death, African American folklore also warns that "it is bad luck to bring a cedar into the house" (Puckett 221). In connecting cedars with the idea of home, this admonition serves as a harbinger of doom for Jason. When he walks out from under the cedars, Jason encounters Caddy and begins thinking about their childhood. He says, "I got to thinking about when we were little and one thing and another and I got to feeling funny again, kind of mad or something" (252). Jason's anger and "funny" feelings in combination with his encounter with Caddy and proximity to the cedars metaphorically recreate the folk belief mentioned above. Instead of bringing cedars into the home, home—in the form of Caddy and thoughts of childhood—is brought to the cedars. What follows for Jason, albeit over several years, is a string of bad luck. Caddy's sudden reappearance in his life brings Jason face to face with the incarnation of all he lost and stands to lose. Although he taunts Caddy with his authority over Miss Quentin, Jason can never fully control Caddy or her daughter. After all, he must still deal with the burden of supporting his family, the constant lack of respect from everyone around him, and the sting of being outsmarted by his niece. Thus, the cedars and their folkloric connotations of bad luck serve, in this instance, as a reminder of Roskus's prophetic complaint, "They aint no luck" with the Compson family.

The connection between African American folklore and feelings of loss and doom is equally strong in Quentin's narrative. While scholars have given significant attention to the role of honeysuckle "as the Southern environmental signifier that stands in for the erotic, sexual mixups he (Quentin) feels for Caddy" (Anderson 38), Quentin's repeated focus on roses has been overshadowed. Like the jimson weed and the camphor tree, roses are linked to African American conjure stories and folk practices. Quentin thinks of roses when he looks back on Caddy's wedding and recalls her fleeing from the house as Benjy bellows. He remembers seeing her run away *"quick, her train caught up over her arm she ran ... her veil swirling ... fast clutching her dress onto her shoulder with the other hand ... the smells roses roses"* (100). Quentin's memory of Caddy and roses shares certain similarities with an African American folktale. According to a story recorded in *Folk Beliefs of the Southern Negro*, roses were used as part of a conjure spell wherein "a girl was given a bunch of roses on her wedding day and her attention was called to their sweet fragrance. That girl fell dead when going into the church" (Puckett 224). While Caddy, like the girl in the story, carries a bunch of roses, it is Quentin who smells "their sweet fragrance" and ultimately ends up dead. The African American association of roses with fatality further emphasizes Quentin's impending suicide. In smelling the odor of roses, Quentin's attention is called to the reality that Caddy is leaving and that his desperate adherence to notions of purity and honor no longer matter. Quentin cannot escape the conjure of the rose bouquet any more than he can escape the sense of helplessness and doom that drive him to suicide.

Quentin's focus on Caddy's wedding bouquet is also noteworthy in light of the connection he draws between roses and dogwood. Recalling the wedding, Quentin obsesses over the idea of virginity: *"Roses. Roses. Mr and Mrs Jason Richmond Compson announce the marriage of.* Roses. Not virgins like dogwood" (95). Roses have long symbolized sexual impurity. Victorian era morals frequently resulted in women being categorized as "either virgins or whores—as the lily or the rose" (Blotner 100). This makes Quentin's association of Caddy's bouquet of roses with her promiscuity almost expected. However, the juxtaposition of roses with dogwood reveals a deeper sense of anguish in Quentin. Certain African American folk practices recommend that women drink tea made from the root of a dogwood tree, which "will not only prevent conception but will also produce abortion if conception has already occurred" (Puckett 332). The medicinal use of the root as a contraceptive/abortifacient highlights Caddy's sexual activity and therein emphasizes Quentin's anger over his sister's sexuality and his inability to control it. Understood in light of African American folk medicine, dogwood reiterates the sexual and fatal implications of roses and reminds Quentin that there is no virginity to be symbolized or restored. Caddy is irrevocably fallen and lost to Quentin completely.

The consuming sense of loss Quentin feels following Caddy's marriage reaches its pinnacle in his suicide. Quentin calmly reflects on his decision to drown himself: "when He said Rise only the flat irons" (139). He then quickly lapses into memories of talking with Caddy about her decision to marry Sydney Herbert Head. Quentin recalls her insisting, "I've got to marry somebody" (139). The juxtaposition of Quentin's thoughts of suicide with memories of Caddy's desperation to marry create a connection between death and marriage that has roots in African American folk culture. Many Southern blacks believed that dreams were a sign of things to come, and "it [was] a widespread belief that a dream of dying or a funeral indicate[d] a wedding, and a dream of a wedding, a funeral" (Puckett 499). Although they are not dreams, Quentin's thoughts of death and memories of Caddy share a similar relationship to African American dream signs. Quentin's vision of the floating flat irons generates memories of Caddy's marriage because her wedding serves as an impetus for his suicide. In this way, his recollections of Caddy function as dreams that foreshadow his death. One begets the other, trapping Quentin in an endless cycle of longing for and dreaming of death and Caddy. In the end, Quentin knows he can never have Caddy, so he chooses death—the other "little sister" (94).

The Sound and the Fury leaves everyone in the Compson family in an ever-increasing state of collapse. As African American folklore intersects with plant imagery, it reveals Benjy's, Jason's, and Quentin's feelings of grief, anger, and desperation following Caddy's loss of innocence. In her absence, the brothers are left to navigate a world seemingly filled with bad dreams, ill luck, and conjure spells. African American conjure practices and folk beliefs infuse the brothers' experiences with a sense of doom, highlighting their inability to conquer their shared yet different pasts. Neither heritage nor hoodoo can be overcome. While the Compson lineage is defeated by social tradition and family pride, the cultural knowledge that is African American folk belief survives in the brothers' stories. When they remember and relive the gradual crumbling of their family legacy of privilege, each brother effectively helps record and therein preserve the rituals and beliefs of the Gibson family and the greater black community. African American folklore endures amidst the demise of white aristocracy, exposing the inherent false-hood of racial superiority. Thus, the fictions contained in *The Sound and the Fury* ultimately reveal the truth that equality between black and white races is just as *natural* as the environment of the South and the folkways that characterize it.

Notes

1. Benjy's identification with the broken narcissus flower, which he holds at the end of the novel, has been the subject of considerable scholarship examining Faulkner's use of plant lore in *The Sound and the Fury*. Because the narcissus only appears at the end of the novel and has already received critical attention, only the jimson weed—which appears in multiple parts of the text—will be examined in relation to Benjy.

2. Peavy cites Edmund Volpe's argument that the strong smell of the jimson weed reflects Benjy's loss of Caddy and her scent, which smells like trees (437).

3. In African American folklore, conjuration refers to the process a conjurer or hoodoo doctor uses to affect or control an individual and often involves the use of a charm, which is a combination of materials connected with the conjurer's intended victim. See Botkin, "Southern Folk Beliefs," 632-33.

4. A type of soda, with or without alcohol, which became popular during the nineteenth century. See Stewart, 191-92.

Works Cited

Anderson, Eric Gary. "Environed Blood: Ecology and Violence in *The Sound and the Fury* and *Sanctuary*." *Faulkner and the Ecology of the South*, edited by Joseph Urgo and Ann Abadie, UP Mississippi, 2005, pp. 30-46.

Bleikasten, André. *The Ink of Melancholy: Faulkner's Novels from* The Sound and the Fury *to* Light in August. Indiana UP, 1990.

Blotner, Joseph. *Faulkner: A Biography.* One-Volume Edition. UP Mississippi, 2005.

Botkin, B.A. "Bayou Pierre Plant Lore." *A Treasury of Mississippi River Folklore*, edited by B.A. Botkin, Crown Publishers, 1955, pp. 422-24.

—. "Southern Folk Beliefs." *A Treasury of Southern Folklore*, edited by B.A. Botkin, Crown Publishers, 1949, pp. 626-35.

Buell, Lawrence. "Faulkner and the Claims of the Natural World." *Faulkner and the Natural World*, edited by Donald Kartiganer and Ann Abadie, UP Mississippi, 1999, pp. 1-18.

Faulkner, William. *The Sound and the Fury.* 1929. Vintage, 1956.

Hazzard-Donald, Katrina. "Crisis at the Crossroads: Sustaining and Transforming Hoodoo's Black Belt Tradition from Emancipation to World War II." *Mojo Workin': The Old African American Hoodoo System*, edited by Katrina Hazzard-Donald, U of Illinois P, 2012, pp. 84-91.

Hoffman, Daniel. *Faulkner's Country Matters: Folklore and Fable in Yoknapatawpha.* Louisiana State UP, 1989.

Middleton, David. "Faulkner's Folklore in *As I Lay Dying*: An Old Motif in a New Manner." *Studies in the Novel*, vol. 9, no. 1, 1977, pp. 46-53.

Peavy, Charles. "Faulkner's Use of Folklore in *The Sound and the Fury*." *The Journal of American Folklore*, vol. 79, no. 313, 1966, pp. 437-47.

Puckett, Newbell Niles. *Folk Beliefs of the Southern Negro.* Chapel Hill: U of North Carolina P, 1926. *Archive.org*, www.archive. org. Accessed 3 March 2016.

Stewart, Amy. "Sarsaparilla." *The Drunken Botanist: The Plants that Create the World's Great Drinks*, edited by Amy Stewart, Algonquin Books, 2013, pp. 191-92.

Notes on Contributors

C. D. Albin is Professor of English at Missouri State University – West Plains. He is the author of the short story collection *Hard Toward Home* (Press 53, 2016), for which he received the 2017 Missouri Author Award in Fiction, and the poetry collection *Axe, Fire, Mule* (Golden Antelope Press, 2018). His articles and reviews have appeared in a number of publications, including *Arkansas Review*, *Georgia Review*, *Harvard Review*, *Philological Review*, *POMPA: Publications of the Mississippi Philological Society*, and *Style*.

Rachel Betts is an adjunct professor at SUNY Geneseo, St. John Fisher College, and Eastman School of Music where she teaches academic writing and English. She completed her B.S. in Biology at Centre College in Danville, KY and her M.A. in English at the University of Rochester. Rachel is interested in environmental equity, policy, and management. She currently lives in Rochester, NY with her adorable, but quite temperamental bunny, Olive.

Joseph Fruscione was an English and Writing professor for 15 years in the Washington, D.C., area. After leaving academia in 2014, he started a freelance career as an editor and proofreader. He's also the cofounder and communications director of PrecariCorps, a nonprofit that supports adjunct faculty financially. He's the author of *Faulkner and Hemingway: Biography of a Literary Rivalry* (Ohio State, 2012), as well as numerous articles on Hemingway, Ellison, and other writers. He edited *Teaching Hemingway and Modernism* (Kent State, 2015), and he coedited (with Kelly J. Baker) *Succeeding Beyond the Academy* (Kansas, 2018), a collection of stories and advice about changing careers. He lives in Silver Spring, Maryland.

Barry Hudek is currently a Lecturer in the English Department at the University of Illinois at Urbana-Champaign. Prior to that, he completed a PhD at the University of Mississippi with a dissertation entitled "Book of Empire: the Political Bible of U.S. Literary Modernism" that explored the use of biblical allusion as critique upon U.S. justifications for imperialism, nation-building, and racial oppression—justifications that often used the Bible in defense of those endeavors.

Andrew B. Leiter is professor of English at Lycoming College in Williamsport, Pennsylvania. He is author of *In the Shadow of the Black Beast: African American Masculinity in the Harlem and Southern Renaissances* (LSU Press, 2010); editor of *Southerners on Film: Essays on Hollywood Portrayals Since the 1970s* (McFarland, 2011); and co-editor (with Christopher Rieger) of *Faulkner and Hurston* (Southeast Missouri State UP, 2017).

Renee Mattos is a lecturer in the English departments at California State University, Stanislaus and Merced College, Los Banos. Her research interests include death and the human body, burial practices, folklore, Southern literature, and William Faulkner.

Pennie Pflueger teaches American Literature, Women's Literature, Film, and Writing at Southeast Missouri State University where she is an Instructor of English.

Han Qiqun is Professor of English at Nanjing Forestry University in the People's Republic of China. She received her Ph.D. degree from Nanjing University in 2013. Her recent publications include "'The Material Unconscious' and William Faulkner's Environmental Writings," published in *Shandong Foreign Language Teaching Journal*, "William Faulkner's Snopes Trilogy: A Material Cultural Perspective," published in *English and American Literature Studies*, and "The Material Turn: A Keyword in Critical Theory," published in *Foreign Literature*. A 2016-17 visiting scholar at the Centre for Faulkner Studies at Southeast Missouri State University, she is currently undertaking a nationally funded project entitled "A Study of the Moral Reconstruction in American Southern Literature."

Carl Rollyson, Professor Emeritus of Journalism at Baruch College, CUNY, has published biographies of Marilyn Monroe, Lillian Hellman, Martha Gellhorn, Norman Mailer, Rebecca West, Susan Sontag, Jill Craigie, Michael Foot, Sylvia Plath, Amy Lowell, Dana Andrews, Walter Brennan, and several studies of biography, including *Confessions of a Serial Biographer*. He is at work on *This Alarming Paradox: The Life of William Faulkner* and *The Last Days of Sylvia Plath*.

Matthew D. Sutton is a postdoctoral assistant in the Department of Literature and Language at East Tennessee State University. His essays on Faulkner have appeared in *Mississippi Quarterly* and the edited collections *Faulkner and Twain* and *Soundscapes and Sonic Cultures in America*.

Terrell L. Tebbetts holds the Martha Heasley Cox Chair in American Literature at Lyon College. His articles on American literature have appeared in journals such as *Steinbeck Review, South Central Review, College Literature, Southern Literary Journal, The F. Scott Fitzgerald Review, Teaching Faulkner, The Faulkner Journal*, and *Philological Review*, as well as in books published by the UP of Mississippi, Auburn UP, Greenwood, MLA, and Southeast Missouri State UP. He regularly co-leads Teaching Faulkner sessions at Ole Miss's annual Faulkner and Yoknapatawpha Conference.

Dr. Michael Wainwright is Honorary Research Associate with the English Department at Royal Holloway, University of London. His five monographs for Palgrave Macmillan include *Darwin and Faulkner's Novels: Evolution and Southern Fiction* (2008), *Faulkner's Gambit: Chess and Literature* (2011), and *Game Theory and Postwar American Literature* (2016).

Eden Wales Freedman is an Assistant Professor of English and the Director of Diversity Studies at Mount Mercy University (Cedar Rapids, IA). She has published articles on reading race, gender, and trauma in the works of William Faulkner, Ernest Hemingway, Zora Neale Hurston, Toni Morrison, Eve Sedgwick, and Lauren Slater. Her book project, *Reading Testimony, Witnessing Trauma*, explores readerly engagement of literary trauma.

Yuko Yamamoto is associate professor of American literature at Chiba University. Her essays on Faulkner and other modernists have appeared in English and in Japanese in such journals as *Studies in English Literature, Studies in American Literature*, and *The Faulkner Journal of Japan*.